The Crucified Book

DIVINATIONS: REREADING LATE ANCIENT RELIGION

SERIES EDITORS
Daniel Boyarin
Virginia Burrus
Derek Krueger

A complete list of books in the series is available from the publisher.

The Crucified Book

Sacred Writing in the Age of Valentinus

Anne Starr Kreps

PENN

UNIVERSITY OF PENNSYLVANIA PRESS

PHILADELPHIA

Published by
University of Pennsylvania Press
Philadelphia, Pennsylvania 19104-4112
www.upenn.edu/pennpress

Printed in the United States of America on acid-free paper
10 9 8 7 6 5 4 3 2 1

Hardcover ISBN: 9780812253870
Ebook ISBN: 9780812298482

Library of Congress Cataloging-in-Publication Data
Names: Kreps, Anne Starr, author.
Title: The crucified book : sacred writing in the age of Valentinus / Anne Starr Kreps.
Other titles: Divinations.
Description: 1st edition. | Philadelphia : University of Pennsylvania Press, [2022] | Series: Divinations: rereading late ancient religion | Includes bibliographical references and index.
Identifiers: LCCN 2021042878 | ISBN 9780812253870 (hardcover)
Subjects: LCSH: Valentinus, active 2nd century. | Gospel of truth—Criticism, interpretation, etc. | Valentinians. | Sacred books—History and criticism. | Books—Religious aspects—Christianity. | Church history—Primitive and early church, ca. 30–600.
Classification: LCC BT1475 .K74 2022 | DDC 273/.1—dc23
LC record available at https://lccn.loc.gov/2021042878

ϩⲙ̄ ⲡⲣⲡⲙⲉⲉⲩⲉ

Fr. David W. Johnson, S.J., Ph.D.

CONTENTS

Introduction

Bibliomorphosis

Romans crucified prisoners naked. Several ancient sources attest to this practice. Dionysius of Halicarnassus and Josephus describe the condemned having their clothing removed before being led away to execution.[1] The Gospel accounts of Jesus's crucifixion report that soldiers divided his clothing at the base of the cross, indicating that Jesus may have died naked. This prospect vexed early Christians who were wrestling with the theological implications of his physically humiliating death. As artistic representations of the crucifixion emerged, a loincloth was placed around the crucified Jesus, thus balancing the physical suffering of a human Jesus with the dignity of divinity. The cross symbolically projects, in the words of Robin Jensen, "significant valence, both positive and negative depending on where or when it turns up, how it is used, what it looks like, and who sees it."[2]

The *Gospel of Truth* clothes Jesus, not to preserve some bit of dignity, but to reframe the entire crucifixion as an act of publication. This second-century text, named after its opening words, "the gospel of truth is joy," was found in two Coptic translations among the Nag Hammadi codices. It exhibits features of Valentinian Christianity and is often attributed to the early Christian Platonist Valentinus himself.[3] The *Gospel of Truth* presents a visually jarring image of Jesus crucified, wrapped in a book, reading aloud from his own heart as he dies. The text reads: "Jesus appeared. He rolled himself up in that book and was nailed to a tree and published the edict of the Father on the cross. Oh! Such a great lesson! Gliding down to death, while eternal life clothes him. After he divested himself of perishable rags, he took on himself imperishability. It is that which is not possible for anyone to take from him. After setting out onto the empty paths of fear, he left the power of those who were naked by the power of forgetfulness. He was knowledge and completion, reading out the contents of the heart."[4] In this passage, the book replaces clothing. Jesus is "divested . . . of perishable rags" while the book is a garment that cannot be taken. As the book covers Jesus, Jesus publishes the book, and the words no longer distinguish the body of Jesus from the book. In the *Gospel of Truth*, Jesus is crucified in a book and as a book, "reading aloud the contents of his heart."

The *Gospel of Truth* provides an intriguing look into the literary landscape of early Christians. It was composed around the time Irenaeus was mounting his defense of a fourfold Gospel. Yet, just as Irenaeus asserted that the number of Gospels could be no greater nor fewer than four, the Nag Hammadi texts, the *Gospel of Truth* among them, demonstrated that for many Christians, the number of Gospels was indeed greater than four. The *Gospel of Truth* invites readers to examine this alternative scriptural world.[5] It is overtly self-reflective about its own textuality. The text is replete with multiple, sometimes bizarre representations of sacred writing, including the description of Jesus wrapped in a scroll, nailed to the cross, speaking.

Ancient Christian documents that narrate Jesus's death each have a different idea about the last words of Jesus. Paul was not interested in Jesus's last words, only the fact that he died. The *Gospel of Truth* continues Paul's focus on the cross, but also includes speech. Why is it that the *Gospel of Truth* is not interested in *what* Jesus says, but simply that he speaks? Why do the specific contents of the revelation remain obscured? Why does the text consider speaking on the cross to be an act of publication? What was a book for its Christian audience that it could be described as an article of clothing? What does the image of Jesus as a crucified book tell us about ancient theories of sacred books?

The Crucified Book addresses these questions. It places the *Gospel of Truth* in the context of discourse about sacred books from the second through the fourth centuries. By documenting the text's unusual representations of sacred writing, it argues that the *Gospel of Truth* promoted the conception of books as living documents, permitting the generation of religious books by multiple authors as new sources of revelatory authority. The *Gospel of Truth*, and Valentinian Christian texts more broadly, offered a definition of sacred book that competed with the fourfold Gospel of nascent orthodoxy. Valentinian Christians endorsed a mode of open authority, recognizing ongoing oral and written revelation, instead of a closed canon of sacred books.

The Material Gospel

In the late nineteenth century, the German philologist Friedrich Max Müller attempted to classify world religions by drawing on the evolutionary model of branching descent. His classification system was heavily influenced by Charles Darwin's new work *On the Origin of the Species*.[6] Müller identified two religious family trees, the Aryan and Semitic, some of whose branches developed sacred books. These religions, Christianity included, he termed "religions of the book" and opined, "how small is the aristocracy of real book religions in the history of the world!"[7] (Ironically, both Christians and their opponents acknowledged the unaristocratic features of Christian books: Celsus criticized the crude koine of the Gospels. Lactantius worried that potential Christian converts would be put off by the Gospel "fairy tales for little old ladies.")[8]

Müller, a devout Protestant, objected to the *Origin of the Species* on theological grounds, even as he adopted its methodology and expressed great personal admiration for Darwin. While scholarship now avoids his language of primitive and aristocratic religions, Müller's classification has had lasting influence. The primacy of the written word for the first Christians is taken *ipso facto*. In *Scripture and Tradition*, Craig Evans asserted that Christianity was "born with a Bible in its cradle."[9] In *Books and Readers in the Early Church*, Harry Gamble claimed, "Christianity was a literary movement from its inception."[10] In so few words, these statements invoke a physical sacred text and a religion that is the progeny of another.

Should we presume the primacy of a physical sacred text in early Christianity? The term for the primary sacred texts for Christians, "gospel," does not naturally connote writtenness. For Ignatius of Antioch, the act of speaking an oral gospel distinguished *Christianismos* from *Ioudaismos*, which centered on the study of scripture.[11] His contemporary, Papias, famously made known his preference for oral over written sources. He imagined that "what was to be got from books was not so profitable to me as what came from the living and abiding voice."[12] Although born before most literary accounts of Jesus's life were written, Papias's life span coincided with the composition of multiple Gospels. The sheer number of new Jesus-centric texts inspired William Harris to diagnose early Christians with "acute logorrhea."[13] In the context of this vast literary production, Papias's comments about a "living and abiding voice" reflect a wider debate in early Christian circles about the role of books in the newest religious movement of the Roman Empire—his own student Irenaeus, in a radical departure from his teacher, preferred to consult texts, not people, and insisted the Gospels could be "neither more nor less than four."[14] While Irenaeus's paradigm prevailed, Papias, together with the *Gospel of Truth*'s crucified Jesus, is residual evidence of an oral revelatory authority that persisted in the second century.

As shown by the latest scholarship, the canonical Gospels came from spoken traditions and were experienced aurally, read out loud, and passed down orally.[15] This can all be gleaned from features of the written text. In the *Gospel of Truth*, scholars have found similar evidence of the performative elements of the text.[16] But this has come at the expense of an appreciation for the materiality of text. Recent years have given rise to a backlash against the presumed oral origins of biblical texts. Larry Hurtado accused New Testament scholars of an "oral fixation" which has obscured the importance of written texts for early Christians.[17] He observed that questions about the physical form of early Christian literature had rarely been raised, with the exception of Gamble's examination of textual references to books and writing to understand how Christian books were composed, published, and disseminated.[18] Gamble's work opened up space for scholars to consider what the physical manuscripts signified to their readers.

Current work in scriptural studies pays increased attention to the material conditions of written Gospels.[19] That is, the manuscripts have more value than mere records of the "original" New Testament texts. As Chris Keith observed, "Whether in modern or ancient times, a book is itself an object whose physical and visual properties are significant, with the result that a manuscript's significance or 'meaning' often extends beyond its content."[20] By abandoning the search for the oral, Hurtado, Keith, and others have focused on what the manuscripts themselves signaled to their contemporaneous audiences. Similarly, we can abandon the common reading of the *Gospel of Truth* as a record of an oral sermon, and question the text's status as a book and the multiple representations of the book within the text itself. What, then, might a manuscript, wrapped around Jesus, have signaled to the audience of the *Gospel of Truth*?

The claim that "Christianity was born with a Bible in its cradle" also presumes a history of the Christian book tethered to the history of the Jewish book. Such a claim is driven by the assumption that the first Christians were Jews, Jews had sacred texts, and therefore the first Christians did too. But should we presume the first Christians imported the sacred book from a Jewish parent? The now vast literature on the so-called parting of the ways has called for an end to the parent-child metaphor when depicting the historical dynamic between the two traditions. Whether these traditions were quarreling siblings, "estranged brothers," or variants of a language family, these models complicate the claim that Christianity inherited a singular Jewish sacred literary world. Guy Stroumsa proposed that the New Testament and the Mishnah were two new literary inventions of two new religions, the product of a shift from a religion of sacrifice to religions of the book.[21] Yet, there is no reason to limit ourselves to nascent orthodoxy. The *Gospel of Truth* should also be counted as a new literary invention, not as a child or nephew or second cousin of the orthodox.

The assertion that the Christian sacred book "came from" Judaism belies a range of Jewish thinking about the role of the written word, and advances a canonical agenda before its time. Most recently, and decisively, Eva Mroczek has documented the various "shapes" scriptures took in antiquity. If Christianity was born with a Bible in its cradle, texts such as *Jubilees*, *Ben Sira*, and *4 Ezra* rob that cradle of a defined set of texts. Maybe we should not say that Christianity was born with a (capital "B") Bible in its cradle. Maybe it was born swaddled in a panoply of texts such as *Jubilees*, *Ben Sira*, and *4 Ezra*, as well as Genesis, Proverbs, and Ezra. In the textual terrain of Second Temple Judaism, we find a land, in Mroczek's words, "before the categories of 'Bible' and 'books' were available concepts."[22]

An Alternate History

This book examines the *Gospel of Truth* through the literary practices of its time, in an era when the categories "Bible," "book," and "gospel" were *debated* concepts.[23] Famously, Irenaeus argued the number of written Gospels "could be neither more nor less than four in number."[24] Such canonical statements and polemical declarations eventually fixed a narrative collection about Jesus and his disciples. At the same time, they promoted an idea of The Book—a finite collection of written works, to be neither altered nor expanded. Irenaeus cited the illiterate barbarians he ministered to in Gaul, who would block their ears if they heard something contrary to the four Gospels even though they could not read the texts.[25] Thus, the idea of a fixed collection of books, iconic and immutable, contributed to the formation of Christian orthodoxy.

Irenaeus's statements have formed a kind of orthodoxy for historians of Christianity. The history of early Christian literature is often told as the history of the Christian canon. The earliest research into the origins of the New Testament argued that the authority of the texts emerged very early. Adolf von Harnack claimed that the earliest Christian reading practices were too diverse for canon to be a natural process, identifying Montanus and his practice of ongoing prophecy as the instigator for the formation of an authoritative collection of Christian scriptures.[26] Hans von Campenhausen argued that the formation of a New Testament was a choice forced by Marcion, who had insisted there could be only one Gospel text.[27] Irrespective of precisely *which* heretic prompted the "closing of the canon," the driving questions remain: why did certain texts become authoritative, and when? In the study of early Christian literary culture, as David Brakke has observed, we "continue to tell a story with a single plot line, leading to the seemingly inevitable *telos* of a closed canon of the New Testament."[28]

This teleological perspective even guides newer work on biblical literature that is grounded in textual history. For one example, in *Gospels Before the Book*, Matthew Larsen has questioned the extent to which the first gospel was even a book.[29] The Gospel of Mark, although a text, was not a stable book with an identifiable author. The innovation of heresiologists such as Irenaeus was to conceive of the gospel in its closed "bookish" sense. I am in full agreement with Larsen's major point: modern ideas of books and authorship have distorted our understanding of ancient gospels. Yet, while no longer presuming the *initial* primacy of biblical texts, *Gospels Before the Book*—even in its title—takes as destined the outcome of a closed canon.

What if such an outcome were not inevitable? What other paths were available? Well into the second century, authors continued to conceive of the gospel as fluid. Origen contended that the role of an evangelist was not merely to retell the events of Jesus's life, "how the Savior cured a man who was blind from his birth, or raised up a dead man who was already stinking, or to state what extraordinary works he wrought."[30] Rather, gospels were "hortatory and intended to strengthen belief in the mission of Jesus." Working with this definition, he reasoned, "whatever was written by the Apostles is gospel." For those who might "object that the Epistles are not entitled 'gospel,' and that we are wrong in applying the name of gospel to the whole of the New Testament," Origen explained, "it happens not unfrequently in Scripture when two or more persons or things are named by the same name, the name attaches itself most significantly to one of those things or persons." Fifty years after Irenaeus had vehemently insisted that there were only four Gospels, Origen mused, many books were gospel but some more so than others.[31]

The different perspectives of Origen and Irenaeus point to a variety of what David Brakke has termed "scriptural practices."[32] He observed that the groups we conveniently refer to as nascent orthodoxy, Sethian and Valentinian Christians, cultivated different approaches to revelatory texts. While a specific set of books eventually prevailed as authoritative closed collection, the ontology of such a collection was not a forgone conclusion. Some Christians emphasized the role of scripture in communal worship and teaching. Others oriented themselves to study and philosophical contemplation of texts. Still other Christians envisioned an open model of sacred book, allowing continued revelation and inspiration.

The arguments of Brakke and others should change the way we read the Nag Hammadi Gospels more than they have at present.[33] While we no longer speak of Nag Hammadi texts as deviant aberrations of normative orthodoxy, the "tyranny of canonical assumptions"[34] (as Robert Kraft identified it) still directs us to evaluate noncanonical gospels in light of the New Testament. Pheme Perkins observed that the Nag Hammadi Gospels are often regarded as a "duelling canon" to the New Testament, at the expense of a fuller understanding of these texts and their engagement with non-Christian and Second Temple Jewish literature.[35] The proliferation of texts titled "Gospel" provokes questions: What kind of significance did these new books carry? What were these other texts for the communities that produced them?[36] If we really want to understand how the sacred book became a defining feature of Christianity in the way that it did, we need to evaluate noncanonical documents as authoritative texts without relying on the orthodox idea of Gospel and our own expectations about holy books.

What Is a Book?

The *Gospel of Truth* joined a contentious literary landscape. Discussing the origins of the Mishnah, Martin Jaffe found "an empire-wide debate over the relative primacy of the sacred book."[37] In Christian discourse, this conversation manifested in disagreements about the nature of gospel. But behind these discussions lay a more basic question: what is a book? In the second century of the common era, the answer to this question was not obvious. Valentinus's book could be wrapped around someone like a garment, published and inherited, and appended in perpetuity. Likewise, the legal definition of "book" was complicated by multiple, rapidly changing formats: the codex, an ancient format resembling the modern paperback, grew more popular than the scroll, and by the end of the second century surpassed the scroll as the dominant format. Papyrus, cheaper and more widely available than vellum, became the material of choice.[38] Books existed in other formats as well, including early forms of codices of wooden and wax tablets.

The physical transformation from scroll to codex introduced practical considerations. For instance, Ulpian (c. 170–223 C.E.), whose legal career roughly coincided with Valentinus's activities in Rome, clarified the definition of a book for inheritance law. Because books were published with a range of materials and multiple formats, an opportunistic would-be heir could exploit the ambiguity of the term "book" to revise the original intentions of the testator. Ulpian aimed to resolve ambiguities and close loopholes attached to bequeathing books and libraries. However, as he clarified a nebulous area of inheritance law, Ulpian provided a legal definition of a book that would have been enforceable when the *Gospel of Truth* was in circulation. Ulpian ruled, "Under the designation of 'books' (*librorum*) all rolls (*volumina*) are included, whether they are made of papyrus, parchment, or any other material whatsoever."[39] His ruling proceeded to argue for the most expansive definition of "book" possible, from a variety of textiles and multiple formats, including the contentious, such as codices, and the rare, such as bark, "as is sometimes done." The *Gospel of Truth* proposed a similarly multiform gospel and drew on other Roman models for authoritative writing, including wills and edicts, to make a case for its own authenticity.

Usually, historians are comfortable teasing out the Roman context of early Christianity, *except* when it comes to sacred books. In part, our reluctance is evidence of Plato's lasting influence. Despite his own prolific writing, Plato argued that written expression was inferior to oral communication. He articulated the dangers of committing thoughts to writing in the *Phaedrus*: "So this is the case with words. On one hand, you would think that they speak intelligently but if, desiring to learn, you ask something of the words, it signifies the same single thing forever."[40] In his estimation, writing was at best an inferior record of oral expression, and at worst an impediment to learning and knowledge. Plato warned authors that their works could never be a reliable or permanent monument, and called any expectations that writing could be something more than a memory prompt "simpleminded." Intellectuals in Valentinus's Rome, including the emperor himself, would have dwelt on Plato's words. Marcus Aurelius ruled an empire swept by a Greek revival.[41] He too mimicked the rhetoric of Greek authors in eschewing the written word;[42] although a prolific reader, writer, and author, Marcus Aurelius derisively likened books to continually regurgitated air.[43]

This unsavory image has contributed to a historical narrative that distinguishes Romans on one hand and Jewish and Christian traditions on the other, on the basis of books. Larry Hurtado asserted that "in the context of the Roman-era religious setting, early Christianity was unusual as a 'bookish' religion."[44] Yet ancient writers described the books that contained the Sibylline oracles with reverential awe; Dionysius of Halicarnassus observed, "In a word, it is said that the Romans guard no item, hallowed or holy, as they do the Sibylline oracles."[45] Their tight control and limited circulation were regarded as evidence of their value. From the monarchy through the imperial era, the books were kept under strict supervision—only four men were allowed to consult them. When one of the men tried to copy the texts for his own purposes, he was sewn into a leather sack with a dog, a rooster, a snake, and a monkey and thrown into the sea. Such severe punishment, reserved for only the worst of crimes (parricide), reflected the deep connection between these books and the Roman *Patria*.

Recent scholarship in the study of Roman book history has corroborated the report of Dionysius of Halicarnassus.[46] Sacred books played a greater role in Rome's literary landscape than previously acknowledged. In particular, Duncan MacRae's *Legible Religion* has changed our understanding of the role writing played in Roman religious practice, demonstrating that civic religion was mediated through writing. Authors such as Cicero and Varro wrote systematic treatments of Rome's deities, while recording rituals and ideas that constituted Roman religion. Later Christian writers—Tertullian and Augustine—devoted considerable energy to refuting these texts, indicating that they were the literary competitors to Christian works. MacRae identifies as apt the comparison of the Mishnah to Roman religious writings from the likes of Cicero and Varro. Both systematically expounded upon legal texts to demarcate the boundaries of rabbinic Judaism and Roman religion, respectively. Both embraced the oral proclamations of living teachers as valid additions to ancient documents. Both, then, will provide important context for Valentinus and his theory of living books.

The *Gospel of Truth*, a True Gospel

One aim of this study is to analyze a noncanonical Gospel without presuming a fixed definition of "Gospel." In doing so, this book aims to contribute to a broader conversation about ancient book history. Scholars such as Eva Mroczek, Jacqueline Vayntrub, and Rebecca Wollenberg in Judaic studies,[47] along with David Brakke and Chris Keith, have endeavored to reconstruct ancient book culture from a native perspective.[48] The Nag Hammadi texts should be more represented in this conversation than they are at present. *The Crucified Book* moves Valentinus from the periphery and presents him as a central figure in ancient debates about sacred books. It places the *Gospel of Truth* in the context of other Jewish, Christian, and Roman ideas about books, without relying on canonical simplification.

What did the *Gospel of Truth* represent for the community that produced the text? In form, the *Gospel of Truth* is more mystical meditation than strict historical narrative. This literary style has prompted scholars to regard the text as a sermon or homily, and not "Gospel" in the sense of a divine, revelatory text.[49] However, the representations of the written word in the *Gospel of Truth*, together with the Valentinian fragments, suggest that the text would be regarded as revelatory for the community. As a promotion of living, sacred books, both person and text, oral and written, the *Gospel of Truth* addressed itself as much as any other book. In its most dramatic scenes, it could be described as an autobibliography—a self-portrait of a sacred text, from which we can understand the broader Valentinian perspective on holy books. In the text, the figure of Jesus appeared as both an oral and written document. He transcribed his textual self onto the hearts of a select spiritual class of people. The elect were invited to read this book, distribute it, and expand it with their own writings. Books manifested in the hearts of the spiritual elect. The many ways Valentinian texts conceptualized the book—as an oral text, book of the heart, embodied scroll, written document—suggest that the *Gospel of Truth* should be thought of not just as a sermon but as one of these expanded books. As Origen said, "there are many things that can properly be called Gospel,"[50] and the *Gospel of Truth*, for some Christians, was one of them.

By placing the *Gospel of Truth* in a wider Mediterranean context, *The Crucified Book* also demonstrates that Valentinus, a marginal figure in the general historical narrative about the development of Christianity, was not historically marginal. His theories about books and the personified written word align with Greco-Roman concepts of text and authorship. In texts such as the *Gospel of Truth,* elements that do not appear overtly Christian are frequently dismissed as Neoplatonic features which provide the text with its "gnostic" flavor. This observation has guided Ismo Dunderberg's recent monograph on Valentinian thought and his illuminating assessment of the problem: "The ways scholars have defined the core of Gnostic thought have guided their reading of Valentinian sources. Because of this approach, topics . . . such as moral exhortation, views about emotions, and critical analysis of power and society, have not received the attention they deserve on the basis of how large they loom in the original sources. None of these features has been regarded as constituting the distinct essence, or the 'spirit,' of Gnosticism: hence the lack of interest in them in scholarship on Valentinian teaching."[51]

Dunderberg persuades us to read the Nag Hammadi texts, particularly those now classed as "Valentinian," in light of Greco-Roman culture, without fetishizing their Gnostic features. This study takes up Dunderberg's suggestion and connects Greco-Roman books to the *Gospel of Truth*'s presentation of the written word.

Valentinus and the *Gospel of Truth* also showcase the complexity of the Jewish/Christian matrix in antiquity. Today, Christianity and Judaism define themselves as separate "textual communities."[52] However, second-century texts, communities, and textual communities were less distinct. The gradual differentiation of Judaism and Christianity,[53] and of Christianity and heresy,[54] played out through a developing self-consciousness over the significance of books: What does it mean for a book to be sacred? Must such a book give us access to the divine intellect? Daniel Boyarin and Eliot Wolfson have argued that as ancient Jewish teachers located the Logos in their sacred Torah, Christians found the Logos in the body of Christ.[55] Must a sacred book make prescribed claims to orality or writtenness? Guy Stroumsa suggested that as Christianity became more literary, Judaism sought distinction by retreating from overt textual production into an oral tradition recorded in writing.[56] Does it need to come in a certain format? Colin Roberts and T. C. Skeat proposed that differentiation between Jewish and Christian books might even be found in the Christian adoption of the codex as a rejection of Jewish preference for the scroll.[57]

These debates shaped later differences between Jewish and Christian, which are painted in simplistic strokes as Jewish (Torah, oral, scroll) and Christian (Gospel, written, codex). Yet, we know both to be much richer, and not so distinct in antiquity. Valentinus and the *Gospel of Truth*, then, can show us the foggy area mixing oral and written, codex and scroll, Gospel and law. Valentinus used many names to refer to sacred book: Gospel, teaching, edict, book of the heart. He did not choose between oral or written format, or even among the many texts in circulation—Jewish, Christian, or other philosophical texts. The *Gospel of Truth* even depicted Jesus's body as a scroll, not a codex. Rather than being on the outer edge of Christianity, a tradition far removed from the discourses that crystalized into Jewish and Christian orthodoxy, the *Gospel of Truth* was in the middle of the conversation. In some respects, as this book demonstrates, the *Gospel of Truth* stands intellectually close to the Mishnah, perhaps even closer than it does to other ancient writings about Jesus. Ultimately, because the *Gospel of Truth* reflects a mind that was at the center of the discursive debates that formed Judaism and Christianity, this project demonstrates the usefulness of so-called heretical texts for discussions on the parting of the ways.

Finally, the Valentinian evidence is compelling because, even as different book traditions eventually separated Judaism and Christianity, the existence of strong book traditions is often used to distinguish Judaism and Christianity from other faiths. The Qur'an distinguished Jews and Christians from others by calling them "people of the book," a phrase acknowledging a value, shared with Islam, for the centrality of written, revelatory text. When Max Müller adapted this phrase for religious studies, he used the phrase "religion of the book" to distinguish religions that consulted divinely inspired writings from "cult religions." The evidence of Valentinus exhibits the breadth of book traditions we must consider when discussing the category "religions of the book." In its time, the revelatory content of books was a chief source of contention among Christian circles. By the fourth century, written Gospels became intrinsically authoritative items of veneration. The holy book evolved from a written record to a vehicle for the sacred, and eventually to the *axis mundi* of Christian existence. As book veneration became the orthodox mode of scriptural practice, the mode of canonicity represented by the *Gospel of Truth* became heresy. *The Crucified Book*, then, does not ignore the orthodox telos, nor does it fixate on how it came to be. Rather, it examines the *Gospel of Truth* as part of a landscape of shifting textualities.

Chapter Synopsis

The evidence for these arguments is laid out in five chapters. The first two chapters study the *Gospel of Truth* as a theory and a practice. Chapter 1, "The Joyful Gospel," examines the self-presentation of the *Gospel of Truth* as a revelatory text. It studies references to books and writing within the *Gospel of Truth* itself and compares them to contemporary Jewish and Roman modes of textual authority. The *Gospel of Truth* joined the Jewish widespread Jewish speculation about proverbial Wisdom, as witnessed by Philo, *Bereshit Rabbah*, and Ben Sira and his self-proclaimed grandson, to imagine its own divine origins. The text describes its divine composition and publication by referencing Roman publication practices and Roman modes of infallible writing. The *Gospel of Truth* envisioned a divine book that circulated through creative acts—the new writings and speeches of an elite class of Christians. The text imagined revelation through both body and book, and drew from both Jewish and Roman ideas about authoritative writing.

How did this theory work? Chapter 2, "The Valentinian Gospel as a Scriptural Practice," takes up this question and examines how the discourse of books as bodies functioned in second-century Valentinian circles. Fragments of Valentinus's other writings corroborate the *Gospel of Truth*'s claim that all humans contained writings of the heart, lying dormant until the heart was pure enough to publish them. These fragments equate such cardiac texts with physical books, a revelatory model found in the contemporary Jewish text *4 Ezra*, as well as Philo and early Christian intellectuals. The writings of two of Valentinus's disciples, Heracleon and Ptolemy, continued this perspective. In his *Against Heresies*, Irenaeus, demonstrating knowledge of the Valentinian theory of the Gospel, argued against the Valentinian idea that people could function as eminent texts.

The extent to which divine revelation resided in books provided a chief source of contention between Valentinian and Irenaeus's nascent orthodox circles.

Chapter 3, "The *Gospel of Truth* According to the Christian Heresiographers," argues that such disagreements in the second century became two distinct, competing modes of canonicity in the fourth century. One mode advocated an authoritative, closed list of inspired texts and a second promoted an open collection of oral and written revelation. Heresiologists from Tertullian to Epiphanius drew the proverbial line in the sand, distinguishing orthodox from heretical based on these types of canon. The idea of a fluid canon was not a theoretical construct of the heresiologists. Nag Hammadi Codex I, one of the codices that contains the *Gospel of Truth*, serves as an example of a fourth-century counter-canon that encouraged readers to find new sources of Gospel within themselves.

Such a notion of sacred book—theorized in the *Gospel of Truth* and practiced in Nag Hammadi Codex I—faded away from early Christian circles. The idea of an open canon did not win the battle to define orthodoxy. However, the Valentinian position should not be considered particularly exotic or doomed to failure. Chapter 4, "Rabbis Who Published and Perished," demonstrates that the closest analogy to this open canon is found in the Jewish concept of a dual Torah. The wide range of sources now grouped together as "rabbinic literature" routinely collapsed the distinction between holy person and holy book to promote an authoritative Oral Torah, initially given to Moses on Sinai and passed down to Jewish leaders. Rabbinic sources defined sacred books by treating Torah scrolls and Torah scholars with surprising parity. As the rabbinic answer to the question of what is a sacred book, the dual Torah provides an important model for Christian debates about the definition and selection of revelatory, sacred, or authoritative books. Ultimately, this chapter argues that if some Christians presumed no boundary between holy books and holy people, rabbinic efforts showcased a way books could become people and people could become books.

The Conclusion, "The Iconic Book," observes how canonical developments gave rise to talismanic uses for books. While bibliomancy had long been an attested practice in Christian and non-Christian settings, the fourth century witnessed the rise of apotropaic uses for books, as evidenced by the new fashion of wearing miniature gospels as jewelry. Church leaders complained about this practice, thus testifying to its popularity. In the fourth century, by the time Christian orthodoxy found its center, new debates about the role of sacred writing arose. Ecclesiastical writers no longer solely focused their attention on distinguishing right books from wrong books; they also addressed the proper format and use of sacred texts. These discussions about books as talismans in antiquity dovetail with modern discourse about how technologies have changed the written word. Just as the move from material to electronic format has provoked our reflection on the authenticity of written sources, the shift from scroll to codex prompted audiences of antiquity to evaluate the authority of their own burgeoning literary production. The Valentinian sacred book was a casualty of this conversation.

Unless otherwise noted, translations are my own. In places where the reader might appreciate the original language—usually quotations with vocabulary related to books, writing, and revelation—I have placed the ancient text in the endnotes.

PART I

Valentinus and the Valentinians

CHAPTER 1

The Joyful Gospel

The Spermatic Book

If the author of the Gospel of John harbored any ambition that his would be one of only four approved accounts of Jesus's life, he gave no such indication in his work. The Gospel ended with the declaration: "Now there are so many other things Jesus did that if ever it was written completely, not the world itself, I suppose, could hold all the books that would be written."[1] These words are jarring to a modern reader, who would, perhaps, expect a canonical Gospel to promote canonical thinking. However, John even seemed to encourage the publication of additional accounts, noting that "Jesus performed many other signs before his disciples, which are not written in this book."[2] John did not just tolerate the existence of other books about Jesus; he presumed the possibility of limitless composition. Thus, at the beginning of the second century, there existed the possibility of a boundless collection of authoritative texts.

Later in the second century, Justin Martyr attempted to make sense of his expanding library as he considered the role of philosophical books for the Christian reader. Justin Martyr was fundamentally a philosopher, and he had to make room for the writings of Plato that had taught him "the reality of the one, unchangeable True and Good."[3] Justin had already championed the Septuagint as the superlative translation of scripture, but, Justin wondered, why did Greek philosophy seem to resonate so well with the Christian message? In an answer to his own question, Justin identified a "spermatic Logos"—bits of the divine Logos that had been scattered (σπειρῶ) among men—in the writings of Greek philosophers, which explained their affinity to nascent Christian morality and theology.[4] Justin argued that the Logos in the Socratic written word was the same Logos incarnate in the flesh of Jesus.[5] The concept of the spermatic Logos allowed Justin to read Greek philosophy as part of a Christian curriculum—although best articulated in the Hebrew Bible and some early Christian Writings, bits of divine truths could be found in any book. For John and Justin, there was room for innovation in the second-century Christian literary imagination.

The *Gospel of Truth* presented a theory of sacred book that continued these ideas. As a text that kept temporal company with John and Justin, the *Gospel of Truth* promoted both John's idea of limitless composition and Justin's texts of diverse provenance. The text made multiple references to books and writing, through which it told a cosmic history of the sacred book, from its divine authorship to publication and distribution. This chapter draws out the mechanisms of divine literary production in the *Gospel of Truth*. First, it examines how the text presented its theory of sacred book, one grounded in a widespread tradition of reading Genesis together with Proverbs 8. Then it unpacks the *Gospel of Truth*'s theory about how the book became accessible to humanity. The text proposed a divine publication process informed by Roman publishing practices and Jewish concerns about the infallibility of the divine book. The *Gospel of Truth* proposed that the divine book was implanted into the bodies of believers, mediated by the crucifixion of Jesus as a book. The divine spermatic book resided both in the bodies of believers and their compositions. New creative acts drove the distribution of the divine book, which circulated through the publication of new texts by an elite class of Christians.

By collapsing the distinction between body and book, then, the Gospel not only explained how the divine book might become accessible to humanity, it ensured the original meaning could not be lost, even as it endorsed new compositions as versions of the divine book. The *Gospel of Truth* presented itself as such a document, thus claiming for itself revelatory status as a version of the divine sacred book. Although the *Gospel of Truth* appears an outlier against the later canonical backdrop, it follows the main currents of the Roman and Jewish book culture in its time.

Before the discovery of the Nag Hammadi library, we knew of a text called the *Gospel of Truth* because Irenaeus reported, "the [Valentinians] call something written by themselves the 'Gospel of Truth.'"[6] Any research on the *Gospel of Truth* necessarily confronts two questions: Are the two Nag Hammadi texts beginning with the words "The gospel of truth is joy" the same text Irenaeus referenced? And did Valentinus himself author this text? The Nag Hammadi text does exhibit Valentinian features: a confused spiritual child of the Father created the material world; the divine plan for salvation is executed though the historical appearance of the Savior; the Savior is both a model and agent of salvation.[7] Although a few scholars have questioned whether the text under discussion is the text Irenaeus referenced, I side with Thomassen's eloquent evaluation: "the probability that there existed two independent works, one entitled 'The Gospel of Truth' and the other accidentally beginning with the same words, and both of them 'gnostic,' must be regarded as very slim indeed."[8]

Unfortunately, Irenaeus's statement does not provide conclusive evidence that Valentinus himself wrote the text. Stylistic similarities between the text and fragments of Valentinus's writings preserved in the works of others suggest the possibility, but it is impossible to confirm.[9] However, for my purposes, the stakes of this question are low. What if the *Gospel of Truth* was written not by Valentinus but by one of his students, Ptolemy or Heracleon? The next chapter will demonstrate that the fragments of Ptolemy and Heracleon's writings indicate that they too acknowledged the insufficiency of written texts to adequately convey divine truths. While this book accepts Valentinus's authorship and will refer to Valentinus as author, the attribution of the *Gospel of Truth* to Ptolemy or Heracleon would not change the understanding of its alternative sacred textuality.

Authored in the Mind of the Father

An untitled tractate from Nag Hammadi Codex I begins with the phrase "The gospel of truth is joy."[10] We refer to this tractate as the *Gospel of Truth* because of this opening. Yet it is not clear whether the word πεγαΓΓεΛιοΝ, as the part of the first line of the work, was also its title, or if the term referred simply to the contents of the text.[11] The wording, then, raises a critical question: did the author of the *Gospel of Truth* set out to write a holy text? That is, was the *Gospel of Truth* meant as Gospel? On one hand, Irenaeus had accused Valentinians of having their own Gospel and particularly a text called the *Gospel of Truth*, which suggests that ancient readers regarded the opening line as a title. On the other, modern readers have interpreted the term "gospel" in the first line of the text as a description of the contents: "good news." In his definitive *The Gnostic Scriptures*, Bentley Layton described the text as a "sermon and has nothing to do with the Christian genre properly called Gospel (e.g. the Gospel of Mark)."[12]

Indeed, the text does not resemble, in either form or content, the linear, narrative structure of the canonical Gospels. Rather, the *Gospel of Truth* begins in mythic time, describing a cosmic disaster in which knowledge of the Father had been lost, then veers into the historical era of Roman Judea, and ends with a series of ethical exhortations to its audience. The text exhibits no interest in the life of the historical Jesus and makes no effort to record his words. Consequently, in the critical edition of the *Gospel of Truth*, Harold Attridge argued, "the term 'Gospel' here, in any case, is not a technical term for a literary genre. Rather it refers to the contents of the work, the proclamation of the revealer's message."[13] Pheme Perkins noted, "The Valentinian entries, the *Gospel of Truth* and the *Gospel of Philip* have no ties to the genre 'Gospel.'"[14]

However, the question should be asked: why would they? Specialists in early Christian studies have long recognized the wide semantic range of the term gospel in antiquity: Justin Martyr had described the Gospels simply as the "memoirs of the Apostles."[15] Ignatius of Antioch used the term "Gospel" regularly to designate both the written documents that competed with Jewish scriptures[16] and also the oral teachings of Jesus, Paul, and contemporary Christian leaders.[17] Ignatius opposed Christians who insisted that if they could not "find it in the archives, they would not believe it in the gospel."[18] For these Christians, whom Ignatius termed Jews, only the Hebrew scriptures could validate the contents of the new Jesus message. Ignatius proposed that if one wanted to consult the "archives," one should look to "Jesus Christ, the inviolable archives are his cross and death and his resurrection."[19] For Ignatius, the Gospel superseded the written scriptures, even as he viewed the Gospel in a corporeal format.[20] Even as the champion of orthodoxy, Irenaeus of Lyon, claimed there were only four Gospels, he did not use term Gospel consistently to designate written texts.[21] When Origen composed his *Commentary on the Gospel of John* in the early third century, he claimed that although there were only four Gospels, all of the writings of the church should be considered Gospel.[22] The *Gospel of Truth* fits neatly into these Christian perspectives.

The *Gospel of Truth* might not have been Gospel in the classical sense of the term, if such even exists, but that does not exclude the possibility that for Valentinus the term "Gospel" signified something more than "announcement." Valentinus's Gospel was not a Lukean corrective eyewitness account or, in John's terms, one of many books about "what Jesus said and did."[23] The *Gospel of Truth* hinted that, for Valentinus, Gospel served a revelatory function. Many religious texts account for their own production: New holy books justify their authority. Newly authored books claiming to be old explain why they appeared. Oral traditions explain their unbroken chain of sources. The *Gospel of Truth* was no different. Every book had its story and the *Gospel of Truth* opened by telling its own.

The Joyful Gospel

The book's subtle etiology reflected its author's position within a Jewish and Christian matrix. On one hand, the *Gospel of Truth* did not claim authority by conventional means. Unlike other texts, it not been narrated secretly to a single person, hidden in heaven or a temple. On the other hand, Valentinus drew on traditional sources to design a textual concept that explained the origins of the Gospel he preached. He utilized a hermeneutical tradition that interpreted the figure of Wisdom in Proverbs 8 as the divine Logos to describe his idea of a heavenly book, which he then subtly equated with his own composition. In the dynamics unfolding below, as the *Gospel of Truth* narrated its own history, the text tied itself to a preexistent, supernatural book and thus claimed for itself the status of holy document.

In Proverbs, the Wisdom figure operates as an eternal mediator between the divine and human. Wisdom is eternal and preexistent, "formed long ages ago, at the very beginning, when the world came to be" (Prv 8:23). Wisdom resides in close proximity to the deity, "brought forth as the first of his works" and "constantly at his side" (Prv 8:22; 8:30). Wisdom carries an abundance of joy, "filled with delight, day after day, rejoicing always in his presences, rejoicing in the whole world, and delighting in mankind" (Prv 8:30–31). Wisdom promises life, and as "those who find [her] find life and receive favor from the Lord." Wisdom, then, is both the means by which humans can know the deity, and the resulting knowledge that marks humans as "blessed" with divine favor (Prv 8:32).[24]

The opening of the *Gospel of Truth*, commonly regarded as a prologue, is an interpretation of Proverbs 8. The text opens: "The gospel of truth is joy to the ones who receive grace from the Father of Truth to come to know it/him through the power of the word, which was cast out from the Pleroma, which is in the thought and mind of the Father. This is he who is called the Savior, which is the name of the work he will do. He is the salvation of they who became ignorant of the Father, while the name of the Gospel is the revealing of the hope, which is the thing that is found for the ones who seek it/him."[25] The *Gospel of Truth* in general, and this passage in particular, have often been read through the lens of what Geoffrey Smith has described as an "unwavering commitment to biblical interpretation."[26] Hans Martin Schneke noted that the description of "joy" appeared in the Odes of Solomon,[27] and must therefore reflect an intellectual kinship. Smith himself found points of contact between this passage and the Gospel of John, *Ben Sira*, and the *Wisdom of Solomon*, and reads the *Gospel of Truth* as an interpretation of John.[28] Yet, it is not evident that the author of the *Gospel of Truth* understood his composition this way or even conceived of something called "the biblical" to interpret. The continued scrutiny of the *Gospel of Truth* as biblical interpretation is representative of the teleological approach Brakke has urged us to abandon.

In light of the widespread hermeneutical fascination with Proverbs 8, shared among John, *Ben Sira*, the *Wisdom of Solomon*, and the *Gospel of Truth*, the similarities can be better understood as part of broader ancient interest in the Wisdom figure from Proverbs. Indeed, from its first words, "The gospel of truth is joy," the text engaged with the Proverbs 8 tradition. Proverbs had described Wisdom experiencing the presence of the Father as "delight" (מעשעים) and "rejoicing" (משחקת).[29] The Septuagint rendered the Hebrew terms as προσχαίρω and εὐφραίνομην, respectively. The Coptic term in the *Gospel of Truth*, ⲧⲏⲗⲏⲗ, was likely a translation from the original Greek εὐφραισύνη, the noun form of εὐφραίνομαι.[30] The *Gospel of Truth* regarded the agent of the deity with the same term Proverbs used to describe Wisdom as the "daily delight" and emissary of the deity.

In its opening, the *Gospel of Truth* also described salvation through a schematic parallel to what we find in Proverbs. Proverbs 8:17 described humanity's quest for Wisdom as a seek/find schematic: "I love the ones who love me, and the ones who seek me diligently will find me." Similarly, seeking as salvation is introduced in the opening lines of the text: "the name of the Gospel is the revealing of the hope, which is the thing that is found for the ones who seek it/him."[31] However, ambiguities in the Coptic left open the precise identities of the actors in this search, and thereby blended the identity of several divine entities—Father, Word, Savior, Gospel. The translations below are all viable renderings of the Coptic, and the dynamics that subsequently unfold in the text indicate that Father, Gospel, name, and word were intertwined actors in the revelation.

Gospel of Truth 16.31

Translation A. The gospel of truth is a joy to the ones who receive grace from the Father of truth to come to know the **Father** through the power of the Word.

Translation B. The gospel of truth is a joy to the ones who receive grace from the Father of truth to come to know the **Gospel** through the power of the Word.

Gospel of Truth 17.1–2

Translation A. The name of the Gospel is the revealing of the hope, which is the thing that is found for the ones who seek the **Father**.

Translation B. The name of the Gospel is the revealing of the hope, which is the thing that is found for the ones who seek the **Gospel**.

Translation C. The name of the Gospel is the revealing of the hope, which is the thing that is found for the ones who seek the **name**.[32]

The pronouns in these passages are enigmatic, possibly purposefully so.[33] The resumptive (ⲛ̄ⲥⲱϥ) could refer to either of the two masculine/neuter nouns in the introduction—Father (ⲡⲓⲱⲧ) or Gospel (ⲉⲩⲁⲅⲅⲉⲗⲓⲟⲛ).[34] This ambiguity was also preserved in the first line, "to come to know it" (ⲁⲧⲣⲟⲥⲟⲩⲱⲛϥ̄), the object suffix pronoun referring to either the Gospel or the Father. Similar vagueness arises in the last line of the prologue; what was the object of the search? As feminine nouns, hope and truth are ineligible, but the gospel/Father/name are all possible objects designating the item "found for the ones who seek it/him." The vague pronouns in the *Gospel of Truth*, perhaps intentionally, left the reader with the sense that divine actors, including the Gospel itself, were inseparably intertwined.

These elusive associations confounded subject and object and eliminated distinctions between divine actors. They suggested that the revelatory message was itself preexistent.[35] Through its ambiguous modifiers, the prologue, as Judith Hoch Wray observed, "created a loose equation between Logos and Gospel,"[36] as both the "Gospel" and the Son (who is termed Logos elsewhere in the texts) served revelatory functions. In its body, the *Gospel of Truth* attached additional several epithets to the person of the Savior—name, word, "living book of the living," or sometimes simply "book." These terms further obscured the boundaries between Jesus, word, Gospel and physical books.

The text assigned qualities to this agent that Proverbs 8 associated with Wisdom. The proverbial Wisdom claimed in Proverbs 8, "Before the mountains were planted, I was produced when he had not yet made the earth and fields."[37] Likewise, the agent in the *Gospel of Truth* preceded creation, as the text asserted: "since before the foundation within the All, it resided among the incomprehensible ones."[38] The "foundation of the All" was a Valentinian term for creation—the *Gospel of Truth* described the aims of Jesus's ministry as a teacher, for example, as "the word of the Father reaching down among the All, which is the fruit of his heart and an impression of his wish. He himself endures the All."[39] The idea of a foundation before the All indicates that the *Gospel of Truth* equated the revelatory agent with the preexistent Logos.[40]

Moreover, both Proverbs 8 and the *Gospel of Truth* described a close physical proximity between their respective revelatory figures and the Father. The proverbial Wisdom resided "beside [the deity] like a little child." In the *Gospel of Truth*, the book was "written in the thought and mind of the Father,"[41] demonstrating physical overlap between the Father and his extraterrestrial book.[42] The Son-as-book resided with the Father, so close that when "the Father reveals his bosom, his bosom is the Holy Spirit, which reveals its secret. Its secret is the Son."[43] In their own readings of Proverbs 8, both the Gospel of John and rabbinic midrashim used that same language to describe the physical closeness between the Father and the revelatory agent: the Gospel of John signaled a comparable relation between the Father and Son, placing Jesus in "the bosom of the Father."[44]

The *Gospel of Truth* shared in this interpretive tradition to offer its readers a primordial etiology of the sacred book. Eliot Wolfson has argued that the ubiquitous references to the book and the "living book" indicate that "the *Gospel of Truth* preserves an alternative incarnation to the Gospel of John."[45] For Wolfson, the alternative Valentinus presented to Logos becoming flesh was Logos becoming book. In the *Gospel of Truth*, though, Valentinus did not present the book as an alternative to the flesh, but a book encompassed in the flesh—Jesus existed as both flesh and book. He was both a "living book" and the "Book of the Living." Whereas Jewish intellectuals transformed Wisdom into the figure of the Torah, and John transformed Wisdom into the figure of Jesus, Valentinus permitted both transformations, invoking the bosom of the Father to describe the location of the divine agent—one represented as both flesh *and* book.

Many circles, diverse in their thinking—*Ben Sira*, *Genesis Rabbah*, Philo, the Gospel of John—had read Proverbs 8 to consider how Wisdom manifested among humanity as a text, as a body, or, in Valentinus's case, both. These sources, some roughly contemporary to Valentinus, provide precedent to interpret the *Gospel of Truth*'s reading of Proverbs 8 specifically as a statement about the source and scope of holy books. For instance, *Genesis Rabbah*, an exegetical midrash from the *amoraic* period, claimed that God consulted the Torah when he created the world, comparing the Torah to instructions that God the craftsman followed:[46]

> Another matter: The word child (אמון) means workman (אומן). The Torah says, I was a tool of the Holy One, blessed be he. As is the custom in the world, when a flesh-and-blood king builds a palace, he does not build from his own mind, but from the mind of the craftsman. Now the craftsman does not build from his own mind, but he has documents and tablets to know how he should make the rooms and doorposts. So the Holy One, blessed be he, looked into the Torah when he created the world. As scripture says, "the Lord made me as the beginning of his way."[47]

In typical midrashic fashion, this passage explains the opening line of Genesis, "In the beginning," by citing an attestation of "beginning" in another Hebrew scripture, in this case Proverbs 8:30–31, which depicts wisdom "at the beginning" in close proximity with the deity. Wisdom describes herself as "a little child" (*'amon*). The midrash observes that an alternative vocalization to "little child" is workman (*'uman*). Thus, the passage posits that Wisdom, identified in the midrash as the Torah, provided instructions for the deity when he created the world. For *Genesis Rabbah*, the Torah encompassed more than the five books of Moses. As Peter Schäfer notes, *Genesis Rabbah* presents a world in which "there is no cosmological information outside the Torah. . . . one needs to take the Torah in its entirety (that is, not only the Torah in the strict sense of the word but also the Prophets and the Writings) into consideration if one wants to discuss and discover the mysteries of creation."[48] The Torah, for *Genesis Rabbah*, included all biblical books, and, perhaps, nonbiblical, oral books.[49]

Philo employed the same metaphor of the deity as the craftsman, spun to reflect different ideas about the Torah as a divine book. Philo posited that the deity, like a craftsman, created a sketch in his mind, built a model, then created a world perceptible to the senses:[50]

> Whenever a city is built for the sake of the great ambition of a king or some ruler making claims to autocratic power, being a brilliant mind and wanting to show off his prosperity, there comes some educated man, an architect, and perceiving the opportunity and perfect timing of the matter, diagrams first in his own mind nearly all the parts of the future finished city. . . . As a good workman does, looking at the model, he begins to construct it from wood and stone, the corporeal parts coming to resemble each part of the incorporeal ideas. One must conjecture similar things about God—when deciding to build the mega-state he first thought of its buildings, from which he made a noetic world, then completed the perceptible one, using the noetic one as a model.[51]

Philo's description of the construction of a city closely followed his ideas about creation. The world was created by the laws of nature. In line with his platonic world view, Philo maintained the existence of noetic ideals and sensible manifestations of these ideals. Unlike other Platonists, however, Philo rejected the notion that the sensible experience was a corruption of the ideal. For Philo, the sensible world was a copy of the intelligible world, which was modeled on the inaccessible, ineffable thoughts of God. Similarly, then, the written law of Moses was a copy of the law of nature, modeled on the image in God's mind.

However, absent in the Philo passage were references to written documents. Instead, Philo thought of creation in terms of images.[52] The architect possessed an impression (τύπους) of the city sealed upon his soul as on wax. Instead of a written document, the architect "carries a picture" (ἀγαλματοφορεῖ) of the city in his mind. As David Runia has noted, this Greek verb invoked the image of statues being carried in processions.[53] When the architect built the sensible city, he conjured up the images (εἴδωλα) of the model (παράδειγμα) engraved in his mind. In this respect, Philo's heavenly Torah matched his own ideology of written Torah. For Philo, the written Torah was not superior to other manifestations: the Law of Nature could be found in the content of Torah and also be found embodied in certain individuals.[54] Key figures in the Hebrew Bible intuitively followed Jewish law despite living before Moses received the law on Mount Sinai. Philo even called these biblical characters "living and rational laws."[55] As such, each patriarch was inscribed with a virtue as an archetypal model of a living law.[56] Enos, for instance, embodied hope, and Noah represented justice. Even Moses, Philo asserted, could not have written out God's law if he did not already possess its innate meaning.[57] The Mosaic writing was simply a copy of the laws embodied in these men. This is consistent with the way Philo presents deity-as-architect consulting a Torah of images, not writing.

In contrast, the deity in *Genesis Rabbah* consulted Torah as a physical book, comparing it to a craftsman's documents (דיפתראות) and tablets (פינקסאות). Burton Visotzky has posited that the dual references to documents and tablets represent the written and oral Torah, respectively.[58] When *Genesis Rabbah* imagined God consulting the Torah, then, it was configured to mirror the rabbinic conception of Torah. In *Genesis Rabbah*, the deity consulted documents to create the world; in the Philo passage, God worked from pictures and models, not texts. While *Genesis Rabbah* and Philo agreed that Torah was a preexistent model for creation, they differed on the physical form the Torah took.

These examples, well known in Judaic studies, should also serve as a backdrop for the *Gospel of Truth* and other texts where a primordial Wisdom drives creation. Philo and *Genesis Rabbah*, two of Valentinus's contemporaries read Proverbs 8 to develop theories of revelatory book. The *Gospel of Truth*'s interpretation of Proverbs 8 proposes its own: the text presents an idea of divine book that is revelatory to be sure, but one where the reader might stumble over the conflation of revelatory agents: father, word, son, and gospel. But this conflation is not due to imprecision in language or fuzziness of Valentinian thought—it is a shape-shifting mode of revelation with Jewish precedent in the *Wisdom of Ben Sira*.

Wisdom of Ben Sira was composed in Hebrew at the beginning of the second century B.C.E., and Ben Sira's grandson later translated the text into Greek.

The textual variants among manuscripts, the addition of new material in Greek recensions, testifies to the popularity of the work.[59] We can surmise that Valentinus would know of the text, even if he did not read it—complete manuscripts survive in Greek, Syriac, and Latin. Quotations of *Ben Sira* appearing in Rabbinic literature from the earliest stratum to medieval thinkers, in addition to the many fragments found in the Cairo Geniza, also attest to its wide circulation. The text presents itself as a collection of proverbial wisdom, as curated by the sage Ben Sira. For the most part, the sayings are generic, conveying values associated with Hellenistic Judaism; for example, "set your heart right and be steadfast, and do not be impetuous in time of calamity."[60]

Yet the text also presents its wisdom as part of the Proverbs 8 primordial tradition, originating with creation and passed down through instruction. Thus, Ben Sira argues, wisdom can be acquired through learning and by following the Torah. He also looked to the wisdom hymn in Proverbs 8 to define wisdom as a primordial entity, emitted from the mouth of God before creation.[61] Wisdom "came forth from the mouth of the Most High." An amorphous Wisdom "covered the entire earth like a **mist**." For Ben Sira, wisdom was a divine gift bestowed on those who loved and feared the deity. Obedience to the Torah was the primary marker of one who possessed these qualities and identified those eligible to receive the gift of wisdom.[62] It was diluted over the whole earth, but was found in concentrate among the people of Jacob. Wisdom described how she flourished after "taking root in a glorified people, in the portion of the Lord, his inheritance."[63] She thrived like observable natural phenomena—likened to growing trees, fragrant temple incense, and fruitful grapevines. Yet wisdom itself was overabundant—Wisdom warned, "the ones who eat of me will hunger still; the ones who drink of me will thirst still."[64] Like wisdom, the book of the covenant was defined by natural abundance. Referring back to the trees, temple incense, and grapevine, Ben Sira claimed:

> All these things are the book of the Covenant of God the Most High, the Law that Moses commanded us as an inheritance for the congregations of Jacob. It overflows, like the Pishon, with wisdom, and like the Tigris at the time of the first fruits. It runs over, like the Euphrates, with understanding, and like the Jordan at harvest time. It pours forth instruction like the Nile, like the Gihon at the time of vintage. The first man did not know wisdom fully, nor will the last one fathom her. For her thoughts are more abundant than the sea, and her council deeper than the great abyss.[65]

Lamentably, the passage is not extant in the original Hebrew. Ben Sira identified the "book of the covenant" with manifestations of wisdom in the natural world. The fruits of wisdom, the trees, sacred incense, the vines, "all these things are the book of the covenant." The book itself could not contain the wisdom it possessed. To extend Ben Sira's metaphor, if wisdom was a flourishing, fertile farm among the people of Jacob, it was an overgrown jungle in the Torah. Wisdom literally overflowed from the parchment. Ben Sira charged himself with making order from the chaos. Ben Sira, an advanced student, could inundate himself with Torah. Comparing himself to a canal, he allowed himself to be flooded through study of scripture until his "canal became a river and river a sea."[66] His own book channeled the flood of Torah to "again make instruction shine like the dawn . . . and pour out teaching like prophecy." His study of diluvian scripture yielded his own work: the *Wisdom of Ben Sira*, a condensed guide for the intermediate student. Divine wisdom might be located in Torah, but the contents of Torah could be distilled into his work that depicted Hellenistic values as the "gist" of Torah. Through his agricultural imagery, then, Ben Sira implied that Torah was too expansive to be contained in a physical book, or even five books. Eric Reymond observed, "Ben Sira reveals a sensitivity to language's inherent imprecision."[67] Wisdom could not be fully contained in books, and human language was insufficient to articulate it. Ben Sira accepted the ambiguity of language, like the *Gospel of Truth*, whose own language represented the ambiguity of its revelatory actors. For Ben Sira, no one could comprehend Wisdom in its entirety: "The first man did not know her fully, nor will the last one fathom her."[68]

The *Gospel of Truth* also agreed with Ben Sira on the role of divine Wisdom in creation. But, perhaps deliberately, it critiqued his theory by providing an adversary—Error—who leaves those humans who misguidedly pursue knowledge in a state of ignorance. Ben Sira proclaimed that Wisdom "came forth from the mouth of the Most High." Similarly, the *Gospel of Truth* stated that the son was "spoken forth" from the mouth of the father. Ben Sira envisioned the Wisdom "cover[ing] the entire earth like a mist." The *Gospel of Truth* also saw the world engulfed in a primordial mist: "As the All was searching for he from whom they came forth, and the all was inside of him, the unthinkable, the unknowable, this one who is better than any thought, ignorance of the Father caused agitation and fear. Now the agitation closed in like a **mist**, so no one could see. Because of this, error became powerful. She performed her empty works, but did not know the truth, that she came into existence as matter, preparing powerfully and beautifully a substitute for truth."[69]

In this passage, the act of seeking out the unknowable caused agitation, engulfing the world in a mist. Geoffrey Smith has argued that the reference to "mist" in this passage illustrates that Valentinus knew *Ben Sira* directly. He observes that in *Ben Sira*, "Wisdom covers the earth as mist and thus illustrates the availability of God's Wisdom to all of her people (cf. 24:1); in *Gospel of Truth* 17:11–15 and 30–31 on the other hand, the mist encompasses the primordial totality so that Error can preserve it in a state of ignorance regarding the Father and begin work on her world of deception."[70] Was Valentinus critiquing the human attempts at gaining wisdom that *Ben Sira* promoted? *Ben Sira* argued that the world overflowed with divine wisdom so that no single person could fully capture it, nor single book contain it. The *Gospel of Truth* argued that efforts to grasp wisdom created an environment for error to flourish, preparing a seductively deceptive "substitute for truth." Whether the mist represented divine Wisdom or divine Error, neither text concludes that revelatory writing should be jettisoned as wrong or incomplete.

The reception history of the *Wisdom of Ben Sira* indicates that later readers interpreted the text to endorse an open theory of revelatory writing. One layer of this reception is preserved Ben Sira's self-proclaimed grandson's ancient introductory essay to the text, composed for the Greek translation of his grandfather's work around 132 BCE.[71] The grandson claimed that salvation was tied specifically to texts; reading allowed one to "make greater progress in living according to the law."[72] The grandson described a threefold division of humankind, based on their ability to read texts: "readers," "lovers of learning," and "those outside." His grandfather was a reader, who could engage directly with the "law, prophets and other writings of our ancestors" (τοῦ νόμου καὶ τῶν προφητῶν καὶ τῶν ἄλλων πατρίων βιβλίων), growing in wisdom by consulting texts. His grandfather's composition was aimed at the "lovers of learning," who required an interpreter (such as Ben Sira) to condense Torah into manageable pieces.

Similarly, the grandson's essay and translation were aimed at lovers of learning who could not read Hebrew. An explanatory prologue to his translation aimed, in Francis Borchardt's words, "to show the importance of translation as a contribution to the life of the law . . . this means that it must contain the same qualities as the Law, the prophets, and other books."[73] The grandson compared his own translation efforts to the Septuagint translation—he asked for his readers' patience with his translation, explaining that no translation is ever perfect, not his nor any translation of "the law, prophets and the rest of the books, which differ not a little read in their original language."[74] Through such a comparison, Ben Sira's grandson implied that his grandfather's work held equal status to other Jewish sacred texts.[75] As Ben Wright asserts, "the grandson was saying to his audience the equivalent of, 'look; if you think I have failed at any point to make a good translation or to get it right, then what about your highly regarded translations; they are just as problematic.'"[76]

Whether the grandson was displaying honest uneasiness at the difficulties of translation, as Wright has argued,[77] or simply seizing the opportunity to promote his own work, as J. K. Aiken has claimed,[78] the grandson implied that if one objects to the Greek translation of Ben Sira, she also should object to Greek translations of the Septuagint. In doing so, he equated his grandfather's work with other sacred texts. For Ben Sira and his grandson, then, no book could comprehensively describe divine wisdom; all texts were deficient. What does this mean for the sacred book? Eva Mroczek states, "Ben Sira does not understand his work as a 'book' in the sense of an original and final composition, but as the malleable and necessarily incomplete continuation of a long tradition of revealed wisdom."[79] This wisdom is to be found by observing nature: "all these things are the Book of the Covenant."

The *Gospel of Truth*, then, like contemporary Jewish texts, finds purpose in human efforts to grasp and reveal divine Wisdom. They share a panoramic view of textuality, admitting Gospels and gospels, complete bauplans and incomplete revelations. The breadth of textuality does not dilute its importance, but reflects the eternal and global reach of Wisdom. As a member of the gospel genre, the *Gospel of Truth* is too nonlinear and self-referential to serve as a reliable witness. But as a revelation on the nature of revelation—a position it claims for itself—the *Gospel of Truth* opens up the genre of gospel and walks right in.

Published on the Cross

How can such a divinely authored book become accessible to humanity? The *Gospel of Truth* presented the manifestation and death of Jesus as a literary link in a chain of transmission of divine knowledge. The knowledge of the Father is transferred gradually from deity to revelatory agent to humankind. Language itself is simultaneously a creative and revelatory mechanism.[80] The *Gospel of Truth* rethinks authorship in a radical continuation of Genesis's creation narrative (אלוהים אמר); the text emphasized that language was a mechanism of creation. The *Gospel of Truth* personified divinity as a talking head, claiming, "Truth is in the mouth of the Father, the tongue is the Holy Spirit."[81] The Father, as the mouth of truth, possessed the physical abilities to "speak forth" the Son, who, described with the epithet "living book of the living," was dictated into physical existence. Throughout the text, several epithets were attached to the person of the Son—name, word, "living book of the living," or sometimes simply "book"—confounding the boundaries between Jesus, Word, Gospel, and physical books. Yet, not only the divine agents were animated through language; the text described the creation of an elite class of humans through the act of composition. The Father wrote the names of the elect into the living book of the living, an act that "caused them to exist" in the presence of the Father. Thus, the text presented the major actors of the cosmos literarily, each a crucial component in generating the divine book. Authorship was not a solitary process for the deity; he empowered other actors to assist in editing and publication.

The text developed its dynamic publication process in its renditions of the life and death of Jesus. The *Gospel of Truth* was not interested in a unique birth story, instead describing Jesus's appearance among humanity as "he entered the midst."[82] The text did not mention miracles he performed, nor did it describe the content of his teaching.[83] Its primary concern lay in recovering the knowledge of the Father, which error had obscured for humanity. The publication is taken to an extreme as Jesus appears among humanity to reveal this knowledge through his crucifixion. The *Gospel of Truth* described the crucifixion as "such a great teaching."[84]

It was such a great teaching, the *Gospel of Truth* described it twice.[85] Two passages referred to the crucifixion, in which Jesus was "nailed to wood" (ⲁⲩⲁϥⲧϥ̄ ⲁⲩϣⲉ). When read together, the passages showcased the dynamics of Valentinian revelation. In one of the crucifixion scenes, the "good news" was communicated orally in a mythic context, and in the second literarily, in historical time. Valentinus's dual crucifixion of the Logos forecasts Origen's dual incarnation of the Logos: the historical event of the Logos "putting on the flesh" of Christ, but also a universal, gradual incarnation, in which the Logos gradually descended from the unknowable Father.[86] As Karen Jo Torjesen has demonstrated, for Origen, the historical incarnation was attested by the Gospels and the universal incarnation was evinced by the writings of Moses and the prophets.[87] Similarly, for Valentinus, the incarnate Logos crucified also became a moment of text production. The *Gospel of Truth*'s representations of good news— revelation of the knowledge of the Father—presented a Valentinian theory of sacred text. The text collapsed the distinction between body and book, arguing that the authoritative good news comprised both oral and written formats and was accessible publicly as a book, but also within the hearts of the spiritually elect. The good news, in the logic of the *Gospel of Truth*, was a book, albeit one published in multiple formats and editions.

The first reference to the crucifixion described an oral publication of knowledge of the Father from the Son to the elect. The scene occurred early in the text and was couched in primeval language. The totality sought to gain knowledge of the Father, which had been obscured by the cosmic antagonist Error. The Son combated ignorance by revealing the Gospel. Because the Son thwarted Error, "Error became angry at him. She pursued him; she was distressed by him. She became idle."[88] Error was combated through crucifixion, the text remarked: "he was nailed to a tree."[89] The text used "tree" or "wood" (ϣⲉ)—not "cross" (ⲥⲧⲁⲩⲣⲟⲥ), as it also did in 18.24—drawing on the tradition of Deuteronomy 21:23, "cursed is one who hangs from a tree." Christian readers often used this phrase to designate the crucifixion.[90] Yet the text chose the verb "nail" rather than "hang," perhaps to be unambiguous about this scene being an act of crucifixion. The potential for confusion lay in Jesus's subsequent transformation into the "fruit of knowledge of the Father."[91] The text alluded to the Garden of Eden, claiming that unlike the Genesis 2:7 stipulations about eating from the tree of knowledge, Jesus "did not cause ruin because he was eaten."[92] In this case, the *Gospel of Truth* joined an interpretive tradition that argued eating from the tree in Eden did not have negative consequences for humanity because it declassified divine knowledge. From the text's perspective, a revelatory act occurred through eating a crucified Jesus-as-fruit: "the ones who ate him, he allowed them to exist. They inwardly rejoiced in the discovery. Now he found them within him and he they found within them."[93]

By joining the crucifixion to the Garden of Eden, the *Gospel of Truth* was able to explain how humankind came to possess knowledge of the Father before the incarnation. Philo had claimed that some patriarchs had followed the law before the events on Sinai.[94] The *Gospel of Truth* similarly explained how certain individuals received knowledge of the Father before the historical life of Jesus. The description of Jesus as "fruit of knowledge of the Father" reflected a Valentinian definition of Wisdom as acquaintance with the inaccessible deity. This interior Wisdom involved perceiving the divine within oneself and recognizing it in others—"Now he found them within him and he they found within them."[95] Wisdom, in this passage, as a private, inner knowledge, was imparted directly from teacher to student. The bizarre scene should be regarded as a "revelatory act,"[96] in which the identity of the Father was made known—on this passage, Kendrick Grobel remarked, "Jesus and the Gospel are one: it is nailed to a tree in his person."[97] Jesus, as the vehicle for that knowledge, functioned as Gospel, which was ingested and published within individuals.

In contrast, the knowledge revealed in the second passion scene took a public, written form. *Gospel of Truth* 20:10–30 described a second instance in which Jesus was "nailed to a tree" (ⲁⲩⲁϥⲧϥ̄ ⲁⲩϣⲉ). This passage moved the *Gospel of Truth* from its mystical meditation on creation to its focus on Jesus's ministry in Roman Judea in its characteristic "blending cosmic history into human history."[98] Jesus appeared as a teacher in classrooms, and instead of being antagonized by Error, "men who were wise in their own minds tested him, but he disturbed them because they were foolish."[99] The antithesis to these foolish ones was the "little children, who possess the knowledge of the Father."[100] Like the ones who consumed Jesus as fruit, the children found themselves in a mutually participatory relationship with the Son: "They knew, they were known; they were glorified; they glorified."[101] The book governed this relationship: the "living book of the living appears in their hearts," the book in which their own names had been inscribed.[102] This was Jesus's act of publication: the text claimed, "nothing could have appeared among the ones who believed in salvation, if that book had not come into the midst. . . . Because of this, he took up that book because he knows that his death is life for many."[103]

In the subsequent passage, the text expounded upon the phrase "Jesus took that book." The crucifixion completed the revelatory act. The Wisdom of the living book became available to everyone, and, significantly, was published in a book medium. Jesus, in this passion, became a living, self-publishing, speaking, physical book:

> Because of this, by his[104] agency Jesus appeared. He rolled himself up in that book and was nailed to a tree and published the edict of the Father on the cross. Oh! Such a great lesson! Gliding down to death, while eternal life clothes him. After he divested himself of perishable rags, he took on himself imperishability. It is that which is not possible for anyone to take from him. After setting out onto the empty paths of fear, he left the power of those who were naked by the power of forgetfulness. He was knowledge and completion, reading out the contents of the heart.[105]

He published the knowledge of the Father, this time not orally and secretly to a few, but publicly to the doubters and believers who witnessed the execution. This episode expanded the audience of the book, growing readership from the small group in the Garden of Eden to a larger assembly.

The text explicitly connects the crucifixion to publication through its representations of Jesus. Instead of wearing a crown of thorns, Jesus was nailed to the cross wearing a book: "He rolled himself up in that book and was nailed to a tree and published the edict of the Father on the cross" (ⲁϥϭⲁⲗⲉϥ ⲙ̄ⲡⲓϫⲱⲙⲉ ⲉⲧⲙ̄ⲙⲉⲩ ⲁⲩⲁϥⲧϥ̄ ⲁⲩϣⲉ ⲁϥⲧⲱϭⲉ ⲙ̄ⲡⲇⲓⲁⲧⲁⲅⲙⲁ ⲁⲃⲁⲗ ⲛ̄ⲧⲉ ⲡⲓⲱⲧ ϩⲓ ⲡⲉⲥⲧⲁⲩⲣⲟⲥ).[106] There are several ways of treating the Coptic ⲁϥϭⲁⲗⲉϥ, and each offers nuance to the crucifixion scene. One option is to amend the verb to ⲁϥϭⲁⲗⲡϥ ("he opened it").[107] However, the sentence makes sense without textual emendation. The verb can be read as a form of ϭⲱⲗ, a technical term that described the action of rolling or unrolling a scroll.[108] Coptic Isaiah 34:4, for example, used the same verb to describe heaven unrolled like a scroll. In this case, Jesus either "rolled" or "unrolled" the book and was nailed to a tree. If the Coptic is translated "he rolled that book closed," Jesus's body became a substitute for the book, as he died "reading out the contexts of his heart." If translated "he unrolled that book," one visualizes Jesus nailed to the cross, arms outstretched, holding open a scroll.

Yet, the surrounding context of the phrase suggests wearing the book, as the act of rolling the book is described as "putting on imperishability" (ⲁϥϯ ϩⲓ̈ⲱⲱϥ ⲛ̄ⲧⲙⲛ̄ⲧⲁⲧⲧⲉⲕⲟ).[109] I have translated the verb ⲁϥϭⲁⲗⲉϥ as a reflexive form of ϭⲱⲗ, "rolling himself in that book," to maintain consistency with the way the text elsewhere describes Jesus as "the living book." Another possibility would be to treat ⲁϥϭⲁⲗⲉϥ as a form of ϭⲱⲱⲗⲉ, "to clothe."[110] The verb is most commonly used to describe ways of dressing that involve "cloaking" or "wrapping." He "wrapped himself in that book and was nailed to a tree." This option yields a similar effect to rolling himself in the book, both imagining Jesus as a human-sized scroll—parchment or papyrus wrapped around the body of Jesus on the cross. Rolled in a book and nailed to wood, Jesus transformed into a scroll of knowledge of the Father, which he published through an oration of its contents.

The image of Jesus as a crucified book also reflected a common concern of ancient Mediterranean literary culture about the defectiveness of written texts. The *Gospel of Truth* described Jesus as "reading out the contents of the heart,"[111] and joined a long tradition of texts that promoted interior writing as a more precise form of communication. Plato had argued that the written word was inherently deficient, lacking the ability to explain itself. For Plato, the written word left understanding and, more often, misunderstanding to the reader.[112] Plato implied that the written word was inferior to a more comprehensible style of writing, oral communication of the "words written in the soul."

In a Jewish context too, interior writing signaled an authoritative form of communication, sometimes even more so than a written text. Philo had looked to biblical patriarchs as living laws. The Jewish teachers who become collectively known as "the rabbis" will promote an Oral Torah of equal status to the written one. Paul replaced what he perceived as the "dead" written law in favor of the living "law of the heart."[113] Colossians conveyed his idea of the dead, written law by nailing it to the cross: "Having wiped out the debt record by ordinance, which was against us, he removed it from the middle, nailing it to the cross. Stripping off the rulers and powers, he exposed them with open speech, vanquishing them with it."[114] The book stood for a debt record of every transgression of the law. Crucifixion expunged the debt record, rendering it obsolete and making way for a new law, expressed with democratic "open speech" rather than through the written word. For Paul, open speech, and the law of the heart, superseded the written version.

The *Gospel of Truth* took this argument in a different direction.[115] Colossians crucified the book to eradicate the law. In contrast, the *Gospel of Truth* crucified the book in order to publish it. Open speech did not defeat written mandate; instead, a public reading confirmed the contents of the book. The book became unrestricted knowledge as an edict on the cross. The text was able to circumvent Plato's original complaints about the written word—the book, a symbolic "thought and mind of the Father," did not leave its own consciousness behind when it adopted its written form. Instead, the contents of the book were insured through a public reading of the text. Plato's concerns about the original meaning of the text being lost also did not apply. The text itself was present to speak, "reading out the contents of his heart." There was no possibility that the text might be lost in transmission or translation; the text was perfectly self-replicating, inscribing itself on the hearts of an elect class of humans. The crucified book represented writing that had significance beyond its written content and historical context.[116] As a symbol, the crucified book could assert its revelatory capacity both visually and aurally, signaling meaning to the audience irrespective of its written content.

The *Gospel of Truth* also presumed a publication process that conformed to contemporary Roman publishing practices. Publishing a book in Imperial Rome was a more involved process than simply putting thoughts to paper (or dictating them to a scribe) and subsequently having slaves make copies. To publish (*publicare*) meant to let go of personal control over one's writing and make it public through a multistage review process involving both written drafts and oral performance. Most authors dictated their thoughts to a scribe then later read over the transcript. After correcting errors, the author would host a gathering of friends to hear the work and provide suggestions. The collaborative publication process helped authors produce a polished text.[117] The thorough vetting, culminating in a final *publicare*, fixed the text.[118] An author had properly "let go" of the composition once it was published. The published book then circulated beyond familiar people to anonymous audiences across the empire.[119] In the *Gospel of Truth*, Jesus the book undergoes a similar process as divine revelation unfolds. The dual publication process mimicked the practice of presenting the work to a small group of friends, then offering the text to a wide audience. The text was authored in the mind of the Father, then dictated as the son was "spoken forth." The Son, the book incarnate, revealed himself first to the elect in a private setting, then publicly on the cross. The book was "published" as it was received on the hearts of the truly wise, who could then distribute their own versions.

The text also drew upon familiar Roman modes of authoritative writing—edicts and wills—to assert this theory of text. Such documents held power not just vis-à-vis their contents but as ritual objects in a way that resembles the significance Christians and Jews began to attach to their sacred texts. They were commonly written on *tabulae*, wooden tablets coated in wax, and possessed unique capabilities and efficacy as objects. *Tabulae* were used in ceremonial contexts. In their earliest attested function, they were primarily used to communicate with gods.[120] In the Roman Empire, this practice then extended into the legal realm. *Tabulae* were used to display edicts publicly, and, in the private sector, used to compose a will (*testamentum*). These documents had final authority in any legal situation and were utilized to address this issue of proof. In such cases, the written documents superseded oral testimony.[121]

The *Gospel of Truth* described the crucified book as "an edict on the cross."[122] This act of taking up the book and being nailed to the cross mimicked the act of nailing up an official edict in the city center. As Karen King put it, "Jesus is . . . the divine Word of revelation, posted like a public notice on a wooden pole and read like the Book of Life."[123] For the author of the *Gospel of Truth*, Jesus on the cross was not simply similar to an edict; Jesus *was* an edict, nailed to the cross, and in Roman antiquity, edicts carried potent authority. As official proclamations, they were considered authoritative, even if illegible, and were considered to administer "an unseen reality . . . authoritatively changed by the act . . . not just undertaken for memory's sake."[124] Edicts also possessed potency beyond publicizing the laws written upon them. The authority of a law was enacted by the act of nailing up of the edict in public. Once an edict was posted, there were multiple ways to break the law. One might disobey the written decree, but one could also physically vandalize the edict. Consequently, a Roman edict was protected as an *Objet de loi*— if someone purposefully destroyed or defaced an edict after it was published, the offender was severely fined. Ancient legal scholars even debated whether a law was valid if the physical edict was destroyed.[125] They were not strictly written documents, nor were they composed only for reading purposes.

Jesus-as-edict in the *Gospel of Truth* conformed to these characteristics, as the text combined a display of Jesus crucified wrapped in a book with Jesus reading a book—the contents of his heart.

In a second reference to types of authoritative writing, the text compared the revelation through Jesus's crucifixion to a "will that is unopened, hiding what is owed of the belongings of the deceased head of house."[126] The Roman will carried a similar authority to an edict as a written document. Wills were considered infallible. Edward Champlin described the ancient will as a "vessel of truth, a document carefully weighed and written free of ordinary constraints . . . since it became public knowledge only when its author was past caring."[127] As the final instructions of a man, the will was a sacrosanct document. Both the image of Jesus crucified as an edict and the comparison of his body to an opened will would have resonated profoundly with the audience of the *Gospel of Truth*. Jesus, the "living book of the living," possessed the infallible, immutable characteristics attached to familiar forms of authoritative writing.

Together, the two passages in which Jesus was "nailed to wood" encoded a complex textuality. On one hand, they can be read sequentially as two crucifixions and two revelations: the contents of the book with cosmic origins were imparted once secretly to a small group in the Garden of Eden, then revealed a second time, this time publicly before a crowd of doubters and believers in Roman Judea. Such a reading makes room for an interpretation that conformed to standard Roman publishing practices. Through its presentation of books, the *Gospel of Truth* mirrored this multistaged process from the original act of composition, in which the deity authored a book, to the intimate scene in which believers ingested the fruit of revelation, to the publication on the cross, in which Jesus read aloud the contents of his heart.

Alternatively, one crucifixion, told twice, sheds some light on the Valentinian nature of revealed texts. In the first instance, revelation was silent, transmitted orally, and preserved internally on the hearts of individuals. In the second crucifixion scene, Jesus externalized the contents of his heart—the living book of the living, dying on the cross, a document reading itself aloud, simultaneously a Roman edict, with its attendant authority. The representations of book indicate that Valentinian revelation included the oral and the written, the author and text, not in opposition but complementary, and even essential to one another. The illusive and allusive language of the text does not permit purchase on any one reading. Yet, Jesus as a "living book" of the knowledge of the Father, and an example of a salvific publication process, provided a model for the text's audience to continue the revelation.

Circulating the Book

Once released to the public, literary creations were vulnerable not just to theft or mutilation, but also to the readers who could do damage of their own.[128] As Plato had observed, good books always manage to find the worst readers, those who would miss the original intent of the writing.[129] How could an author ensure her text would be understood correctly and remain unaltered? Authors often attached pleas, threats, or curses to their documents to discourage readers with editorial urges from making changes. At the end of the Book of Revelation, for example, John threatened any reader tempted to amend the text with plagues in an effort to discourage this common practice.[130] Martial, on the other hand, was so accustomed to his work being stolen, he wrote a poem about it: Martial taunted a book thief to steal his manuscript while it was still "without a cover" and publish it under his own name. "Go ahead, take it," he urged, "no one will know a thing."[131] The *Gospel of Truth* offered a different model, one that is fundamentally about people as texts, authorship as the creation of a new text/person, and publication as the new person/text becoming potentially a new author.

The *Gospel of Truth* drew on images of corporeal text to compare the Valentinian congregation to Jesus, the living book. Early in the text, the *Gospel of Truth* provided an extended meditation on those whose names were written in the living book of the living. The text described them as a congregation of human books: "each alone a fulfilled truth . . . writing like a book that is perfect."[132] These books were not documents. They were "not places of voice (vowels), nor writing cut off from sound (consonants) so that one reads and thinks of emptiness."[133] Instead, they were "texts of truth"[134] superseding any particular format, neither oral nor written. The elect were described as "writings written by the one whom the Father wrote for the aeons in order that through his writings the Father is known."[135] In this run-on phrasing characteristic of the *Gospel of Truth*, the text described the creation of an elite class of humanity as an act of writing performed by the Son. This composition mimicked the creation of the Son, who himself was written in the mind of the Father. Just as the Father authored the Son, the "living book of the living," the Son authored the true believers, the "living written in the book of the living."[136]

Other parallel structures between the Son and the elect abounded in the *Gospel of Truth*. In this text, Jesus was not only the savior of humanity but, since he himself had been separated from the Father and sought to return, also modeled the salvific process.[137] Those who shared qualities with the Son became recognizable to him. For example, when Jesus was consumed as the fruit of knowledge of the Father, the result was that Jesus "found himself within them, they found themselves within him."[138] Similarly, during Jesus's ministry, the "little children" received teaching, this time not by eating fruit, but by becoming students in the classroom of Grammaticus Jesus. As recipients of knowledge, they did as Jesus did: "they became knowledgeable, they taught others, they received glory, they gave glory,"[139] reproducing in their relationship to other students the same dynamic as between themselves and the Son. In the relationship between Father, Son, and humanity, the *Gospel of Truth* foremost depicted the replication of knowledge: Jesus disseminated the knowledge of the Father as a "living book of the living." As he "read out the contents of his heart,"[140] his interior book became inscribed on the hearts of those willing to listen. The text suggested a definition of Gospel that was almost Pauline—knowledge of God was communicated orally, and circulated through the hearts of its listeners.

At the same time, by referring to books and writing, the text also "textualized"[141] the oral Gospel. The text transformed a common ancient trope, "books of the heart," to locate knowledge of the divine within the heart.[142] In the *Gospel of Truth*'s account of Jesus's ministry, those who were "wise only in their own hearts"[143] were resistant to the teachings of Grammaticus Jesus. Other students were more receptive, and it is these, the text claimed, who already "possessed knowledge of the Father." Subsequently, the "living book of the living, that which was written in the thought and mind of the Father, revealed itself in their hearts."[144] Their innate knowledge of the Father made them eligible to publish the ultimate knowledge—the book inscribed on the heart.

In contrast, the text claimed that the ones not truly wise were unqualified to publish the book because their hearts were unprepared. The text thus ensured the accuracy of its contents by conflating book and body: at the time of authorship as the Father spoke forth the son, at the time of publication, when Jesus's body morphed into a book, and when the book was made accessible to humankind. Publication becomes procreation—the Father and Jesus as a model *par excellence*—for the reproduction and circulation of the divine book. The *Gospel of Truth* joins a long tradition of authors describing books as offspring. Clement of Alexandria, for instance, writing around the time Valentinus was beginning his own career, described the *Stromateis* as his "progeny of the soul," a living text birthed, raised, corrected, and left as a legacy.[145] But the Roman Empire was a dangerous place for children, especially when they left the protection of home.[146]

The Incorruptible Book

Authors fretted over releasing a literary progeny. Like orphans without parental supervision, they might wind up a pet (*deliciae*) of a household, a temple prostitute, or a slave.[147] Horace (65–8 B.C.E.) wrote a letter to his own book eager to be published and "go abroad," and described, in sexually suggestive language, what his book could expect if it were set out for sale.[148] If the book traveled to Rome, it would spend its youth "caressed" and "groped by the hands of the rabble" until worn out and left to be eaten by "feasting, lazy grubs." After a time, the book would be set aside, ignored. If the book was lucky, it might spend its old age "teaching boys the basics," in Utica, Ilerda, or some other remote Roman colony.[149]

Martial (c. 40–104 C.E.) imagined a similar fate for his own book as he looked at his final manuscript.[150] Unlike Horace, who imagined his work as innocent offspring finding itself in compromising situations, Martial's book-child could not wait to leave home and be corrupted. Martial described his book as properly "dressed"— pumiced, hammered, and decorated—garb that made a work seductive to readers. Martial asked, "Where, oh, where are you going, my book, garbed in Sidonian refinement?"[151] He predicted his books would find readers in reputable temple libraries, such as the shrines of Europa or Jason. However, these readers would probably open the book only to shake out its worms and only after gossiping about Scorpus and Incitatus, the champion charioteers of the day.[152] His books, plied with wine and greased with the fragrant oils of a famous perfume maker, would "play with boys, and to make love to girls."[153] Martial could be characteristically wry about the fate of his own writing.[154] However, books authored in the "thought and mind of the Father" should not be abused or forgotten.

The *Gospel of Truth*'s divine book was particularly at risk, published, dying on the cross. In the Roman literary world, it was precisely when an author passed away that a work became most vulnerable to corruption. The Roman Jurist Ulpian excluded unfinished books from an inheritance, breaking with legislative practice, which typically protected the claims of the heir and not the deceased. Galen of Pergamum (129–217 C.E.), Valentinus's contemporary in Rome, wrote a treatise titled *On My Own Books* to document his literary output. In this little essay, Galen listed all the texts he authored, explaining the reason he wrote them, naming his intended audience, and noting any subsequent editions. He was able to trace the origins of any corruptions, explaining how readers in other countries published his books under their names and "mutilated" his work, adding, changing, and excising as they wished.[155] Without fail, textual corruption occurred when Galen's unpublished works passed from deceased student to heir. At least three of his works were altered and misattributed at time of the owner's death.[156]

The *Gospel of Truth*'s Jesus and his deathbed bibliomorphosis guarded against such corruptions. Jesus-as-book represented an accurate copy of a heavenly book, and the audience as texts suggested that their reading of Jesus's teaching was the correct one. This extended metaphor of book-as-body provided a way for the author and readers to mediate between the original meaning and the comprehension of the audience. A written document could preserve the thoughts of the author only if it were understood correctly. In the commercial book industry, books as commodities were valued through the language of the body. Books vulnerable to misunderstanding were compared to bodies vulnerable to misuse.

On the other hand, an understanding reader insured the immortality of the author, able discern the original intent and "wear" the book well. The best readers were depicted as indistinguishable from the book; Martial found such a reader in one Pompeius Auctus, who knew Martial's works by heart, down to the letter. Subsequently, Martial declared Pompeius Auctus "was not a reader of my works but the book itself."[157] Pompeius Auctus's bibliomorphosis indicated that there were no contradictions between Martial's authorial intent and Pompeius's understanding. Such mastery of a particular work signified that one had subsumed the book into his being and had, quite literally, become the book. Similarly, Jesus's own bibliomorphosis expressed anxieties about the ability of humans to understand the written word and accurately transmit it, this time with the added complexity of divinely authored books. The *Gospel of Truth* acknowledged the common authorial concern about the way immortal books could be compromised and comprehended, and sidesteps the possibility of corruption by positing a model where the book is transferred from the mind of the deity onto the hearts of believers.

CHAPTER 2

The Valentinian Gospel as a Scriptural Practice

The appearance and death of Jesus as a book in the *Gospel of Truth* anticipated Origen's theology of the incarnation half a century later. Origen theorized that the Son manifested among humanity in a myriad of aspects, as evidenced by the myriad titles attached to him in the scriptures. He proposed that Jesus shape-shifted, adapting his form to assist individuals as they progressed spiritually. The spiritual Christian would see written text as the highest incarnation of Christ: "the Word made flesh was garbed in a fabric of passages joined with passages and sounds joined with sounds."[1] And, just as the Son could customize his appearance, so too "the gospel is set before each individual as it suits him," Origen explained to his pagan adversary Celsus.[2] On this Christology, Corine Milad observed, "Origen likens Christ's theophanic appearance to spiritual interpretation of scripture."[3] The more spiritually a Christian could read the Gospels, the more Christ appeared as a book.

Origen's ideas about the incarnation shaped the way he approached holy books: scriptures were not simply receptacles of information but texts to be deciphered. He proposed a threefold method of reading scripture that mapped onto his threefold progression of the soul: through reading and interpreting one could advance from the flesh to the soul to the spiritual.[4] Through increasingly allegorical reading, a reader could become filled with the Logos, and books mediated this transformation. For Origen, Karen Jo Torjesen notes, "the usefulness of the Gospels is to be found in the fact that they produce the presence and coming of the Logos in the souls of those who desire to receive him."[5] In an inversion of the incarnation, in which the Logos descended into flesh cloaked in scripture, through reading scripture, the reader transcended the flesh and ascended spiritually.

Origen's approach to scripture made room for multiple authoritative texts. Torjesen identified at work a "universal pedagogy of the Logos," an eternal mediator who gradually descended, guiding the hand of Moses as much as the body of Christ. Origen proposed that any writing that resembled the body of Jesus contained sparks of the Logos. For instance, a spiritually advanced reading of the transfiguration would understand that "the garments that Jesus put on are the sayings and letters of the Gospels. Now I think that the words of the Apostles that clarify matters concerning him are also the garments of Jesus."[6] Just as he advanced the idea that more books should be considered Gospel than bear that title, Origen argued for the spiritual authority of the "sayings in the Apostles" based on their likeness to the body of Jesus.

Like Origen, Valentinus represented Jesus as a book, signaling his own peculiar approach to scripture. But while Origen was driven by *interpretation* as a process of spiritual ascent, Valentinus endorsed the *production* of new texts by the spiritual elect. The *Gospel of Truth*'s two passion scenes, representing the publication of divine knowledge, provided a blueprint for what David Brakke has termed a "scriptural practice," a group's answer to the following questions: "What are the characteristics of the reader(s) around which a group gathers? To what kinds of written and oral texts does the reader appeal? What norms are invoked for reading? What forms of behavior and group adherence do the group's reading practice promote? What new authoritative texts does the group produce?"[7] As the *Gospel of Truth* proposed, new texts circulated portions of the divine book, as the Valentinian Christian community published their own books of the heart. Valentinian sources, some directly attributed to Valentinus, preserved in other Christian writings, developed this concept of "living scripture," in which certain Christians were eligible to publish new expressions of knowledge of the Father.

This chapter examines these sources. It demonstrates that the *Gospel of Truth*'s model of the divine book informed a coherent scriptural practice that drew on contemporary ideas of interior sacred textuality: from the very anatomy of a scroll, to the bodies of Isis priests, to the hearts of Valentinian Christians, the conflation of books and people made its way into daily life. Fragments of Valentinus's own writings, preserved in Clement's *Stromateis*, demonstrate how the *Gospel of Truth*'s "books of the heart" become equated with physical books. An eligible heart could receive the divine book, and, as a revelatory agent, produce a written version of itself. Taken together with the *Gospel of Truth*, the Valentinian sources transformed the symbol of the heart into a statement about human access to and dissemination of divine revelation.

The chapter then places the Valentinian concept of heart-as-composition in conversation with Philo and *4 Ezra*. Both of these authors also envisioned an interior revelatory system in idealized scriptural communities, communities that produced new revelatory texts. Finally, the chapter demonstrates that this theory of sacred writing can also be found in the writings of two Valentinian acolytes, Heracleon and Ptolemy. Heracleon's fragments, preserved in Origen's commentaries, detail the spiritual progression of an individual as a literary construction. Likewise, Ptolemy, in his *Letter to Flora*, argued that the imperfect texts of extant scriptural books made room for new revelatory compositions.

The Practice of Books as People

A range of authors, from the deity of the *Gospel of Truth*, who conceived his own son as a book, to Martial and Horace and their paternalistic poems to their own books, spoke to the way authors regarded their books as progeny. While such a metaphor certainly captures the level of investment an author has in her work, it also was not a big conceptual leap from common practice. At the most basic level, the terms for various parts of a book drew from anatomy. Romans named parts of scrolls for parts of the human body: in addition to the *membrana libris* (skin of the book), a book had a *frontis*, its face, which was polished with pumice, and decorative knobs attached at the end of scrolls, *umbilicis* (navel). In the Roman context, one could not speak or write about the physical book without participating in a metaphorical system of books as people.-

In a sacred context too, the language of books as people dictated how devotees used their holy books. The cult of Isis, for one, envisioned the bodies of its priests as sacred texts. Isis worship was tremendously popular during Valentinus's life. Lucian wrote *The Golden Ass*, which provides the one in-depth look at the ancient Isis mysteries, around the time Irenaeus composed *Against Heresies*. Plutarch had also written a treatise on Isis, and, in his analysis, the cult of Isis maintained a close association between body and book. Plutarch recalled the legend of Isis and Osiris, and how Typhon tore Osiris to pieces, which Isis collected and reassembled. Likewise, just as she had carefully put Osiris back together after he had been dismembered by Typhon, Isis routinely reassembled the sacred writings Typhon tore to pieces and gave them to her priests. These Isis priests, Plutarch explained, were called "bearers of the sacred vessels" and "wearers of the sacred robes" not because of their distinctive white garments, but because "these are they who carry in their soul, as though in a casket, the holy words of the Gods, devoid of all superstition and overelaboration."[8] In Plutarch's estimation, the bodies of the Isis priests were envisioned as caskets of sacred writings. The act of tearing up the sacred writings and piecing them back together translated the mythic-time narrative of Isis and Osiris into a ritual practice of Roman Isis worshippers, body and book interchangeably regarded as sacred vessels of the cult. In the Isiac ritual context, the scroll represented the body of Osiris, as the priests' bodies themselves bore the scrolls.

The cult of Isis claimed that the contents were "planted" directly from author to the "soul" of the priest, no written intermediary required. In the *Gospel of Truth*, Jesus the book is transcribed directly into the hearts of his audience. The heart should not be read simply as a rhetorical marker of interiority. It formed the core of Valentinian scriptural practice. Just as Jesus published the book of his heart through a public reading, the *Gospel of Truth* similarly instructed its audience to "Speak the from the heart" and "Speak the truth,"[9] and publish their own interior books. Mirroring the actions of the Son, who recited the first edition of the living book of the living on the cross, the elect were also urged to "speak" as living books. Anyone who possessed a book written on the heart had the authority to disseminate this knowledge of the Father—the contents of the Gospel, in written or oral form. The *Gospel of Truth*'s arguments about language as revelation encouraged the generation and publication of divine revelation by members of the congregation who possess books etched on their own hearts. Consequently, the text suggested its own form of *imitatio Christi*, not through the act of suffering martyrdom, but through the production of revelatory knowledge.

Would anyone "speaking from the heart" be considered an author of the knowledge of the Father? Another Valentinian text, credited in Clement's *Stromateis* to Valentinus himself, provides a perspective that limits authorship to a select circle of individuals (likely Valentinian Christians). This passage argued that adequate preparation of the heart was essential if one wanted to receive the knowledge of the Father. In what is now referred to as Valentinian fragment 2, Valentinus wrote:

> One is good, whose open speech is on account of the appearance of the Son. Now through him alone does the heart become clean, every evil spirit being expelled from the heart. For the many spirits dwelling in it prevent it from being cleansed, each of them bringing about their own agenda, often insulting with unspeakable wishes. . . . This is also the way of the heart. As long as it is not looked after, it is unclean and houses

> many demons. Now, when the singularly good Father examines it, it becomes holy and brightly illuminated and in this way, the one possessing such a heart will be blessed, because he will see God.[10]

This passage sits at the center of scholarly debates about determinism in Valentinian thought. On one hand, the ability to speak was a result of the appearance of Jesus, who purified demon-possessed hearts. On the other, only those hearts that the Father had chosen to guard and illuminate would become capable of encountering the deity face-to-face. Read together with the *Gospel of Truth*, this passage suggested that election was a self-selecting process: those "wise in their hearts alone" were unlikely to be receptive to the message. Yet the "little children" who already possessed some knowledge of the Father were eligible to receive "the teaching from the Father"[11] and have the living book of the living etched upon their own hearts,[12] or, in the words of the Valentinian fragment, those with illuminated hearts "will see God." Such a dynamic has suggested that this fragment demonstrated a theory of open revelation—Valentinus insisted revelation was available to every attentive heart.[13] Should one choose to heed the Son and his manifestation, his heart would become pure and receive knowledge of the Father.

This Is the People

The idea of a "book of the heart" might sound like an abstraction or literary embellishment, but it referred to physical manuscripts in a Valentinian context. Another fragment attributed to Valentinus and preserved in Clement's *Stromateis* associated the book of the heart with books—both philosophical writings and the writings of the church. This passage reads: "Many of the things written in public books are found in the writings of God's church. *For these common matters* are the words from the heart, the law that is written in the heart. This is the people of the beloved, the one who is loved and which loves him."[14] In part, this fragment reflected a popular solution for Jews and Christians looking to reconcile Greek Wisdom texts with their theological systems. Justin could read both Greek philosophy and scripture, because he saw the Logos scattered throughout the works of many authors. Josephus argued that Greek literature contained a deficient form of Wisdom, because Plato had studied the writings of Moses.[15] It was to be expected that an attentive Jewish or Christian reader would find glimmers of Wisdom imbedded in Greek philosophical texts. However, unlike Josephus, who argued the Wisdom of Plato was inferior to that of

Moses, Valentinus claimed that some of the contents of both the public books and the church books preserved the contents of a third category of book, an even more authoritative one—the "words from the heart, the law written on the heart," scattered among various public and church texts. Church texts and non-church texts, then, are placed on equal footing, all incomplete versions of a more authoritative law written on the heart. Not unlike Isiac priests, who bore the sacred texts in their bodies, Valentinian Christians possessed a dormant text of the heart, suppressed until Jesus could make known its contents.

The phrase "this is the people of the beloved" (οὗτος ἐστιν ὁ λαὸς ὁ τοῦ ἠγαπημένου) has presented interpretive challenges for the modern reader. Here, οὗτος does not seem to have a logical referent. Proposed scholarly solutions include amending λαὸς to λόγος, to read, "This is the word of the beloved," or suggesting that οὗτος refers forward either to the "one who is loved and loves him" or abstractly to the Valentinian spiritual church."[16] Because Clement provided no context for the quotation, it is also possible that there was a break in the quotation, and the meaning is unrecoverable.[17] The lack of context means that any attempts to make sense of this fragment are speculative. However, it is possible to resolve the textual problem without emendation, by assuming some consistency in Valentinian writings. In light of the way Valentinian sources routinely brought together flesh and book, there seems to be no reason not to accept the original and natural reading of this fragment. That is to say, "This is the people of the beloved" refers back to the elect as "laws of the heart." In this case, the gist of the fragment would read: "[the law written in the heart] is the people of the beloved, the one who is loved and which loves him." This interpretation of the fragment preserves the same blending of book and person as authoritative sources extant in the *Gospel of Truth*. The *Gospel of Truth* did not confine the Wisdom of the Father to flesh or book and visualized the Logos as both a man and a book. Fragment 6 also maintained the closeness of the book, the literary heart, and the author herself. Thus, the *Gospel of Truth*'s descriptions of humans as eminent texts, together with the Valentinian fragments, presented the generation of new literary works as an act that circulated portions of the divine book.

If this is an accurate interpretation of fragment 6, Valentinus was being less radical than he might sound. Philo made a similar rhetorical move in his interpretation of biblical verses that mention books known only by their titles.[18] The Pentateuch mentions a "Book of Generation of Heaven and Earth" and a "Book of Generations of Man," and Philo found himself explaining what Moses must have meant by these books.[19] Modern scholars have argued that these titles referred to actual documents that once existed separately and were subsumed into the Genesis text.[20] When Philo confronted these books, he indicated that they were not physical books. In his exegesis of Genesis 2:4, which mentioned "the Book of Generation of Heaven and Earth," Philo argued that this book was not really a book at all:

> '**This** is the book of the generation of heaven and earth, when they came into being.' **This** is the perfect logos creating according to the number seven. It is perceptible by the senses as the beginning of the creation of the mind arranged according to ideals and the intelligible arranged according to ideals, as much as it is possible to say so. And he [Moses] called the logos of God a little book, in which it happened that the formation of all other things is written and inscribed.[21]

Philo claimed that Moses was being metaphorical when he called the logos a "book." Playing on the polysemous meaning of logos, as divine active reason and also meaning simply "word," he implied that creation was similar to the process of composition. Both transferred intellectual ideas into sensible experiences. He used the word "συστάσεις" (to create or compose) to describe the logos, suggesting that the act of creation was an act of writing—The Book of Generation of Heaven and Earth was the logos "composing" the cosmos.

Philo made a similar argument concerning the "Book of Generation of Man" mentioned in Genesis 5:1. The Book of Generation of Man was not a physical book. Philo described, "being desirous to deliver an admirable panegyric on the hopeful man, the sacred historian tells us first, 'that he hoped in the father and creator of the universe,' and adds in a subsequent passage, 'This is the Book of the Generations of Men.'"[22] By men, Philo argued, Moses meant "men of hope," a virtue that described certain men who followed the law spontaneously. Philo imbued this Book of Generation of Man, like the Book of Generation of Heaven and Earth, with a metaphorical sense, signifying the offspring of these men: "Not inappropriately, but entirely correctly, he called it the Book of Generation of True Man because one of good hope is worthy of being written and remembered, not on pages to be ruined by bookworms, but in the one of immortal nature, in which excellent deeds are written and collected."[23] In this way, Philo redefined the Book of Generation of Man—the book itself signified the lineage of the patriarchs, not books but people who could not be ruined by bookworms.

Philo pointed to living examples of these such books. He directed the "nations" to look to the Jewish people for a living example of living laws because they "accept the words of law as divine oracles and, being taught this lesson from an early age, they bear a stamp of the ordinances on their souls."[24] Among the Jewish people, Philo described "some who are as icons of the archetype of scripture, modelled from the beautiful and good virtue of wise men."[25] He imagined a community of these embodied laws in the Therapeutae, whom he depicted in detail in his treatise *On the Contemplative Life*. The historicity of this movement is questionable—Philo envisioned the workings of an ideal philosophical community governed by Jewish law.[26] In Philo's understanding of the movement, this Egyptian ascetic group living on the shores of Lake Mareotis practiced a version of living scripture. In their desert monastery, the Therapeutae studied "the laws and divine oracles given through the prophets and hymns and all kinds of other things with which knowledge and piety are increased and perfected."[27] This practice translated into an extensive library: "Also they have writings of ancient men, who, being leaders of the sect, left behind many monuments of nature in allegorical form, which they treat as some sort of archetype, they mimic the manner of this similar sect, with the result that they do not just contemplate but create odes and hymns to God in all kinds of meters and melody, which they inscribe with the grandest rhythms."[28]

The Therapeutae possessed books unique to their community and composed additional texts as well. The group composed during their Sabbath celebrations, which Philo depicted as highly idealized symposia that replaced academic ego and opulent feasting with genuine intellectual inquiry and simple fare. During these dinner parties, "explanations of the sacred scriptures are delivered by mystic expressions in allegories, for the whole of the law appears to these men to resemble a living animal, and its express commandments seem to be the body and the invisible meaning concealed and lying beneath the plain words resembles the soul."[29] For the Therapeutae, scripture blended text and interpretation, the oral and the written, into what Philo could describe only as a living, breathing beast. Allegorical readings uncovered the "soul" of the text that no single document could contain, suggesting that scripture included not only the written text but also allegorical readings. Linking the soul to the allegorical, Philo implied that these interpretations were a better representative of scripture than scripture itself.

The evidence from Philo provides a fuller picture than the fragmentary Valentinian evidence of scriptural practices that included the bodies of righteous individuals, as well as their writings. This model invited the production of more manuscripts, more iterations of the "law of the heart." In this regard, it is interesting that Valentinus calls the interior book a "law of the heart"—and not, for instance, "gospel of the heart." Valentinus's student Ptolemy's *Letter to Flora* shows a Valentinian acolyte struggling to understand the relationship between the Torah and the "words of the Savior." Valentinus's fragment 6 can also be read as: "Many of the things written in public books are found in the writings of God's church. For these common matters are the words from the heart, the **Torah** that is written in the heart. **This** is the people of the beloved, the one who is loved and which loves him."[30] Philo is not a perfect predecessor of the Valentinian scriptural model. He likely imagined the Therapeutae producing writings that explicitly expounded on the text of Torah, as his own writings did, while the Valentinian evidence suggests that new writings were revelatory and original, not simply interpretive. Philo and Valentinus also differed in that Philo envisioned the entire body as a living law, whereas Valentinus placed emphasis on the heart as the textual locus. Nevertheless, the similarities reveal that Valentinian scriptural practice, no less than other Christian Gospels, could arise organically from Jewish scriptural models rather than as a distortion of what later became canonical scripture.

In Your Heart a Lamp of Understanding

The heart also emerges as a revelatory center—a revelatory center tethered to book production—in *4 Ezra*, a Jewish text roughly contemporary to Valentinus. Although *4 Ezra* was written by a Jewish author, the manuscript tradition indicates that it was transmitted primarily through Christian circles.[31] *4 Ezra* imagines the heart as a revelatory center to signal the restoration of the written Torah after the Babylonian exile, and also to promote the inclusion of additional books as revelation. *4 Ezra* itself is a retelling of the Ezra–Nehemiah, the biblical books that inspired a scholarly narrative where the books of the Hebrew Bible became canon. Biblical Ezra–Nehemiah recounted the gradual return of the Jewish elite from exile in Babylonia: the Jews began to rebuild Jerusalem and the temple that Nebuchadnezzar had destroyed fifty years earlier.[32] A century later, with the construction complete, the Second Temple provided a visible marker of renewed Jewish presence in Jerusalem. To mark the occasion, Ezra read aloud the entire Torah in the presence of the nation as a reaffirmation of the covenant with its deity. With this reading, the *Oxford Annotated Bible* claims, "Israel reconstitutes itself as the 'people of the book,' with scripture, specifically the first five books of the Bible . . . becoming authoritative for communal and personal life."[33] So goes the common account of how Jews became a people of the book.

While recent scholarship has effectively shown that the process was far more complicated and gradual, the author of *4 Ezra* pounced on the narrative of the rededication of Torah, turning one of many political events of Ezra–Nehemiah into the cornerstone of his new composition. Like Ezra, *4 Ezra* is set in the aftermath of the destruction of the first temple, although it was penned in the wake of the destruction of the second temple.[34] The text is organized as a series of seven apocalyptic visions of Ezra as a captive in Babylon. In these visions, Ezra wrestles with questions of theodicy through debates with the angel Uriel. The temple has been destroyed, the scrolls of the law burned, and Ezra wonders to what extent the deity could have such control over the world. In the seventh vision, Ezra hears God speak from a burning bush, commanding him to restore the Torah. Thusly anointed as the new Moses, Ezra is told by God to sequester himself with "many writing tablets" for forty days. The deity promises to "light in your heart the lamp of understanding"[35] that will enable him to write. Like Moses, Ezra too will make some writings public, and others will be "delivered in secret to the wise."[36] Ezra appointed five scribes to copy down his words. They produced ninety-four books—twenty-four books for everyone and an additional seventy only for elite readers.

The references to books in *4 Ezra* are often cited as a data point in discussions about canon formation, as the twenty-four books correspond to the number of books in the Hebrew Bible.[37] Hindy Najman has catalogued the various efforts made to link the seventy books to other textual corpora[38]—the seventy books have been theorized to be "the pseudepigrapha," perhaps the books of Enoch, as Tertullian suggested. However, there are good reasons to resist linking the number of books to specific texts. As Mroczek has demonstrated, these numbers are typological and are not necessarily indicative of contents.[39] Moreover, while *4 Ezra* exhibits knowledge of the contents of Jewish scripture, scripture itself is paraphrased rather than cited.[40] Hindy Najman observes that Torah has been "detextualized" in *4 Ezra*. In what she calls "Torah rebooted," although the physical text of the Torah has been destroyed, according to *4 Ezra*, it can always be retrieved.

Thus, *4 Ezra* envisions the Torah as the "Law of Life"—a text that is continually generated.[41] The esoteric revelation is reserved for "the wise among your people. For in them is the spring of understanding, the fountain of wisdom, and the river of knowledge."[42] While *4 Ezra* may not have been referring to specific texts, it seems to address practical concerns about book production. As Michael Stone observes, the goal of *4 Ezra* was to:

> explain in "naturalistic" terms how the revelation was recorded and also distinguish Ezra from Moses in spite of the similarities between them. Moreover, perhaps these elements gave a measure of verisimilitude to the story of Ezra. After all, the production of ninety-four books in forty days without scribes would have demanded a very great miracle. So this

> incident reads as if it were an answer to rationalist objections to the Sinai story. Admittedly, even in 4 Ezra, the writing had miraculous elements to it, but its basic mechanism was explained and comprehensible.[43]

4 Ezra, then, as a rough contemporary to the Valentinian sources, expounds on the practical mechanics of supernatural revelation. *4 Ezra* described his heart as illuminated by the deity, allowing him to produce ninety-four books in forty days. Valentinian fragment 2 promised that when a heart "becomes holy and brightly illuminated . . . , the one possessing such a heart will be blessed, because he will see god." *4 Ezra* and the Valentinian sources are clear that their contents are to be found in books: Valentinus's "law of the heart" could be found in public books and books of the church; *4 Ezra*'s revelation of the heart produced ninety-four books—twenty-four for everyone, and seventy for the wise.

Similarities between *4 Ezra* and the *Gospel of Truth* proper are also difficult to ignore. Both texts present the world engulfed in moral crisis: Ezra perceived that "the world lies in darkness, and its inhabitants are without light."[44] The revelatory environment of the *Gospel of Truth* is a world "engulfed in error." This state has caused humanity to forget the "knowledge of the Father." In *4 Ezra*, the Father's "law has been burned, and so no one knows the things which have been done or will be done by you."[45] These narrative backdrops set the stage for new revelation, which is a restoration of divine knowledge. The revelation in both texts is two-tiered. Ezra receives twenty-four "books for the worthy and unworthy," as well as seventy books only for the "wise." Similarly, the *Gospel of Truth* upholds a model of revelation where Jesus speaks plainly to the "ones in the middle," then reserves secret teachings for the elite members.

Both texts also designate the heart as the primary revelatory agent: the deity "lights in [Ezra's] heart the lamp of understanding," which allows him to speak for forty days and forty nights, while five men transcribed his words in letters they did not know. In the *Gospel of Truth*, Jesus "reads out the contents of his heart," which are subsequently inscribed on the hearts of spiritually elite individuals. Yet, although both texts place an emphasis on the act of revelation itself, the contents of the revelation are never specified. While *4 Ezra* mentioned the number of books, their contents are left vague. Similarly, in the *Gospel of Truth*, Jesus speaks on the cross, but his words are never recorded. The text will also insist that the elect are texts of truth, but these living texts are "texts without vowels or consonants." The *Gospel of Truth* even rejects texts with sounds as "vain empty thoughts." Thus, both *4 Ezra* and the *Gospel of Truth* see revelation, in the words of Najman, as "detextualized." *4 Ezra* knows traditions of the Torah, but never quotes text. Instead it summarizes. The *Gospel of Truth* also exhibits knowledge of biblical texts—Proverbs, letters of Paul—but it too paraphrases instead of quoting directly. This model of holy text, which Mroczek describes as a model where "not exegesis is the solution, but more revelation,"[46] offered a revelatory paradigm for readers of *4 Ezra* and the *Gospel of Truth* to follow.

The Evidence of Heracleon and Ptolemy

These ideas are also found in the writings of two others associated with the Valentinian school: Heracleon, known through the writings of Origen and Clement of Alexandria, and Ptolemy, as preserved by Epiphanius of Salamis. Both Heracleon and Ptolemy dwelt on the insufficiency of human language to convey divine revelation. Both offered hierarchies of the sacred built on human ability to articulate holy words. Heracleon and Ptolemy implied a theory of sacred text that supports the model presented in the *Gospel of Truth*—humans have an imperfect ability to represent the divine mind. In this logic, all human-authored books would be imperfect, but imperfection did not make books worthless. While these similarities have suggested to Christoph Markschies that Heracleon or Ptolemy, and not Valentinus, wrote the *Gospel of Truth*, they also may be indicative of continuity in Valentinian scriptural practice.[47]

Heracleon's works are now lost, but fragments of his thought were preserved in other Christian sources. According to Clement of Alexandria, Heracleon was the most distinguished in the school of Valentinus.[48] Origen was less enthusiastic about his reputation, describing Heracleon as a "familiar" of Valentinus.[49] While Clement carefully pointed out where he and Heracleon agreed and where they parted ways, Origen was overtly hostile to Heracleon's ideas, criticizing his poor research methodology and superficial inquiry.[50] Nevertheless, Origen was compelled to take him seriously enough to quote forty-eight sections of Heracleon's *Commentary on John* in his own commentary on the Fourth Gospel, thereby preserving the vast majority of fragments of Heracleon's writings that exist today.

According to Origen, Heracleon found scriptural support for the insufficiency of written scripture in the Gospel of John, claiming, "the Savior is the Logos, and that signified by John is the voice in the desert, and the whole prophetic order is an echo."[51] While the full meaning of this passage, without the context of Heracleon's original writing, remains obscure, Origen interpreted it to mean that Heracleon had demoted the status of written scripture. Origen argued, "if the prophetic voice is nothing other than an echo, how is it that when the Savior refers us to it, he says, 'Examine the scriptures, because you think you have eternal life in them.'"[52] If we take Origen at his word, for both Heracleon and him, written text (the books of the prophets) preserved the "prophetic voice." However, by designating the "prophetic order" an "echo," Heracleon implied scripture was a deficient version of the Logos, not unlike the sparks of the Logos Justin had identified in Greek philosophical works. For Heracleon, as Origen reported it, the books of the prophets were not a clear voice, but a distorted sound: the echo preserves the general contours of the original, but the sound heard is delayed, fragmented, and warped.

Like the *Gospel of Truth*, Heracleon identified the spiritual elect, the *pneumatikoi*, by their relationship to the Logos, and suggested that they too could function as revelatory bodies. To place the spiritual beings into a hierarchy, Heracleon organized them into a gradation of oral authority: on top, the word, the *Logos*. Next the *voices*, and then below, the *echoes*. With this in place, Heracleon described the path of spiritual promotion for humans, whereby those represented by voice might mutate into Logos: "the voice which is more related to the Logos became the Logos, also as a woman is changed into a man."[53] This path resembled other early Christian claims about spiritual transformation. The Gospel of Thomas also expressed spiritual advancement as "the female making herself male."[54] Though his purpose might be to place humans along a spiritual path, Heracleon in effect ranked bodies through verbal authority: "sounds can be changed into voice, and the voice, which is changed into speech . . . speech is in the position of a disciple, while sound passing into voice is that of a slave."[55] The placement of Logos above voice recalled the *Gospel of Truth*, in which the spiritual elite were neither "voices of sound or voices cut off from sounds, rather they are texts of truth."[56] In this fragment, Heracleon placed humans in a hierarchy of sound, with those at the top, the *pneumatikoi*, as "voices" verbally closer to the Logos than the spiritually inferior, who were merely sounds. In this model, like the *Gospel of Truth*, Heracleon, too, did not maintain a rigid distinction between text and orality, sometimes collapsing the two among holy bodies.

Ptolemy

A similar position was articulated by Ptolemy, another student of Valentinus. Ptolemy, according to Irenaeus, was a popular gnostic teacher whose school was described by Epiphanius "as a bud from that of Valentinus."[57] His *Letter to Flora* took up the question of the ability of written texts to represent divine revelation.[58] This neat little letter, dated approximately between 155–170 C.E. but preserved in

Epiphanius's fourth-century heresiography *Panarion*, endeavored to explain the status of the "law put down through Moses"[59] to a female acolyte named Flora. His letter sought to establish which portions of the Pentateuch were divinely revealed law and which parts were invented by humans. Ptolemy took for granted what Bill Schniedewind has termed the "textualization"[60] of divine law, referencing "that whole law that is contained in Moses' Pentateuch."[61] Yet, while he claimed the law contained in the Hebrew Bible was divine and complete, he also maintained that it was corrupt. However, it was not an anti-canonical letter that rejected Jewish law. Rather, it presented a perspective where books could be beneficial even when corrupt. In his schema, one portion of Jewish law was spoken by the demiurgical deity, other parts were necessary inventions of Moses, and still other sections were corruptions of elders. Ptolemy further divided the portion of law spoken by the demiurgical deity into three parts: the law "pure and uncomplicated by hands,"[62] law "mixed with injustice,"[63] and a spiritual law that required ritual commandments to be interpreted allegorically. In these divisions, Ptolemy's taxonomy of divine law exhibited similarities with Philo and other Hellenistic Jewish ideas about the law.[64] Removed from his problematic "gnostic" context, we can see Ptolemy engaging in a not uncommon practice—explaining the relationship between Torah and other books of divine wisdom.

In reading his *Letter to Flora*, one could even say that Ptolemy deliberately entered this conversation.[65] The letter opened by observing that "disagreeing opinions"[66] circulated about Jewish law and by acknowledging that the concept of law was a confusing topic that most had failed to understand properly. Ptolemy initially positioned himself between those who claimed the Pentateuch "was given by God and Father" and others who insisted that it was given by the "devil, maker of destruction."[67] For Ptolemy, the five books of Moses were imperfectly divine. Because Ptolemy explained that those who view the law as evil "attribute the creation of the material world to him, saying he is the Father and maker of everything,"[68] several scholars, Markschies and Campenhausen among them, have attributed Ptolemy's polemic as a direct response to Marcion.[69] Certainly the identification of an evil deity with an evil law represents the position of Marcion; however, Marcion was not the only Christian to posit malevolent origins of the Pentateuch.[70] Moreover, those identified at end of the spectrum, the ones who ascribed the law to God the Father, lack a clear referent in the *Letter*. It is possible, as Harnack suggested, that Ptolemy was referring to Jews,[71] or perhaps, as Gilles Quispel posited, a form of Ebionite Christianity, or, more broadly, to a solidifying Christian orthodoxy.[72] By nestling his own position between these polarities, Ptolemy placed himself at the center, and as the *centrist*, in a broad debate about the divinity of the law. For Ptolemy, the law, as represented in the Pentateuch, comprised a nebulous combination of the divine, spiritual, and corrupt. However, his conception of divine law and its inherent corruption did not diminish the status of the law. Rather, it presented a unique solution to the relationship between law, revelation, and sacred books.

Ptolemy structured his letter to invite the attentive reader to reflect on the definition of law and the extent of its divinity. The body of his letter was built around three systematic expositions on the definition of the law and its characteristics.[73] In the first (4.1–11), he argued that the law of God was divided into three: the law of God, Moses, and Elders. The words of God were discernable in the text of the Pentateuch as the direct speech of the deity. He also claimed that some of the law was legislated by Moses, and by this Ptolemy did not mean the content surrounding the direct speech of the deity that Moses composed for context.[74] According to Ptolemy, Moses added laws, such as laws of divorce and personal injury, based on the needs of a generation. The third category of Torah comprised "certain traditions of the elders." While in other circles "traditions of elders" came to designate rabbinic practices that were not contained in the Torah, Ptolemy viewed the "traditions of the elders that have been mixed with the law"[75] as malicious additions to the Pentateuch. For Ptolemy, the traditions of the elders were a corruption of the law of God, and, unlike the law of Moses, possessed no authority. In the second exposition (5.1–6.6), Ptolemy divided the law of God itself into three subcategories: law comprising the perfect, unadulterated law of God (as represented by the Decalogue) and the laws that had been corrupted by unspecified causes, which the Savior must fix. He created a third category of "spiritual law" consisting of the legislation that required interpretation. These included laws about ritual practices—laws of sacrifice, temple operations—that need to be read allegorically. In the third portion of the letter (7.1–7), Ptolemy abruptly changed the subject, moving away from a discussion of the law to a discussion of the divine agents at work in the world. These agents, like the law, were also three, and consisted of the supreme, unknowable Father, the demiurge, and the adversary.

This tidy, tripartite composition addressing tripartite concepts appears purposeful. Markschies has suggested that "topics of the theory of principles and the theory of legislation are closely connected and thus that the text is a perfect ring composition."[76] That is, Ptolemy divided the law into threes to match the division of the three divine agents, which in turn was represented by the "threeness" of his own literary composition. However, this leaves open a question: if

Ptolemy intended for his divisions of the law to correspond to divisions of divine agents, why did Ptolemy attribute the "pure law" (τὴν καθαρὰν νομοθεσίαν) of the law of God to the middle character—the demiurge—and not the "perfect God and Father" (ὑπο τοῦ τελείου θεοῦ καὶ πατρὸς)?

One answer to this question might be found in how he viewed the relationship between divine law and divine book. In Ptolemy's logic, the deity who authored the law, though a demiurge, was best characterized as "just," not evil as other sources on gnostic Christianity suggest.[77] Morally, his demiurge stood closer to the unknowable Father than to the "devil, the adversary." In fact, although Ptolemy demurred to fully explain the nature of the divine agents to Flora, he did indicate that the identity of this middle deity was to be equated with the Savior.[78] Thus, for Ptolemy, the Savior was both author and editor of divine law. To demonstrate how the Savior edited the law, Ptolemy directed Flora to the discrepancies between the divorce laws of Leviticus and the claims in Matthew 19:8 that prohibited a man from divorcing his wife. Ptolemy saw the contradiction between Matthew and Leviticus as evidence that the Levitical laws could not have been legislated by God. They had to have been the laws of Moses because he saw no contradictions in God's law.[79]

For Ptolemy's definition of divine law, the implications are two: First, Ptolemy insinuated that the law of God contained in the Pentateuch was incomplete. Second, by citing what the "Savior said" in the Gospel of Matthew, Ptolemy expanded the definition of the "law of God" to include content from Gospel books, even as he reduced the content of the law of God within the five books of Torah. His taxonomy of law in the *Letter of Flora* indicated that, for Ptolemy, the words of Jesus superseded the Pentateuch as a source of divine law. This, however, did not mean that he found the Pentateuch evil, or worthless, but simply imperfect.

Ptolemy presumed that the divine law was contained in the books of the Pentateuch. Yet, as he expanded the definition of law to include the "words of the Savior," he did not insist that these words be written down. Although Ptolemy made references to the content of the Gospels of Matthew and John, he never once used the term "Gospel" in either its textual nuance nor its general meaning of "good news." Instead, he cited Gospel traditions as oral sources, as did his contemporary Ignatius. For instance, when referencing the tradition in Matthew that revised Mosaic divorce laws, Ptolemy referred to the source as "the apostle says." Likewise, even when quoting a Gospel source verbatim, he cited the source as "the apostle says."[80] Perhaps anticipating Origen's broad definition of Gospel that included both the Gospels and Epistles, Ptolemy cited Paul as an authority in the same way he cited the Gospels—"the apostle says."[81] Likewise, Ptolemy cited content from the Gospels as oral traditions, even as he was probably reading the Gospels as books: when quoting any direct speech of Jesus, Ptolemy consistently cited the "words of the Savior" rather than the books containing these words.[82] By including the words of the Savior in the category *nomos*, Ptolemy indicated that he did not consider the law to be only a text. The law also comprised oral proclamations.

In effect, Ptolemy's theory included the words of the Savior as part of perfectly just divine law, which was imperfectly represented in writing. Consequently, the words of the Savior possessed the ability to improve the laws of the Pentateuch. However, Ptolemy also acknowledged the flaws of the words of the Savior. These words could only serve as a deficient "guide to the grasping of the truth"; they could not accurately duplicate truth.[83] This position on the value of the words of the Savior was congruent with Ptolemy's other ideas about divine law: both the Elders and Moses had corrupted the law of God as contained in the books of the Torah. This did not render the Pentateuch obsolete. Rather, these corruptions made room for additions and emendations through a new source of law—the words of the Savior. Similarly, the words of the Savior, while they could improve the Pentateuch, possessed their own deficiencies as Platonically flawed "grasping of the truth." Such shortcomings of the words of the Savior allowed for the accommodation of the scriptural practice promoted in the *Gospel of Truth*. Ptolemy's model of an imperfect law contained in imperfect writing provided license for the continued generation of other authoritative imperfect texts, namely Valentinian compositions.

In rejecting the perfectness of Jewish scripture, Ptolemy participated in contemporary Jewish and Christian speculation about its capacity to perfectly record divine law. Rebecca Scharbach Wollenberg has investigated rabbinic and Christian exegesis on Ezra's renewal of the Torah at the end of the Babylonian exile.[84] The Book of Ezra described the reception and rededication of the Torah, which had been destroyed in the Babylonian conquest. Later Jewish and Christian readers recognized that the renewal was not a perfect reconstruction of the original given to Moses. Yet this realization did not lead to a rejection of the Torah. Rather, as Wollenberg observed, rabbinic interpreters pointed to Ezra's Torah as evidence of the historical contingency of the law.[85] Christians interpreted Ezra as an example of "inspired textual reconstruction."[86] These interpretations supported their own respective compositional practices—Jewish readers saw validation of the rabbinic project to make the Mosaic law relevant to late antique Jews, and Christians found claims of supporting the inspired nature of new writings. Ptolemy, in detailing the historical context of the Torah, as well as its inspired parts, saw both.

Ptolemy's Law and Valentinian Scriptural Practice

When thinking about the relationship between divine law and Gospels, Ptolemy's ideas dovetailed with contemporary Christian thinking. As Ptolemy had referred to Gospel as the "words of the apostles," Justin Martyr had classified the Gospels as "memoirs of the apostles."[87] Both viewed Gospels as human accounts, and this matched their view of the Mosaic Torah. Ptolemy, like Justin Martyr, saw the Pentateuch as an aggregate of God's law and Moses's law. While for Justin, the author of the law was the supreme deity, not the demiurge, he agreed with Ptolemy that it was imperfect. Justin too expected the Logos, through the "words of the savoir," to amend laws of Moses that had expired. For some Christians, the imperfection of the Mosaic Torah made room for the creation of newer texts. But how could a second-century Christian have evaluated the authority of new revelation?

If previous authoritative (if imperfect) revelations contained the Logos, then "sparks of the Logos" could serve as marks of authority. Justin had seen such sparks of the Logos within works of Greek philosophy. Valentinian sources identified something analogous, a "spiritual seed," within human bodies.[88] In fact, their heresiographic opponents, adversaries of Ptolemy, identified the "spiritual seed" as a distinct trait of Valentinian Christianity. They satirized the theology of a "spiritual seed" as a chaotic form of revelation. Irenaeus strenuously objected to this revelatory "truth residing at one point in Valentinus, and then in Marcion, then in Cerinthus, then afterward in Basilides."[89] Tertullian satirized the fluid nature of their revelation, likening it to "a female prostitute who is accustomed to changing her garment daily . . . with that spiritual seed of theirs passing through each man in such a way."[90] The polemics of Irenaeus and Tertullian displayed remarkable awareness of their Valentinian opponent's revelatory epistemology. As they mocked the role of the spiritual seed in revelation, the heresiologists actively rejected the notion that humans could function as eminent texts.

When we consider the *Letter to Flora in situ*, preserved in the *Panarion*, Ptolemy's second-century theory of divine law collides with Epiphanius's fourth-century canon. Epiphanius's rebuttal of Ptolemy shows a confrontation between fourth-century orthodox ideas of holy books and the fluidity of Valentinian sacred text. As he studied the *Letter to Flora*, Epiphanius was vexed by Ptolemy's claim that the words of the Savior were to be considered law. He asked Ptolemy, "Your words charm but where are they? They appear nowhere in the Pentateuch, so you have expounded to your foolish fan Flora in vain."[91] In his complaints, Epiphanius sounded like one of the *Iudaios* Ignatius complained about who would not believe the Gospel unless they could find it in the "archives of the nation."[92] Epiphanius understood the term "law" in its textual sense. Law meant the five books of Moses and only the five books of Moses, and Epiphanius found no quotations of Jesus in these texts. Epiphanius wanted to present Ptolemy as an obscure example of deviant scriptural practice. We should not be convinced. Rather, his assumptions about Ptolemy reveal how much scriptural practices changed over two centuries.

PART II

Irenaeus, Epiphanius, and the Rabbis

CHAPTER 3

The *Gospel of Truth* According to the Christian Heresiographers

If individuals were eligible to receive unique revelatory messages, what if these messages disagree? Fragment 6 of Valentinus's writing suggested one solution. By grouping the shared content between books into a single category of "books of the heart," he implied that the conflicting content should be ignored. Christian heresiographers opposed this solution, finding disagreement among sources to be evidence of their falsity. Yet their objections indicate knowledge of the Valentinian theory of revelation: Irenaeus associated Valentinianism with the acceptance of diversity of doctrine.[1] Valentinians, he argued, not only deviated from the original, orthodox teachings of the primitive church, they also they disagreed among themselves. Such allegations have typically been attributed to a combination of the rhetoric of orthodoxy and the heresiographers' own ignorance of Valentinian Christianity. However, in light of the theory of text put forward in the *Gospel of Truth*, it appears that these polemics were a negative evaluation of a feature of the Christianity that the *Gospel of Truth* promoted—an open collection of continuously revealed Gospel.

This chapter examines these negative voices. It discusses how heresiologists from the second through the fourth centuries described the Valentinian sacred book. The heresiographers, despite their overt polemical aims, are useful for understanding the *Gospel of Truth* in its intellectual environment if they are read as a coherent community with common goals. The chapter proceeds to examine how Irenaeus and Tertullian imagined the heretical sacred book as they defined the orthodox scriptures. In the rhetoric of orthodoxy, the many books of the Valentinians deviated from the singular message of the church and its four-Gospel canon. Yet the complaints of Irenaeus and his successors indicate that they had some knowledge of Valentinus's spermatic book, which they claimed led to intellectual chaos. While one prominent marker of orthodoxy became the acceptance of a four-Gospel canon, ancient heresiographers also sought to define the sacred book through other characteristics. We find that, while Valentinus presumed no distinction between oral and written texts, Irenaeus sharply separated the written tradition from oral traditions of the church.

The chapter demonstrates that the differing orthodox and Valentinian scriptural practices that second-century heresiographers identified became two modes of canon in the fourth century. Epiphanius's *Panarion* offers us a glimpse of these second-century developments through fourth-century eyes. For Epiphanius, the history of heresy narrated the struggle over the nature of sacred book. Epiphanius relied on the distinction Irenaeus had made between orthodox and heretical holy books in order to construct his genealogy of heresy. He defined Valentinian heresy through a living, mutating canon that was passed around orally. The Jung Codex—one of two fourth-century manuscripts containing the *Gospel of Truth*—can be read as one of these living canons. The way the Jung Codex was organized, inviting readers to seek new revelatory material, indicates that the Valentinian counter-canon was not an invention of the heresiologists, but rather a viable scriptural practice that faded away as orthodoxy crystallized.

Heresiography as an Intellectual Tradition

While accounts of deviant Christian beliefs and behavior were popular in the second century, their antagonistic style of argument has left doubts about their historical validity. Epiphanius's *Panarion*, for one, as Andrew Jacobs notes, has been read as "a monument to his narrowness and intolerance."[2] Irenaeus, as a "theological innovator,"[3] has not been as easy to dismiss, but his vituperations are politely ignored in studies of theological development. From the early works of Adolf von Harnack and Walter Bauer, through more than sixty years of work on the Nag Hammadi codices, scholars have cast doubt on the value of the heresiographers for understanding Gnosticism. The difficulties surrounding the term Gnosticism are well known and do not need to be rehashed in detail here, except to note that Valentinianism and Gnosticism sometimes operate as separate heuristic categories in scholarship, and sometimes do not.[4] Michael Williams called for abandoning the category of Gnosticism altogether, as the term had become inseparable from its ancient polemical context. Currently, some scholars will only use the term in scare quotes;[5] others eschew it all together. Williams also extracted

Valentinus and his school from the Gnostic category—Valentinian Christianity became a unified tradition, separate from the "Gnostics." While Williams's work has certainly drawn attention to the fact that the theologies of the Nag Hammadi texts are diverse, it does not account for the fact that although his work is directed against the overthrow of "falsely so-called Gnosis," Irenaeus aimed his invective chiefly against Valentinus. It is clear that whatever Irenaeus meant by the term, he saw significant overlap between Gnosis and Valentinus. For this reason, some scholars refer to the tradition of Valentinus as "Valentinian Gnosticism."

The discrepancies between heresiological portrayals of Valentinians and the extant Valentinian also call into question the usefulness of heresiological sources. Irenaeus, Hippolytus, and Tertullian all provided detailed cosmologies they attribute to Valentinus that do not appear in his writings. These cosmologies resembled the *Apocryphon of John* and other Sethian texts far more than any Valentinian speculation. For instance, the *Gospel of Truth* 16:35 introduced the Son "who is in the thought and mind of the Father." In *Adversus Haeresis*, Irenaeus had presented the Valentinian concept of "thought" (Ennoia) and "mind" (Nous) of the Father as distinct cosmological hypostases.[6] However, in the *Gospel of Truth*, these terms were used as abstractions, describing attributes of the Father. This kind of theological "contradiction" between the Nag Hammadi and catholic writings has been the basis for arguing that the heresiologists are of limited value for understanding the *Gospel of Truth*.[7]

A second example, the *Gospel of Truth*'s claim that "the thing that is hidden is the Son,"[8] also raised suspicions about Irenaeus's accuracy. Irenaeus said that Valentinus claimed that the Father was comprehensible only *through* the Son.[9] Although it does seem that the *Gospel of Truth* later stressed the revelatory abilities of the Son, this line has presented some problems. How can the Son be the vehicle of revelation when he is hidden? Philip Tite has used the seeming contradiction of the comprehensible yet hidden Son to demonstrate that the Nag Hammadi text was not the same text Irenaeus referred to when he mentioned the Valentinian *Gospel of Truth*.[10] Kendrick Grobel called for textual corruption; this phrase must have a later addition, a parenthetical statement not attributed to Valentinus.[11] In light of such discrepancies, it can be a frustrating exercise to reconstruct a Valentinian systematic theology by data mining the heresiographers for details about Valentinianism or Gnosticism.

The overlap among the sources, signaling prolific borrowing from source to source, also diminished the historical integrity of the heresiologists. Heresiology developed as a coherent tradition largely because later authors recycled large amounts of material from their predecessors. Irenaeus's *Against Heresies* (c. 180) likely followed Justin Martyr's earlier lost heresiological treatise, and Tertullian (160–220) and Hippolytus (170–235) were heavily influenced by Irenaeus's widely circulating work. Tertullian's *Against the Valentinians* and large sections of Hippolytus's *Refutation of All Heresies* summarized many of his points. Almost two centuries after Irenaeus penned his polemic against Valentinus and his followers, Epiphanius lifted from this work for his own anti-Valentinian invective, rather than write his own account. Irenaeus's heresiological monograph circulated widely and was soon translated into Latin.[12] His work is better known through its Latin title *Adversus Haeresis*, or *Against Heresies*, because the original Greek is lost, only reconstructed through fragments quoted by later authors, such as Irenaeus's self-proclaimed intellectual heir,[13] Hippolytus of Rome. Hippolytus composed two heresiological works, *Refutation of All Heresies* and an earlier *Syntagma* against the Heresies noted by Eusebius, now lost. The *Refutation of All Heresies* began with polemics against Greek philosophy, worked its way through the mystery cults, then focused on detailed descriptions of thirty-three Gnostic heresies, including Valentinus. This work is dated after 222 C.E., as Hippolytus indicated that his enemy Pope Callistus had finally died.

His Latin writing counterpart, Quintus Septimius Florens Tertullianus (155–220) of Carthage, wrote prolifically after his conversion to Christianity in 193. He was a Roman citizen, the son of a high-ranking aide to the Proconsul of Carthage, and (possibly) educated as a lawyer and ordained as a priest. He composed his *De Praescriptione Haereticorum*, a legal treatise against all Christian heretics, applying the legal maneuver of *praescriptio* to extinguish any claims of ownership heretics made for Scripture. The content was freely borrowed from Hippolytus's and Zephyrinus's earlier treatises, and his *Against the Valentinians*, composed after his conversion to Montanism, depended entirely on Irenaeus.

Such dependency has suggested to some that these works are not accurate but are instead repackaging of earlier information for rhetorical purposes. For example, Adiel Schremer disregarded them because they contain "polemical rhetoric." This suggests that a serious reading of the Nag Hammadi material must come at the expense of the heresiologists.[14] Explaining why he did not utilize any of the heresiological sources, Schremer explained his focus on Valentinus's own writings by claiming, "these texts (NHL) were written by real people to real people within historical contexts and evidently with specific rhetorical goals in mind."[15]

However, the heresiologists were no less real and their historical contexts no less relevant. Irenaeus, Hippolytus, and Tertullian shared a common vision of the past and future of early Christianity. As Todd Berzon has observed, these authors struggled to make sense of the plurality they encountered in the Christian landscape. They all described a unified catholic church, which presented a consistent and singular teaching from its inception. They certainly would have disagreed among themselves about the content of the singular teaching, but they all agreed that the church taught only one doctrine. They further agreed that the unified catholic church was under attack. Their writings convey concerns about the constant threat of corruption; heresy required vigilance and preparation.

These rhetorical goals were not separate from their historical realities. In their lifetimes, Christianity *was* under attack of sorts, and each heresiologist confronted persecution and opposition. While these persecutions were not widespread, each author was personally involved. Irenaeus's own teacher Polycarp had been martyred. Irenaeus himself was arrested and knew other Christians who suffered martyrdom in his outpost Gaul as well as in Rome during the Aurelian persecutions. He owed his own position as bishop of Gaul to the martyrdom of his predecessor, Pothinus. Both Tertullian and Hippolytus would have been targets during persecutions against Christians under the Emperor Severus (c. 193–211) and Emperor Maximinus's hunting of the clergy (c. 235–238). Their anxieties are evident through their writings. Tertullian addressed his own congregation in Carthage about the virtues of martyrdom and issued an *Apologeticus* to the Roman Senate and an instruction manual on martyrdom, *De Corona,* in the face of persecutions. Maximinus exiled Hippolytus to Sardinia, where he died in the mines. The point is that, for these authors, the stakes of their arguments were high and not just debates on what Schremer describes as "mere theology"[16] or freewheeling polemics. Their agenda to delineate a singular belief from a pluralistic Christianity did not spring from a spontaneous urge to standardize and regulate. To draw on Rodney Stark's terms, their compositions reflected the level of commitment they were forced to make to be Christians in times of persecution.

Moreover, as Alain Le Boulluec has persuasively demonstrated, the heresiographers' orthodoxy was a discourse, not a doctrine. This point is underscored by the observation that Irenaeus, Hippolytus, and Tertullian all would be considered heretics by the standards of Constantine's Christian Empire. Hippolytus and Tertullian were even considered heretics in their own time. By the end of Hippolytus's life, he was one of the leading voices against the centralizing church leadership in Rome, headed by Callistus. Although there are legendary accounts of his martyrdom,[17] during his life and for two centuries after his death, Hippolytus remained out of favor with the central church in Rome. In part, this was a result of Hippolytus's own convictions. He was a heresy hunter and vigorously opposed to modalism, a popular view of the trinity as three aspects of a single God rather than three distinct beings within the godhead. This view of the trinity was so widespread that it was not immediately clear to Pope Zephyrinus that modalism *was* heresy, as later church councils declared, and so he permitted its teaching.[18] Hippolytus charged the future Pope Callistus, a deacon at the time, with bribing and manipulating Pope Zephyrinus into protecting and furthering the modalist cause. When Callistus took over for the martyred Zephyrinus, Hippolytus accused him of usurping the office and declared himself the antipope. Ironically, it was Hippolytus's trinitarianism that later prevailed as orthodox doctrine.

Hippolytus's vociferous dissent aside, it is not clear whether he was in a position of much influence at all. He had his own group of followers but noted bitterly that Callistus's school was "crowded."[19] Eusebius was not quite sure of his origins, noting he was a "bishop from somewhere."[20] Although praising his zealous writing style and factual reporting, Jerome did not know much about him either.[21] Hippolytus upheld stringent expectations for Christian behavior that included permanent excommunication for Christian *lapsi* who avoided martyrdom. Prudentius reported that Hippolytus had advocated such puritanical Novatianism, which excluded the *lapsi* from the church, but recanted before he died.[22] Pope Damasus's fourth-century inscription on the grave of Hippolytus indicated that he had been a Novatian until he died, but should still be regarded as a holy martyr.

Hippolytus was not the only heresiographer to be classified as a heretic before becoming a martyr. Although he wrote stridently against false beliefs, Tertullian also found himself at the receiving end of such polemics. A decade after Tertullian's conversion to Christianity, he became a follower of the Phrygian prophet Montanus. He was vocal about his own acceptance of Montanist teachings, which accepted new prophecy from individuals inspired by the Holy Spirit. In Carthage, he sat on a council that debated and authorized the authenticity of these new prophecies.[23] Even though excommunicated, he continued to write against Christian heretics, particularly Gnostics. The biographies of the heresiologists indicate that heresy lay in the eye of the beholder—even Irenaeus would have had to recant his claims that Jesus lived until the age of fifty![24]

Thus, against the backdrop of a diverse, primitive Christianity, the heresiographers' call to guard against heresy points to efforts to delineate, rather than protect, the catholic church. Their literary projects aimed to manage the diversity within early Christianity and, by ruling out variations of doctrine, reveal the content of orthodoxy. Their ambitions to define the boundaries of orthodox Christianity hinged upon amplifying small differences they perceived among the many varieties of Christianity. Their project, as Todd Berzon points out, grew out of a need to make sense of diverse Christian beliefs as they argued for the unity of the Christian tradition.[25] Their complaints about Valentinian instruction were part of these efforts. So how should we read them?

More charitably than we do now. As Andrew Jacobs pointed out, the heresiographers were influential in their own times, so we should try to understand the appeal of the writings. Todd Berzon has argued that, despite the polemics, their writings are better understood as ethnography, as a genuine effort to understand other people. In this logic, their writings should be read as a way to organize that knowledge. However, the ethnography model does not fully explain the invective toward the ethnographic subject that runs through these texts. If Irenaeus's *Against Heresies* is ethnography, it is in the evolutionary model of E. B. Taylor, rather than the cultural relativism of Margaret Mead. While Berzon's approach invites a sympathetic reading of these texts, taking the heresiologists seriously means taking their invective seriously too.

The polemical nature of their works tells us as much about the authors as the subjects. As put by Michael Bérubé, "What, in other words, actively makes sense to people whose beliefs you do not share?"[26] This question invites us to examine the heresiographers based on their own internal logic. What did they perceive as the difference between themselves and the Valentinians? David Brakke has observed that "heresy was indeed an invention, but it was not created by rhetoric alone. It was created also through practices such as excommunication, ritualized condemnation, and silencing of texts."[27] The subject of sacred texts provokes some of the strongest invective of the heresiographers. This was not just an effort to silence certain texts, but a sign of deep disagreement on how such texts operate.

Speaking Similarly, Intending Differently

In the history of research of the canon, Irenaeus is a compelling figure for scholars who wish to define canon as a self-consciously created collection, rather than one that emerged spontaneously and gradually. His Gospel defense is also invoked to pinpoint when the term Gospel became defined as a written text rather than oral proclamation—his Gospel defense is, as Matthew Larsen puts it, the first time the term appears in its "bookish" sense.[28] Yet his account also raises the question: was Irenaeus being innovative in his proposition, or was he following popular reading practices that favored four texts? As Henry Gamble observed, even if Irenaeus were following popular opinion, he certainly felt compelled to defend the idea of four Gospels vigorously enough to indicate there was opposition.[29] While Marcion is typically named the opponent, Valentinus and his gospel presented another source of contention, and Irenaeus's fourfold Gospel might be considered equally a response to it.

Irenaeus's heresiological project, when it came to Valentinus, was to make difference obvious where it was not apparent. Irenaeus wanted to make clear that Valentinus's Christianity was not orthodoxy. Yet the potential for confusion was evident. For instance, although Irenaeus mentioned that Valentinus claimed there "were more Gospels than there really are," they both adopted multiple Gospels, and also shared a theological vocabulary.[30] Consequently, when Irenaeus endeavored to distinguish between his orthodoxy and the wide range of heresies, he struggled to make sense of the naturally shared language.[31] We can almost sense an unease about the potential for confusion. Irenaeus warned that heretics "speak similarly to us, but intend differently."[32]

Irenaeus's diatribe about the number four remains the most famous example of this shared language. Irenaeus accused Valentinus of shoving whatever he could into the number four, noting, "if there are any such things laying in the scriptures to be thrust into the number four, [the heretics] say it is from their tetrad."[33] Yet just a few pages later, Irenaeus drew on the very same logic. Although faulting the heretics for applying numerological exegesis to sacred writings, he reverted to the same hermeneutical techniques to explain why the number of written Gospels "could be neither more nor less than four in number."[34] Based on the "four regions of the earth," the "four universal spirits," the "four-faced Cherubim," all "four-footed living creatures," and the "four covenants of the human race,"[35] Irenaeus deemed it "fair that the church have four pillars" of the fourfold Gospel.[36] He defended his fourfold Gospel based on patterns in nature that also attest to the number four. This is often regarded as a slipup on Irenaeus's part—he was being hypocritical at best, idiotic at worst, and embarrassing either way.[37]

And yet, what if Irenaeus were being clever? Irenaeus had identified this type of scriptural exegesis as Valentinian, yet fell back on the same methods, ironically to assert the orthodoxy of a fourfold Gospel.[38] Irenaeus attempted to differentiate between Valentinus and himself, arguing, "A principle does not come from numbers, but numbers from a principle."[39] Irenaeus argued that his own approach to numerological exegesis was fundamentally different: "[the Gospel's] words served both ancient things and, also, our times and therefore they should not connect [its words] to the number thirty, but connect them with argument or more accurately, with correct reason."[40] After all, Irenaeus explained, when listening to music, each note does not necessarily have meaning in itself, but has to be understood in the context of the entire composition.

Another instance of potential confusion between Irenaeus's and Valentinus's Christianity concerned the number of Gospels. When Irenaeus remarked that the Valentinians "possess more Gospels than there really are,"[41] it had not escaped his notice that others calling themselves Christian could make the same accusation against Irenaeus himself: Marcion had claimed there was only one written Gospel; Irenaeus was arguing for the primacy of four written Gospels.[42] Compared to Marcion, who emphasized absolute unity with a single written Gospel, Irenaeus's multivolume Gospel might seem almost Valentinian. Irenaeus solved his problem by turning his idea of a fourfold Gospel into the moderate position—not too few, not too many books. On one hand, Irenaeus claimed, "Marcion throws out the whole Gospel. Moreover, cutting himself off from the Gospel, he boasts that he possesses a part of the Gospel." On the other, "those who are from Valentinus, being completely without fear, produce their own compositions, boasting that they possess more Gospels than there really are."[43] Irenaeus's novel proposition of a fourfold Gospel, then, becomes the reasonable choice among a few second-century models of sacred text, rather than a singular reaction to Marcion's single Gospel.

In Irenaeus's estimation, the Valentinians, who "put forward their own compositions, and boast that they possess more Gospels than there really are, . . . have come to such boldness as to title the composition that they wrote not long ago the Gospel of Truth, even though it is in no way in harmony with the Gospel of the Apostles, so that their Gospel is utter blasphemy. For if what they have published is the Gospel of Truth . . . the one handed down from the Apostles is no longer the true gospel."[44]

Irenaeus played on the polysemy of the term "gospel" and the natural ambiguity of the phrase "gospel of truth" to distinguish his fourfold written one from the Valentinian version. He observed that those who claim there are more Gospels than four are claiming to possess "more than is of truth." The Valentinians "produce their own writings" (ἴδια συγγράμματα ἐκφεροντες), including their own writing the "'Gospel of Truth'" (ἀληθείας εὐαγγέλιον). The phrase "Gospel of Truth" is indeterminant. It might have referred to the Valentinian text under discussion. In lower case letters, the gospel of truth could simply mean a veritable proclamation. The Greek phrase could be translated in an adjectival sense—the "true gospel." Irenaeus viewed the Valentinian *Gospel of Truth* as a direct challenge to his "canon of truth" and "gospel of truth" comprising the four Gospels.[45] "For if what has been produced by them is the *Gospel of Truth* (Εἰ γὰρ τὸ ὑπ᾽ αὐτῶν ἐκφερόμενον ἀληθείας ἐστὶν εὐαγγέλιον), . . . that which has been handed down from the apostles cannot be the gospel of truth" (μηκέτι εἶναι τὸ ὑπὸ τῶν ἀποστόλων παραδεδομένον ἀληθείας ἐστὶν εὐαγγέλιον).[46] For Irenaeus the "Gospel of *Truth*" subverts the authority of the "Gospel of the *Apostles*" (and not the Gospel of Matthew, Mark, Luke, and John). And Irenaeus is correct: the *Gospel of Truth* did not embrace apostolic succession.

In addition to the book the "Gospel of Truth," Irenaeus perceived a more general similarity with the Valentinian theory of sacred text. A moment recorded within his four Gospels suggests that the Valentinian mandate to generate new compositions had apostolic precedent. The events of the Pentecost, as described in Acts, indicated that the spirit could descend on individuals and give them license to deliver new revelations. The story of the apostles speaking different things in different languages challenged the notion of a unified "canon of truth" consisting of a single apostolic message and a fourfold Gospel. Irenaeus circumvented this potential point of contact with Valentinus's school by explaining that the Pentecost simply could not have taken place had Valentinus been around to corrupt the Gospel message. According to Irenaeus, Valentinians were claiming that the apostles were not told everything, and began to preach before they possessed "perfect knowledge."[47] Irenaeus cited the Pentecost, when the spirit descended and "filled each one of them with perfect knowledge" to go out and preach to the ends of the earth. Irenaeus paired this event with the composition of the four Gospels to demonstrate that between the spirit and the books, the apostles did indeed have "perfect knowledge." The Pentecost created a distinction between his singular message and what he perceived as Valentinus's promotion of plural preaching—Irenaeus argued that the disciples all spoke the same message in different languages, in contrast to the Valentinians, who all preached different things in familiar language. Irenaeus's choice is telling—the Pentecost suggested that individuals could receive and deliver new revelations. For Irenaeus, there existed a potential comparison between the spirit descending upon the apostles at Pentecost and Valentinian scriptural practices—which suggests that Irenaeus well understood the Valentinian theory of open revelation that included individuals and texts.

Irenaeus also found similarities in the metaphorical language used to describe holy texts. Irenaeus and Valentinus both described a garden of sacred writing. In the *Gospel of Truth*, Valentinus had envisioned the tree of knowledge of good and evil as a kind of scripture. The text described Jesus as the fruit of this tree, and, when ingested, he operated as a conduit for divine knowledge transfer. Those who consumed the fruit then became eligible to publish the contents of their own hearts as books. The presentation of revelatory text in the *Gospel of Truth* allowed for a dual Gospel, at once both oral and written, which originated from the fruit of the tree of knowledge.[48] In a second section of the *Gospel of Truth*, Valentinus offered a description of paradise that extended his allegory of scripture as fruit: "He knows his plantings because he himself planted them in his paradise. His paradise is his place of rest. It is perfect in the thought of the Father, and they are the plants of his thought. Each one of his sayings is the work of his desire, and revelation of his speech."[49]

In the logic of this passage, paradise represented the mind of the Father, and the trees tangible articulations of his thought. But the passage also personified these trees. It described them as acquaintances of the Father, and thus connected them to the Valentinian congregation. These trees, thoughts of the Father, became manifest through speech. Thus, scriptures, for Valentinians, were verbal expressions of the trees in paradise, and the specialized knowledge of the Father came from a special tree in paradise, the tree of knowledge of good and evil.

In Book Five of *Against Heresies*, Irenaeus proposed a similar agronomical model of scripture. He warned his readers to avoid heretical doctrines and to find "nourishment" in the fruit of true scripture. Irenaeus envisioned the church as a garden, with the writings of the church as its vegetation. The same commandment given to Adam and Eve applied to holy writings—"For the Church has been planted as a paradise in this world; therefore says the Spirit of God, 'From every tree of the garden you may freely eat,' that is, eat you may from every scripture of the Lord; but you shall not eat with an hyper-inquisitive mind, not touch any heretical sedition."[50] Irenaeus's interpretation of Genesis 2:16 is a direct, and perhaps deliberate, inversion of the model proposed in the *Gospel of Truth*. Valentinian wisdom originated with a bite of fruit from the tree of knowledge of good and evil. Valentinus and Irenaeus agreed upon that. However, unlike Valentinus, Irenaeus was not promoting this scriptural fruit, but emphasized its ruinous capabilities. He compared all heretical writings to the fruit of the tree of knowledge of good and evil, suggesting their singular destructive character. The trees of paradise represented all the scriptural texts ratified as "of the Lord," whereas the tree of knowledge of good and evil represented heretical scripture. As the *Gospel of Truth* had proposed that the fruit of this tree was a form of true scripture, it appears that Irenaeus was directly rejecting that claim. This does not mean that Irenaeus had read the *Gospel of Truth*, or was familiar with its specific contents. How could it? The image of sacred text as fruitful plants is found elsewhere, from *Ben Sira* 24, which imagined Torah as a fecund, overabundant garden, to Origen, who compared scripture to a seed that multiplies.[51] Valentinus was not speaking an exotic, gnostic language when he described scripture as a fruit and imagined the plants of paradise as the verbal expression of the Father's thought. Both Irenaeus and Valentinus drew on this widespread image. However, Irenaeus's use of this common metaphor appears to be a direct inversion of the *Gospel of Truth*'s model, suggesting that Irenaeus possessed general knowledge of the Valentinian allegory and used it to define the orthodox position on scripture.

Irenaeus exhibited further knowledge of Valentinian scripture, observing that Valentinus's doctrine had been "scattered" (διέσπαρται) among many sources: "the heretics . . . blind to the truth . . . walk in various roads; and the footsteps of their doctrine are scattered here and there without agreement or connection."[52] Irenaeus perhaps alluded to Valentinus's interpretation of the Logos inscribed on the hearts of many.[53] For Valentinus, the Logos explained how a variety of human writings could all express divine truths. Valentinian fragment 6 argued that overlap between books both "public" and "writings of the church" contained fragments of the book of the heart. This fragment indicates that Valentinus would have been a prolific reader of all types of books. Irenaeus spun this concept differently; for him Valentinian theology was scattered so fragmentally among his followers that it made no sense at all. This negative judgement of scattered, contradictory texts resembled Josephus's complaint about Greek writers who provide "conflicting accounts of the same things."[54] Yet, despite Josephus's objections, from the perspective of Greek tradition, to provide multiple, contradictory accounts of an event was to follow Herodotus's method of historical inquiry. Similarly, while Irenaeus viewed variety as weakness and evidence that these books "without connection or agreement" were heretical, he did provide a description, albeit a pejorative one, of a viable textual practice.

In a third example of "speaking similarly but intending differently," Irenaeus and Valentinus both used the phrase "book of the heart" to signify their separate theories of sacred text.[55] Valentinus used the phrase to describe a category of sacred book that superseded any human publication. Valentinian fragment 6 referred to "books of the heart" that included the "shared matter" between public and ecclesiastical books. The *Gospel of Truth* described individuals who could publish the texts of their heart, just as Jesus had done on the cross. For Valentinus, then, books of the heart included both humans with interior texts, and physical books. He was not compelled to limit revelatory material to books, let alone a fixed set of books. Irenaeus, on the other hand, did not use the phrase "book of the heart" to refer to written texts. A heart recorded the "ancient tradition" (τὴν ἀρχαίαν παράδοσιν), the preaching of the apostles *without* the need for the written documents.[56]

Irenaeus described the book of the heart's relationship to the written text by posing the question: what if the Gospels had never been written down? How would one know what Jesus said and did, and, more importantly, how would one know how a good Christian should believe and behave? As a case study, Irenaeus pointed to illiterate barbarian Christians, who

> having come to believe in Christ without papyrus and pigment, they have salvation written on their hearts through the spirit, and, carefully guarding the ancient tradition, believe in one god. . . . If ever someone should preach to them the inventions of the heretics, associating with them in their own dialect, they would instantly plug their ears, and run far away, not enduring even to listen to the blasphemous homily. In this way, through the ancient tradition of the apostles, they do not accept in their mind any of their marvelous tales. For neither community nor instruction has been established among them.[57]

For Irenaeus, then, the contents of the book of the heart provided authoritative information in the absence of written sources. Illiterate barbarians were able to discern true belief from false belief even without being able to read the Gospels, because they had the contents of the Gospel written in their hearts. The book of the heart could confirm correctness in the absence of a physical text.

The book of the heart could also confirm correctness in the absence of a physical person. In a letter to an old friend, Florinus, preserved in Eusebius's *Historia Ecclesia*, Irenaeus scolded his correspondent for his interest in the "error of Valentinus."[58] Florinus and Irenaeus had met in Smyrna when Irenaeus was a child and Florinus resided in the royal court trying to impress their teacher Polycarp. Using his closeness with Polycarp to his advantage, Irenaeus explained to Florinus that their old teacher would be horrified to hear the doctrine Florinus was espousing. Irenaeus declared himself an apostolic-like authority on the teachings of Polycarp, adding that he had recorded Polycarp's lessons "not on paper, but in my heart, and always through the grace of God genuinely I reflect on them."[59] Like his barbarian friends who possessed an innate sense of the Gospels as books of their heart, Irenaeus became a written repository of Polycarp's teaching—not just the things Polycarp said, but "the way he carried himself, and his character." Carrying the teaching of Polycarp in his heart gave Irenaeus interpretive authority to speak for Polycarp in the absence of Polycarp himself. One might even speculate that Irenaeus used the phrase "book of the heart" deliberately here, and not just for metaphorical flourish. Irenaeus had expressed concern that Florinus was keeping company with Valentinians. What if Florinus was going around spouting off the contents of his own heart as a Valentinian? The historical record did not record Florinus's position in his own words. However, Irenaeus's critique almost sounds like a rebuttal of such a claim, and in the context of Irenaeus's other polemics against the Valentinians, it is tempting to regard it as such.

From this comparison, two different interpretations of the book of the heart emerged in second-century Christian circles. For Irenaeus, the books etched on the hearts of illiterate barbarians contained the gist of the four Gospels and confirmed the inerrancy of these written sources. In the absence of the written Gospels, illiterate barbarians were still able to discern correct doctrine from heresy, thereby ratifying the four Gospels. In the absence of Polycarp, Irenaeus knew what behavior his teacher would and would not approve. The category "Books of the Heart" permitted Irenaeus to limit himself to a fixed number of authoritative texts, because books of the heart could always interpret existing books. Irenaeus equated the book of the heart with the concept of paradosis—traditions passed down from apostolic times. The concept of paradosis allowed Irenaeus to restrict the source of "good news" to text, while giving authority to rituals and Christian behavior that were not specifically outlined in the written text.

The book etched on the heart of each Valentinian, on the other hand, refuted the concept of a fixed set of revelatory texts, and explained conflicting matter between sources. He collapsed both written and oral book into his Gospel. His book of the heart subsumed public books and books of the church, and also designated the amorphous teaching delivered to the elect, first in the Garden of Eden and then from the cross. In the *Stromateis* fragment, Valentinus had made clear that the contents of the "book of the heart" were to be found in physical, published books of all philosophical orientations.[60] Thus, for Irenaeus, the openness of the Gospel canon and the nature of sacred texts were at stake. Valentinus was no straw man in his heresiography. Their shared language and mythical history allowed Irenaeus to engage in this conflict, and identifies for us the points of disagreement.

Tertullian, New Prophets, and New Revelation

Valentinians were not the only Christians who claimed access to current, living knowledge. The New Prophets movement arose in Phrygia roughly contemporary to Valentinus. The New Prophets moved west quickly, perhaps even coinciding with Valentinus's career in Rome. The New Prophets, originating with Montanus and his prophetesses Maximillia and Priscilla, claimed to be recipients of direct divine revelation that could clarify issues left ambiguous by scriptures.[61] Like the term "Valentinian," these "Montanists" probably did not call themselves such.[62] It is possible that they referred to themselves as "New Prophets," aligning themselves with the emerging "New Testament" tradition. Equally possible is that "New" was a derogatory designation (implying fabrication), and the early followers of Montanus simply referred to themselves as "the Prophets." It is clear that the New Prophets did not view themselves as heretics. In fact, Tertullian stressed that they agreed with the church in all things except for the validity of second marriages, and they accepted the continued emergence of prophecy.[63] Christians contemporary to the first New Prophets also did not seem to have much of a problem with them: the earliest written polemics against the movement were not strident enough for Eusebius's taste.[64] Although he knew of the treatise Apollinarius wrote against the Montanists, he cited later, more vituperative sources in his own account.[65] As Turid Karlsen Seim has observed, the disagreement emerging between the New Prophets and nascent orthodoxy was not doctrinal, but rather revolved around the extent to which divine prophetic gifts were still accessible in the second century.[66] According to Montanus, revelation was open, new prophets were to be found among the congregation, and it was possible to generate new authoritative material. These prophecies were written down and purposefully ordered, as Hippolytus mentioned the New Prophets had many books that had subsequently been destroyed.[67] The New Prophets, then, in arguing for the legitimacy of their mantic revelations, also claimed authority for their written versions.

Consequently, the Montanist heresiographer Tertullian can offer a unique perspective on the problem of textual proliferation within early Christianity. Laura Nasrallah teaches us to consider Tertullian's defenses of new prophecy as reactions to ecclesiastical crackdowns on such activities.[68] In his later writings, Tertullian's priorities shifted to explain the role of new prophecy in the face of Church disapproval. As Tertullian had been an active heresiographer before the New Prophets faced scrutiny, he must have been self-conscious about becoming the target of similar polemics. Tertullian had to create difference between the diversity he had condemned in the Valentinians and the diversity he embraced as a Montanist. As Tertullian reportedly headed a council in Carthage devoted to determining the veracity of new prophecies, what was the difference between what he described as the "endless essays" of the Valentinians and the revelations of the Montanists, which were written down and purposefully arranged?[69] Before Tertullian's Montanist leanings became problematic, he defined heresy through dogmatic features. In his *Prescription Against All Heresies*, "heretical" was a cohesive category. That is, for Tertullian's purposes, there was no difference between the teachings of Marcion and Valentinus. He grouped them together, often referring to what the "Marcionites and Valentinians" believed. One of the chief concerns for Tertullian was heretical use of scripture. Heretics "preached a spurious Gospel."

Significantly, Tertullian classified his treatise against heretics as *praescriptio*. In Roman legal procedure, a *praescriptio* allowed a defendant to limit the scope of the case before arguments began. It was a "juridical objection with which the defendant wishes to bar the suit in the form in which the plaintiff enters it."[70] Tertullian, who oddly viewed himself and the catholic church as the defense in his polemical treatise, invoked *praescriptio* to bar heretics from using the scriptures.[71] However, it also suggested that he viewed heretical readings of scriptures as physical threats to the integrity of scriptures themselves, not only, as David Rankin has argued, that "some more 'certain' process of interpretation was desirable."[72] Thus Tertullian escalated Irenaeus's defense of a fourfold Gospel laid out in *Adv. haer.* 3.11.9 against Marcion and Valentinus:

> One man perverts the Scriptures with his hand, another their meaning by his exposition. For although Valentinus seems to use the entire volume, he has none the less laid violent hands on the truth only with a more cunning mind and skill than Marcion. Marcion expressly and openly used the knife, not the pen, since he made such an excision of the Scriptures as suited his own subject-matter. Valentinus, however, abstained from such excision, because he did not invent Scriptures to square with his own subject-matter, but adapted his matter to the Scriptures; and yet he took away more, and added more, by removing the proper meaning of every particular word, and adding fantastic arrangements of things which have no real existence.[73]

Like Irenaeus, Tertullian argued that the proper number of Gospels lay between the extremes of Marcion and Valentinus. Irenaeus maintained that the "Valentinians bring their own compositions." Tertullian interpreted Valentinian additional texts as "laying violent hands" on the scriptures. For Irenaeus, Marcion "uses the knife" eliminating texts, and by doing so cuts himself off from scripture. Tertullian, on the other hand, stressed the physical cutting element of Marcion's knife, an act of violence done to the text through "excision." In light of these changes, Tertullian's invocation of *Praescriptio* makes sense. In his logic, heresy was an act of physical violence done to scripture; consequently, heretics should not be allowed to use it.

In his defense of a fourfold Gospel, Tertullian invoked the perfect overlap between body and book. If Valentinus and the *Gospel of Truth* compared the body and book to emphasize the diversity of scripture, Tertullian claimed perfect unity in scripture was the same as perfect unity of the church. Tertullian suggested that perfect scripture reflected the perfect self—"The fact that what we ourselves are also the scriptures are and have been from the beginning. From them, we are, before there was any other way than we are, before they were interpolated by you."[74] Tertullian asked rhetorically, "for indeed what is contrary to us in our [scriptures]?"[75] He argued that the teachings of the church perfectly aligned with scripture—"What particular to us have we brought in so that, detecting something contrary and in scripture, we must fix it by detraction, addition or alteration?"[76] An internally consistent collection of scripture was a sign of its correctness, but also a sign of an individual and a church's orthodoxy. Holy writing in its primordial state embodied the primordial church and perfect Christian. For Tertullian, scripture was singular, like the unified catholic church.

This position allowed Tertullian to avoid any debate about interpretation of scriptures. Indeed, in the treatise he avoided discussion of biblical texts and focused on differences of doctrine. One of the features he identified as distinctively Valentinian was the practice of seeking, which recalls the seek/find schematic that opened the *Gospel of Truth*. The entire premise of the Gospel is that knowledge of the Father has been lost, and humankind needs to seek it out. In Tertullian's logic, such seeking disqualified them from identifying as Christian: "For since they are still seekers, they have no fixed tenets yet; and being not fixed in tenet, they have not yet believed; and being not yet believers, they are not Christians," he claimed.[77]

A second difference Tertullian identified was the heretical disregard of apostolic authority. Instead, Tertullian observed, they claimed either that the apostles were not told everything or that they were told everything but did not get the message out to all persons.[78] "During the interval the Gospel was wrongly preached; men wrongly believed; so many thousands were wrongly baptized; so many works of faith were wrongly wrought; so many miraculous gifts, so many spiritual endowments were wrongly set in operation; so many priestly functions, so many ministries, were wrongly executed; and, to sum up the whole, so many martyrs wrongly received their crowns!"[79] Instead, "truth awaited some Marcionites and Valentinians to liberate it."[80] Tertullian tethered the heretical dismissal of apostolic authority to their approach to sacred books. Differences in their teaching indicated that heretics possessed corrupt scriptures—a sure indication of their moral defectiveness as "haters of the apostles." He noted that Valentinus emended scripture with "other expositions and obvious changes."[81] He also accused the Valentinians of "palming their essays off on to us." Tertullian insisted that nothing was held back from Peter, John, and the other apostles. They were told everything. Moreover, they did not keep back anything that they were told. There was no new revelation to be expected. Tertullian mocked heretics for claiming to possess revelatory gifts because it suggested that, in the meantime, Christians had been practicing Christianity incorrectly.

However, the Montanist Tertullian held different concerns. Unlike his comprehensive work against *all* heresies, his heresiological work focusing only on Valentinus was likely written after his adoption of Montanist concepts of continued revelation. In *Adversus Valentinianos*, he endeavored to make a distinction between himself and Valentinus when outsiders might not have been able to tell the difference. One can sense the anxiety of Tertullian's own predicament in his description of Valentinus. He noted that Valentinus was a "brilliant and able man," and part of the inner circle of Rome's church.[82] Tertullian indicated that Valentinus's departure from the church was driven primarily by pride and personal ambition—he was irritated that another member was chosen as bishop based on his status as a "confessor." Valentinian teachings sprung from this, as Valentinus was a spirit "roused by ambition and inflamed with the desire for revenge."

Tertullian might have written these same words about himself. He had a reputation for belligerence: Jerome referred to him as a "man of impetuous temperament,"[83] and in the introduction to *Da Pentientae*, Tertullian described himself as "always burning with the fires of impatience." Like Valentinus, Tertullian also had a reputation for brilliance. According to Jerome, Cyprian read his writings every day and referred to him as "the master." Jerome attributed Tertullian's interest in Montanism as the result of "envy and reproaches of the clergy of the Roman church." Tertullian, it seems, was a brilliant personality who clashed with bureaucratic authorities.

As a Montanist, Tertullian was challenged with the problems of newness of the New Prophecy while embracing a fixed set of scriptures. He even possessed a book of the recent prophecies of Priscilla and Maximillia, which were not included in the scriptures. Consequently, he was less interested in Valentinians "palming off their essays" than he was about other issues—fabrication, secrecy, and disagreement—because these were the very accusations leveled against the New Prophets. In *Against Valentinians*, Tertullian's primary concern about the

Valentinians was not their composition of new teachings and texts, but the fact that all their new teachings contradicted one another. Tertullian accused the Valentinians of having a "propensity for fables," which they taught as secret doctrine. Montanists insisted that mantic activity be done in public. On the Valentinians, Tertullian insisted that "it is their secrecy that is a disgrace."[84] He compared them to followers of the Eleusinian mysteries, who "hide divinity in secret recesses." Valentinians too, Tertullian argued, "consecrated their mysteries in profound silence." He complained, "If you propose to them inquiries sincere and honest, they answer you with a stern look and contracted brow and say 'the subject is profound. . . .' If you intimate to them that you understand their opinions, they insist on knowing nothing themselves." In contrast, Tertullian's revelations were "always in high and open places, and facing the light! As the symbol of the Holy Spirit, it loves the radiant East, that figure of Christ. Nothing causes truth a blush, except being hidden."[85] Montanist revelation happened in public. In *On the Soul* 9.4, Tertullian described the mechanics of these new prophecies. He mentioned a woman in his congregation who habitually received revelations "experiencing ecstatic visions during the sacred rites" on Sundays—in a public, crowded setting. "After the people are dismissed at the conclusion of the sacred services, she is in the regular habit of reporting to us whatever things she may have seen in vision (for all her communications are examined with the most scrupulous care, in order that their truth might be probed)." For Tertullian, any new revelation was accessible and available for scrutiny.

If Montanism revelation existed to clarify, Valentinian revelation purported to obscure. Tertullian accused the Valentinians of speaking in "double tongue." Their obscure readings "fabricated out of suggestions of holy scripture." Tertullian considered diversity to be characteristic of Valentinianism—"We know, I say, knowing best their own origin, why we call them Valentinians, although they seem not to be. Indeed, they have separated from the founder, but the origin is by no means effaced; if ever it differs, the very difference is the testimony."[86] Disagreement itself, Tertullian argued, was a distinctive feature of Valentinianism. He saw "innovation stamped on the very face of their roles," and diversity "concerning even the Lord Jesus, into how great a diversity of opinion are they divided!"[87] Such diversity of opinion corresponded to diversity in revelation: "This heresy is permitted to present itself pleasingly many ways, as prostitute who customarily changes her dress daily. Why not? With that spiritual seed of theirs passes through each man in such a way. Whenever they have add anything new, immediately they call the presumption a revelation, and ingenuity a grace, and never unity, only diversity."[88]

Tertullian claimed that the individual and discordant teachings of Valentinians were by-products of their teachings about the spermatic Logos residing in individuals, likening these revelations to the spiritual "seed" encountering a prostitute. In contrast, Tertullian insisted that New Prophets were in perfect agreement with the catholic church. The revelatory spiritual gifts received by New Prophets were in full accord with the doctrine of the catholic church. Tertullian was adamant that Montanists "only disagree here, that is, we do not acknowledge second marriages and we do not ignore Montanus' prophecy about future judgment."[89] The novelty of the New Prophecy and new prophecies was not the introduction of new doctrine, but spiritual guidance on how to make old doctrine relevant for the modern age.[90] Thus, Tertullian wrote *Adversus Valentinus* to distinguish Valentinian and Montanist theories of open revelation.

Epiphanius's Gnostic Gospels

Epiphanius (ca. 310–404) offers a retrospective on this discussion.[91] His heresiological compendium, the *Panarion*, provided a genealogy of heresy, recording eighty heresies from primordial times to those of Epiphanius's own times. Epiphanius wrote his heresiography in markedly different conditions than his predecessors. Christianity was no longer illegal. Epiphanius did not need to adopt a defensive strategy, nor did he risk execution for his public position. Instead, Epiphanius grew up in a Christian cocoon. He was raised in a wealthy Christian home in Palestine and left this life of luxury to become an ascetic Christian monk. Because of his learned, multilingual background, Epiphanius rose in the monastic ranks and later became bishop of Salamis.[92] He also traveled extensively in the eastern Mediterranean and encountered a variety of Christianities, thus inspiring the composition of the *Panarion*.

However, his *Panarion* has never been taken particularly seriously as a reliable source for the ancient heresies Epiphanius claims to know firsthand. An early twentieth century article reflects some attitudes about his writing that persist: "His erudition is outweighed by his prejudice, and his inability to recognize the responsibilities of authorship makes it necessary to assign most value to those portions of his works, which he simply cites from earlier writers."[93] Epiphanius's sweeping arguments, sensational eyewitness claims, and inaccessibility to the modern reader have not championed his historical usefulness.[94] Like his forerunners, he borrowed liberally from Irenaeus, and he was not always compelled to cite his sources.

However, Epiphanius was also more systematic than often recognized. As Young Richard Kim and Andrew Jacobs have argued, the *Panarion* was not incoherent rambling, but Epiphanius's effort to display his own vast learning ranging from the sciences to literature to history. As Andrew Jacobs has characterized him as a "celebrity icon," famous because of his fame, Epiphanius captured the popular feeling of his times.[95] Therefore, Epiphanius's writings tell us how fourth-century Christians perceived the difference between Valentinian Christianity and Orthodoxy. One of the differences that emerged revolved around scriptural practice.

Epiphanius's career also coincided with imperial efforts to define Christian reading practices. In 362, the Emperor Julian ruled that only Christians could teach Christian texts and pagans were to teach pagan texts. Julian's rescript against Christian teachers transformed teachers into religious figures, and, as C. Michael Chin observed, "directly connected the teaching of reading to the religious persona of the teacher."[96] Some Christians must have agreed with Julian. Jerome, for one, asserted that reading non-Christian texts was tantamount to denying Christ. Thus, in the fourth century, Chin writes, "the act of reading pagan or Christian texts marked the reader's cultural and religious identity."[97] This position would have frustrated second-century readers, such as Justin, who saw bits of wisdom scattered even among the Greek philosophers. In the fourth century, books marked one's allegiance to pagan or Christian religious tradition.

Epiphanius also presumed a theory of the written word in which books had curative and injurious properties. He offered his own writing as a cure for lethal heretical books and teachings. The title, *Panarion*, reflected this notion. *Panarion*, or "breadbasket," is typically translated "medicine chest." Epiphanius's *Panarion* was designed as preventative and curative medicine. Epiphanius compared the eighty heresies he catalogued to various poisonous snakes and offered curative theology as the anti-venom. The *Panarion* recorded a history of heresy from the creation of the world to his own era. He homed in on names, places, and dates to fill in details of his historical narrative. Epiphanius was methodical in his descriptions and wrote systematic expositions of each sect: he would explain its geographical and intellectual origins, outline their key beliefs and name major leaders, making note of deviant ritual traditions, and subsequently offer his refutation.

In the logic of the *Panarion*, the creation and dissemination of books drove human history, and the moral world of humans was inextricably linked with books.[98] Consistently, Epiphanius commented upon a group's use of the written word, noting any abnormal textual behavior—if a heretical group disregarded a sacred book, excised a sacred book, or composed a sacred book. In this narrative, the misuses of books began with the first humans. According to Epiphanius, illicit composition practices originated among the five earliest heresies—Barbarism, Scythianism, Hellenism, Judaism, and Samaritanism.[99] Barbarism, the primeval heresy existing from the time of Adam to the flood, was marked by an absence of sacred text. Instead, "there was no difference of doctrine yet, no different ethnic groups, no name for a heresy, neither was there idolatry. . . . Each person followed his own ideas."[100] Barbarism, in Epiphanius's taxonomy, was not technically a belief system. It marked an era of moral decline from Adam's disobedience and the first murder. However, Epiphanius carefully noted that Barbarism did not constitute systematic heretical thought. Perhaps drawing a comparison to the morally ambiguous biblical era of Judges, Epiphanius characterized the age of Barbarism too as a time when "everyone did what was right in their own eyes."[101] Thus, human reliance on instinct as a moral code flourished in a time marked by absence of books.

The choice of Barbarism as the first heresy, as Young Richard Kim noted, may have been a deliberate move to signal that Greek culture was a further distortion of an ideal age.[102] Epiphanius, like his predecessor Eusebius, had imagined the first humans as the first Christians, living before the law was given on Sinai, well acquainted with the deity, whom they worshipped without idolatry.[103] In the era of the first heresies, Barbarism and Scythianism, humans were divided into categories of "pious" and "impious." Epiphanius defined the age of Scythianism, a heresy widespread after the flood, as an era that continued the Barbarian period of no "learning from teaching or books."[104] In these instances, Epiphanius was more concerned with demonstrating that Christianity had been practiced before Adam's disobedience and the world's descent into moral cloudiness.[105] The absence of systematic heretical thought reflected an absence of books.

In the narrative of the *Panarion*, heresies proliferated once knowledge became disseminated through teaching and books. After the Tower of Babel fell, and humanity scattered across the world, the Hellenism "error" was propagated by Egyptian, Babylonian, and Phrygian authors—historians and chronographers—who spread "erring mythology . . . giving rise to sorcery and magic arts."[106] These foreign books became vectors of heresy. By the age of Epicurus (c. 340–270 B.C.E.), the whole world was divided into two religious inclinations—Hellenism and Judaism. With these two groups came two competing canons: followers of Hellenism read the "poets, prose writers, historiographers, astronomers."[107] Jews, on the other hand, read twenty-seven books, in addition to two "in dispute," along with "some other secret books."[108] The number of books in the canon, irrespective of the particular contents, had a history of being used as a "quantitative expression that is qualitative in meaning."[109] Josephus had claimed there were twenty-two books, corresponding to the twenty-two letters of the Hebrew alphabet exclusive of the final forms, symbolically representing the twenty-two patriarchs from Adam to Jacob. While Josephus was not interested in the bibliographic content, Epiphanius did list the twenty-seven books, and named the two—the *Wisdom of Solomon* and Sirach—that were in dispute. Yet his choice of twenty-seven was also symbolic, corresponding to the twenty-seven letters of the Hebrew alphabet, inclusive of the final form of five letters. If the number of books represents, as Mroczek has phrased it, "completion and coherence,"[110] Epiphanius's observation that the number was "in dispute" signaled a defect in Judaism.

Indeed, Epiphanius observed that in the hands of certain circles, these texts were abused, misinterpreted, and rewritten inspired by "the stupid ideas of individuals," thus giving rise to new heresies.[111] Novel textual combinations produced new heresies, such as the Samaritans' combination of Jewish and Greek scriptures. Scribes, which Epiphanius named as one of fifteen heretical Jewish sects, possessed four versions of the Torah.[112] Another sect of the Jews, the Nasaraeans, claimed all five books of Moses were fabricated.[113] The Osseans, he noted, also rejected the books of Moses, and one of their teachers composed his own book of proper praxis.[114] As Epiphanius enumerated the many Christian heresies sprouting in his own time, he consistently delineated heresies by their mistreatment, ignorance, and illicit creation of books.

The textual aberration of the Valentinians, according to Epiphanius, was their tendency to "take an impression of the Greek poets and myths."[115] While Epiphanius quoted some Valentinian texts, they are not known to us from the NHL or any other source. Nevertheless, they do contain thematic overlap with the *Tripartite Tractate* and the *Apocryphon of James*. However, Epiphanius was not really that interested in the Valentinians. He quoted large portions of Irenaeus's *Against Heresies*, and consequently did not attempt to delve deeply into the Valentinian heresy, except to note that it bore genealogical and intellectual proximity to the Gnostics. Consequently, because Epiphanius emphasized the connection between the Gnostic heresy (a term he assigned to a specific sect and also a term he would use interchangeably with ten other sects) and the Valentinians, his report on the book culture of the Gnostics is relevant for his portrayal of the Valentinians.

Epiphanius continued the complaints of earlier heresiologists that the Gnostics possessed too many books. He noted that some Gnostics fabricated a work called the "Gospel of Perfection" (which Epiphanius renamed the "dirge of perfection"), and others read a "Gospel of Eve." These compositions reflected their concept of Gospel, which Epiphanius described as "moronic visions and testimonies, which they claim is Gospel."[116] To describe the content of "visions" and "testimonies," Epiphanius quoted one of their ritual chants, in which they conversed with spirits. The divine spirits imparted divine revelation, and the ritual saying observed that the visionary and the spirit became one: "I stood on a high mountain and saw a big man and a short man. And I heard a voice like thunder and went near to hear it and the voice spoke to me and said 'I am you and you are me and wherever you are, I am there. I have been sown in all things.'"[117]

Epiphanius's description of the Gnostic revelatory experience has several points of contact with the Valentinian model. He indicated that revelation was an individual experience inspiring a Pentecostal glossolalia/glossography. The divinity and human resided within one another, the visionary figure was "sown" (ἐσπαρμένος), perhaps like a spermatic Logos, everywhere. This dynamic allowed for individual revelatory experience. Epiphanius described the ensuing act of publication as "spewing out moronic visions and testimonies, which they proclaim as Gospel."[118] Thus, for Epiphanius, the Valentinian Gnostic Gospels comprised both written texts and not-necessarily-written visions.

The Valentinians, Epiphanius maintained, were an offshoot of the Gnostics. In fact, he noted, the Valentinians often referred to themselves as "Gnostics." While today we find the doctrinal differences between Gnostics and Valentinians insurmountable, Epiphanius saw a connection between them:

> For this man, sowing his dreams in many people, calling himself a Gnostic, as it is said, has tied together many scorpions, into one chain. As the ancient, distinct parable holds, that scorpions bind together in a chain, one after another, until ten or even more, letting themselves down from a roofed chamber or house and thus create pain for humans with cunning. Thusly also this man and his students, called Gnostics, have become architects of error and each has been taught by another coming before him, adding to the error after his teacher, and creates yet another heresy, coming from the one before it."[119]

The image of a chain of scorpions projected the model of succession, albeit pejoratively, laid out in the Valentinian sources. Perhaps referencing Valentinian stylistic tendencies as displayed in the *Gospel of Truth*, Epiphanius also railed against convoluted language and argued that true teachings were narrated by apostles "in plain language."[120] From his depiction of Gnostic and Valentinian textuality, then, Epiphanius saw a fundamental difference between orthodox and Valentinian sacred writing. He echoed the objection of Irenaeus, who objected to the Valentinian convoluted writing style. He upheld the complaints of Tertullian, noting that "their own ideas differ."[121] He was adamant their "myths" were wrong because "no scripture said these things—neither the Law of Moses nor any prophet after Moses, neither the Savior or his Evangelists, and certainly not the apostles."[122] The singularity of written scripture demolished the continuing revelatory claims of the Valentinians and the *Gospel of Truth*.

The Jung Codex as a Valentinian Book

The only extant copies of the *Gospel of Truth* are from a pair of fourth-century Egyptian codices from the Nag Hammadi library. One copy is badly damaged. The more complete manuscript is the third text comprising codex one (now called the Jung Codex, named after the institute that eventually purchased it). The Jung Codex, and the way it was organized, demonstrates how the *Gospel of Truth* might have been interpreted by later readers. The *Gospel of Truth* was the third of five texts in the Jung Codex, which included the *Prayer of Paul, Apocryphon of James, Gospel of Truth, Treatise on the Resurrection*, and the *Tripartite Tractate*. The order of the texts comprising the Jung Codex and the *Gospel of Truth*'s placement within it suggested that its fourth-century audience read this second-century text as a book about books, endorsing a theory of open revelation.

Recent efforts in codex criticism have tried to explain why the texts in the Nag Hammadi library were grouped the way they were.[123] Analyses of the codex has demonstrated that looking for intention behind the organization of the Jung Codex is not simply idle speculation. The collection of texts and the sequence in which they were ordered was purposeful. As Michael Kaler has shown, two scribal hands copied the texts comprising the Jung Codex. Scribe A initially copied the *Apocryphon of James, Gospel of Truth,* and the *Tripartite Tractate*, leaving seven pages for scribe B to copy the *Treatise on the Resurrection* between the *Gospel of Truth* and *Tripartite Tractate*.[124] Scribe A subsequently copied the *Prayer of the Apostle Paul* into the introduction.[125]

Michael Williams suggested that the order of the texts promoted a chronological history of revelation from a rewritten Genesis to witnesses of a risen

Christ.[126] The specific combination and order of the texts of the Jung Codex might be explained by the compiler's efforts to mimic the layout of the New Testament. Following this theory, the *Gospel of Truth* would have been regarded as epistle, or explanatory essay, which certainly guides how modern readers have approached the text.[127] Alternatively, Michael Kaler argued that the evidence shows that the *Prayer of Paul* and the *Apocryphon of James* were included in the Jung Codex as an afterthought.[128] This indicated that the compliers were trying to invite as many holy figures into the collection as possible.[129] It also suggests that the compilers invited as many modes of revelatory authority as possible: the codex included named apostles such as James, who knew the historical Jesus personally; Paul, who claimed a revelatory apostleship; and unnamed spiritual authorities.

If this is the case, the placement of the *Gospel of Truth* within this context may have been considered an invitation for others to join the apostles' literary activities. The opening text of the Jung Codex invoked the reader's capacity to function as a text. Kaler has argued that the *Prayer of the Apostle* "implicitly argues in favor of prioritizing revelatory, esoteric knowledge over exoteric knowledge conveyed through physical means, thus again validating the reader of codex I and her reading experience."[130] However, the reception of revelatory, esoteric knowledge was not necessarily limited strictly to "validating the reader. . . . And her reading experience." The text reads: "Give me your power, when I make a request of you. Give healing for my body, as I request of you through the evangelist. . . . Bestow that which no angelic eye has seen, nor archonic ear hears, and that which has not gone into the heart of men who have become angels."[131]

If we are to imagine that, as a prayer, this text was spoken aloud by the reader, these requests were removed from the mouth of Paul and given new meaning in the mouth of the supplicant. These words uttered by the supplicant requested completely new revelation, a revelation new not just to humanity, but to the entire primordial cast—archons *and* angels. Paul, who, like the second-century supplicant, never met the savior but experienced a supernatural vision of his own, was an ideal candidate for pseudepigraphy. The compilers of the Jung Codex opened with Paul, a historical voice, but a historical voice historically separated from the historical Jesus.

The second text in the codex, the *Apocryphon of James*, gave voice to the disciples who knew the historical Jesus. Yet, the author of the *Apocryphon of James* seemed to think that disciples who knew the historical Jesus were overrated as spiritual authorities. The portrayal of the disciples and the placement of this text within the Jung Codex anticipated further the call for continued generation of new revelatory texts by authors who, like Paul, were not historically linked to Jesus. In the *Apocryphon of James*, the disciples were engaged in the business of textual production. The text is a response to a letter from an unnamed student requesting "an apocryphon, which was revealed to me and Peter through the Lord." James obliged and sent the text, "in Hebrew writing . . . sent to you, and only you." He advised his correspondent, whose name was obscured from damage to the manuscript, to "be careful about reciting this book to many, this is that which the savior did not want to say to all of us, his twelve disciples."[132] The *Apocryphon* also revealed that this was not the first secret book James had sent this "servant of salvation," nor the only apostle to compose one. This particular text was revealed to James when the twelve disciples were sitting around and "bringing to mind the things the Savior had said to each one of them, whether secretly or publicly, and arranging them in books."[133] According to this letter, all the disciples were actively writing books. The text acknowledged that the revelations in the books were unique to each of them. Just as James had explained to his correspondent that the contents of his particular revelation were not for everyone, the other disciples were also recording the things the Savior told them, "secretly or openly."

The text also anticipated new revelatory information. By the end of the *Apocryphon*, James, Peter, and the other disciples had fallen out of favor, and the Savior informed them they were saved only for the sake of the "children coming after us." As James explained to the others, "He has . . . given us an assurance and promised life to us all and revealed to us children coming after us, having commanded us to love them as we will be saved because of them."[134] The text explained that those who wrote during the incarnation of the Son had the least clout among three groups of people—the ones who predicted his incarnation were once blessed; however "blessed three times were they who have already been ordained by the Son when they had not yet existed."[135] The apostles were not happy that these future sons usurped their authority as the elect. James mollified them all by sending each to a different section of the world and turned his attention back to his correspondent. James abdicated his authority, "offering a prayer that the beginning come into existence for you," and concluded, "Now we proclaim a part with these ones, the proclamation being made for them, these whom the Lord has made his sons."[136] Francis Williams has explained this obscure ending indicated that James made a partial revelation in collaboration with "those for whose benefit the proclamation was made (i.e., the Gnostics)."[137] In other words, James's proclamation was not complete, and awaited completion by "those about to be born."

The ending of the *Apocryphon of James* left the "proclamation" unfinished and in the charge of "those to be born." The three texts placed after the *Prayer to Paul* and the *Apocryphon of James* conspicuously lacked pseudepigraphic authorship. The *Gospel of Truth*, the third text in the codex, separated the historical voices of Paul and the twelve apostles from the anonymous author instructing Rheginus in the *Treatise on the Resurrection* and the author of the *Tripartite Tractate*, the texts comprising the rest of the codex. The purposeful arrangement of the texts in this order is suggestive. An introduction in the voice of Paul, who never met Jesus the man and argued that "knowledge of Christ and of the mysteries of the cosmos that Christ reveals comes from revelation," coupled with a second text that censured Jesus's apostles, invited the next three texts, presumably written by authoritative authors who never met Jesus during his lifetime.[138] The compilers indicated that the traditional authors of the authoritative texts, the apostles, were no longer the only keepers of knowledge about Jesus. The three texts that follow aligned themselves with the voice of Paul, who opened the codex. Paul never met Jesus; neither did the authors of the last three texts of the codex. The order of these texts in the Jung Codex, and the exhortation that opened the collection, may have suggested to the fourth-century reader that he or she was also part of a revelation tradition, and a living text herself.

Another fourth-century text supports this reading— a new fragment of Athanasius's thirty-ninth *Festal Letter* found in the archives of Moscow's state museum and published in 1994.[139] This letter recorded the first list canonizing the twenty-seven books comprising the New Testament, setting them apart from noncanonical and apocryphal texts. Yet, it also suggests that the Christians whom Athanasius called heretics understood textual authority in a fundamentally different light, a light apparent in the request in *Prayer of the Apostle Paul* to "bestow that which no angelic eye has seen, nor archonic ear hears, and that which has not gone into the heart of men who have become angels." This prayer revised a line from Paul's first letter to the Corinthians, in which he described "what no eye has seen, nor ear heard, nor the human heart conceived."[140] David Brakke has argued that certain fourth-century Egyptian Christians cited this verse to endorse their own use of noncanonical texts,[141] and Athanasius did complain in his *Festal Letter* that heretics "write such books whenever they want."[142] The new fragment of the *Festal Letter* explicitly states that heretics have "said that Paul presented evidence from hidden sources when he says, 'what no eye has seen, nor ear heard, things that have not occurred to the human heart.' I [Athanasius] will answer him that this method is the manner of argumentative people. Paul does not contrive his words through other words, but with the things which are written in the Scriptures."[143] Paul, Athanasius contended, composed using the text of Scripture, not through revelatory, new "other words." Athanasius, it appears, was reporting a specific scriptural practice, even as he railed against it. He complained that some misused Paul's legacy to promote their own words.

CHAPTER 4

Rabbis Who Published and Perished

Books of the Heart and Books of the Mouth

Rabbinic tales attest to at least two instances of Jewish sages mutating into scrolls upon their untimely deaths. In the *Gospel of Truth*, the sage Jesus and text are juxtaposed on the cross in a syzygy of readers, dying and publishing. Similarly, the bibliomorphoses of sages in the Talmud fit a broader pattern of scholar and scroll becoming legally interchangeable—in rabbinic material, they are accorded equal respect in burial or carried side-by-side, sometimes so close that one cannot *be* without the other. Consequently, the rabbinic discussions about the sacredness of Torah scrolls can be illuminating for understanding Valentinian scriptural practice.

Rabbinic scriptural practice is distinct for its theory of a dual Torah—a written Torah and an oral Torah. Mishnah Avot described the sayings of sages as part of an oral tradition that could be traced all the way back to the revelation Moses received on Mount Sinai: "Moses received the Torah from Sinai and transmitted it to Joshua, Joshua to the Elders, the Elders to the Prophets, and the Prophets transmitted it to the Men of the Great Assembly."[1] The Mishnah introduced the idea that the words of contemporary teachers could be part of a more ancient wisdom tradition. Later rabbinic teachings transformed this idea further. *Sifre Deuteronomy* argued that since the wisdom of these teachers originated on Sinai, they too constituted Torah. This legal midrash described two Torot that Moses received on Sinai—a written law and an oral law.[2] In the Babylonian Talmud and amoraic midrash from Palestine too, the sayings of the sages became codified further as the "Torah of the Mouth," one part of a dual Torah that comprised the written Pentateuch and a second oral version, passed down through the mouths of Jewish leaders. By doing so, the Talmud articulated an idea the Valentinian sources only hinted at: the words of certain teachers could be classified as divine law.[3]

As the rabbinic answer to the question of what is a sacred book, the dual Torah provides a useful comparison to understanding the *Gospel of Truth* as a sacred text. In the context of ancient debates about the selection of revelatory, sacred, or authoritative books, Valentinus's "book of the heart" most closely resembled the Oral Torah.[4] As the category "books of the heart" permitted Valentinus to embrace many forms of revelation, the concept of "Torah of the Mouth" permitted rabbinic circles to generate new material which they could include in the category "Torah."[5] Yet both Valentinus and the Rabbis shared more in common than the construction of new texts. With traditions of living canons, books of the mouth and heart respectively, the Rabbis and Valentinus blurred distinctions between teacher and text. If Valentinus presumed no boundary between holy books and holy people, rabbinic efforts showcased a way books could become people and people could become books.

This chapter examines rabbinic legal comparisons between human bodies and Torah scrolls to understand how, theoretically, a scroll and person could function together as a sacred book. Just as Valentinus had promoted a living document perspective on the written word, Jewish sages argued that Torah could reside not just in a scroll but in the mouths of certain teachers. The chapter analyzes how the Mishnah and Tosefta develop a legal language to treat Torah scrolls and Torah scholars with parity.[6] These legal discussions belonged to the same disagreements witnessed between Valentinus and Irenaeus about Gospel: What is Gospel? Is it the oral proclamations of a living body? Is it a written text? If so, how should the written text be valued? Then, the chapter turns to the way the legal equivalence between text and scholar translate to equivalent practice. Rabbinic burial practices placed a Torah scroll in the tomb of a Torah scholar to represent their equal status.

After looking at legal discussions that defined the rabbinic sacred book, the chapter turns to a practical problem presented by living documents. Irenaeus had objected to the pandemonium resulting from each "preaching his own opinion." Despite his overt bias, Irenaeus raised a valid point; what happens when living sacred texts disagree? Extant Valentinian sources did not address this problem, but Talmudic tales that recount the deaths of Rabbi Hanina, and Rabbi Eliezer presented a solution that relied on the same scholar-as-scroll motif appearing in the *Gospel of Truth*, to "canonize" Oral Torah, namely, certain sages whose teachings were suspect.[7] Just as Valentinus's Jesus published the text of his heart as a crucified scroll, in Talmudic narratives, Torah scholars were described as scrolls to ratify their own oral teachings at the very moment they were in doubt and to symbolically conveyed the inadequacy of human language to convey divine concepts.[8] These stories, to borrow Rodney Stark's language, indicate that Valentinus's ideas were not in tension with the ideas of his contemporaries.[9] Although ejected from a coalescing Christian center, Valentinus's views about the relationship between the oral and the written dovetailed with contemporary Mishnaic views. These views gradually became the trademark of Rabbinic Judaism as codified by the Babylonian Talmud. However, the dual Torah might have met the same fate as Valentinian Christianity. As Martin Jaffee has observed: "If the rabbinic movement had not survived the third century, had it reached the end of its literary life in the *tannaitic* compilations, historians would have no reason to think that the notion of an Oral and Written Torah enjoyed particular prominence among Sages."[10] Instead, Valentinus has been relegated to the intellectual margins of Christianity, but if the Rabbis considered his perspective, they might have considered him mainstream.

Torah Scrolls Defile the Hands

Jewish and Roman legal scholars puzzled over the question: what counts as a book? In a Roman legal context, to execute a will, to interpret a declaration such as "I bequeath my son 100 books," jurists had to make precise the phrase "one book." For this, the jurists approached questions of wide relevance; they considered material books in every possible form: complete books, books with no ending, books not yet begun, books with many parts, books owned by the deceased, and books written by the deceased. Ulpian, the second-century Roman jurist whose career coincided with Valentinus in Rome, provided such a legal opinion, preserved in Justinian's *Digest*:

> Under the designation of "books" (*librorum*) all rolls (*volumina*)[11] are included, whether they are made of papyrus, parchment, or any other material whatsoever; even if they are written on bark (as is sometimes done), or upon any kind of prepared skins, they come under the same appellation. If, however, they are in codices (*in codicibus*)[12] of leather, or papyrus, or ivory, or any other substance, or are composed of wax tablets, will they be considered to be due? [Let us see.] Gaius Cassius says that where books are bequeathed, the skins (*membranas*)[13] are also

> included. Hence, it follows that everything relating to them will be due if the intention of the testator was not otherwise.[14]

This ruling was not simply an attempt to explain the difference between a book and a manuscript.[15] Ulpian's edict took up the legal challenge of explaining the general concept of book in light of diverse examples. Ulpian began with the easiest case: *liber* designated *volumina*, or rolls—the most recognizable form of a book. Rolls could be made from a variety of textiles, which Ulpian listed: Rolls made of papyrus (*charta*), parchment (*membrana*), and various bark products (*philyra* and *tilia*) all counted as liber. His list of textiles moved from the common to the rare, evidenced by his own aside, "sometimes scrolls are made of bark."

Ulpian's legal opinion provides important context for similar discussions in rabbinic material. Roman jurists detailed physical characteristics that made a document a book in the context of inheritance law;[16] Jewish jurists outlined the features that distinguished a Torah scroll from other scrolls. They were asking questions about materiality: What kind of ink should one use to copy out a scroll? What other materials can be used? What language should it be written in?[17] How should it be rolled? How big should it be?[18] How many books can be included in the scroll?[19] Jurists from both traditions explored the physical boundaries of the book. Ulpian asked whether book covers, scroll cases, book boxes, and book cases were included in an inheritance of a personal library;[20] rabbinic scholars asked whether scroll straps, boxes, and sleeves possessed the same characteristics as the scroll itself.[21] They even evaluated whether the blank spaces of a scroll carried the same sanctity of the letters themselves. These discussions aimed to make precise the characteristics that made a Torah scroll a Torah scroll.

Roman jurists had demarcated the boundaries of "book" for the purpose of inheritance. Rabbis demarcated the boundaries of "scroll" to locate sanctity and cleanliness. As the document God consulted to create the world, the Torah was considered a sacred book *par excellence*. But if so, how should the sacredness be quantified? For instance, the Mishnah passage below asked, is a Torah scroll holier than the Sabbath?

> A. If a man was reading in a scroll upon the threshold and the scroll rolled from his hand, he may roll it back to himself.
>
> B. If he was reading on top of the roof and the scroll rolled from his hand, if it does not reach ten handbreadths from the ground he may

> roll it back to himself. But after it has reached ten hand breadths, he turns it upon the written side.
>
> C. Rabbi Judah says, "Even it is not suspended from the ground except for the width of a needle, he may roll it back to himself."
>
> D. Rabbi Shimon says, "Even if it is upon the ground itself, he may roll it back to himself, because no prohibition overrides the holy writings for you."[22]

This passage explored how a potential problem associated with scrolls should be addressed by Sabbath law. Since rabbinic regulations prohibit the transport of an object between private and public domains on the Sabbath, what should be done when a Torah scroll rolls from one domain to another? The first pericope explored the horizontal limits: if a reader is positioned on the border of the public and private domain, the threshold, and a scroll rolled into the public domain, may one roll the scroll back? The second pericope explored the vertical limits of the Sabbath boundary. If the scroll rolled down from the roof, at what point had it crossed the Sabbath limit? The general rule was ten handbreadths, after which the scroll rolled into public domain. In the third pericope, Rabbi Judah argued that as long as the scroll did not touch the ground, it remained in the private domain and may be rolled up. Yet, a modern reader, familiar with the veneration of the Torah scroll, might be surprised that a Torah scroll could be left hanging from a rooftop at all! Rabbi Shimon agreed. He placed the Torah scroll above the Sabbath in his hierarchy of holiness, arguing that its protection superseded the preservation of Sabbath boundaries.

The classification of a text as sacred or not was further argued by a counterintuitive proxy: sacred texts would defile the hands and everyday texts would not. This classification-by-proxy points to a conceptual worldview in which special books possessed the qualities of people, not other books. Rabbinic discussions measured the sanctity of a book by its capacity to impart uncleanliness. A Mishnah passage classified Torah scrolls as objects that defile the hands: "The harps for singing are unclean; but the harps of the sons of Levi are clean. All liquids are unclean but the liquid in the slaughtering house [of the temple][23] is clean. All the scrolls defile the hands except the scroll used in the Temple Court."[24]

An object that defiles the hands makes one ritually impure and therefore ineligible to participate in ritual life.[25] But why should an object of ritual power be a vessel of ritual impurity? Jacob Milgrom, Shamma Friedman, and Timothy

Lim have demonstrated that "defiling the hands" touched on notions of authority and canonicity.[26] The Tosefta ruled, "the Gospels and heretical books do not defile the hands,"[27] and indicated that they were to be avoided. Mishnaic sources debated whether the Song of Songs, Esther, and Qoheleth defiled the hands. These discussions indicated that scriptures that defiled the hands did so because they were inspired by God and not humans. BT Megillah 7a similarly proposed that Esther defiled the hands because it was composed under divine inspiration.[28] It also added the qualification: "composed to be read, not composed to be recited," meaning, unlike with certain "texts" repeated but not written down, one should be looking at the parchment when reading from Esther. This has suggested that a book that defiles the hands was a book read for liturgical purposes. In contrast, books that were supposed to be recited would be regarded as memory aids and not texts used in a ritual setting.

But why should texts inspired by the holy spirit or read in a ritual setting defile the hands? Why should uncleanliness in particular be a marker of that authority? After all, many ordinary objects carry the same degree of uncleanliness as Torah scrolls and other books of scripture do, yet, as M Yadaim 4.6 below indicates, the ability to defile the hands described the extraordinary when applied to books:

> The Sadducees say, "We accuse you, Pharisees, on the charge that you say, 'the holy writings defile the hands, the books of Homer do not defile the hands.'" Rabbi Johanan ben Zakkai said, "Do we not have anything against the Pharisees but this alone? Look, they say the bones of a donkey are clean, but the bones of Johanan the high priest are unclean." They said to him, "corresponding to our love is their uncleanliness, for no one makes utensils of the bones of his father and mother." He said to them, "So it is with the holy writings, our love is their uncleanliness. Now the books of Homer, which are not beloved, they do not defile the hands."[29]

Here, the Mishnah constructed a debate between Sadducees and Pharisees about the relative sanctity of a holy book. The Rabbis of the Mishnah distinguished heretics on the basis of what they perceived the book to be: the "heretical" Sadducean position compared books of scripture to other books. Their view might be summarized: if the books of scripture, which are precious to us, defile the hands, how much more so should the books of Homer, which are not precious. For the Sadducees, the capacity to "defile the hands" described ordinary objects, such as books. In contrast, the "orthodox" rabbinic position, argued through the mouths of the Pharisees, claimed that a book that defiles the hands was extraordinary.[30] The pharisaic outlook, using the Sadducees's ruling about the relative value of bones to their own advantage, compared books of scripture to bones, not to other books. By placing scripture into a category apart from books, they argued it deserved not the casual treatment reserved for Homer, but the reverence one should show toward human bones.

The rabbinic material also placed Torah scrolls and bones in the same category in other legal discussions. For instance, a *baraita* ruled: "Someone who is carrying bones from place to place may not put them in a saddlebag, set them on a beast of burden and ride upon them because one would be treating them with contempt.... And as they said about bones, so they said about Torah scrolls."[31] The comparison with human bones, which could be both unclean and objects of reverence, supports the argument for what Jacob Milgrom called "sacred contagion"—a Torah scroll's ability to impart uncleanliness as a ritual object.[32] Sacred contagion describes the transfer of holiness from one object to another—the sanctification of priestly garments when sprinkled with the blood of sacrifice in the temple, for example.[33] However, in addition to imparting holiness, a sacred object could kill those ineligible to handle it. The ark of the covenant was thought to possess such lethal capabilities, striking dead two Israelite brothers who accidentally touched the ark after retrieving it from the Philistines.[34] Various Jewish traditions also connected the ark of the covenant with sacred writing: the ark was said to contain the tablets of the ten commandments[35] and the book of Deuteronomy,[36] and the Damascus Document mentioned a "book of the law" residing in the ark.[37]

M Yadayim 3.5 also made an explicit comparison between Torah scrolls and the ark of the covenant, insinuating that Torah scrolls possessed similar attributes that imparted uncleanliness to all who touched it: "A book that was erased but eighty-five letters were left—as many as in the paragraph, 'It came to pass when the ark set out,'—defiles the hands. A scroll on which eighty-five letters are written—as many as in the paragraph, 'And it came to pass when the ark set out'—defiles the hands."[38]

The underlying question posed in this passage asked: when is a Torah scroll still a sacred book? Ulpian tried to clarify how much writing must be on a document before it counted as a book for inheritance purposes, and here the Mishnah quantified how much writing must remain on a Torah scroll for it to defile the hands. The ruling was derived from counting the number of Hebrew letters in a passage of Torah describing the ark as it traveled through the wilderness with the Israelites. This passage hinted at an association between the ark and Torah, suggesting that the same abilities of the ark to impart sacred contagion applied to Torah scrolls too.

Rabbinic circles measured sacredness by a book's ability to defile the hands. Yet, this presents a difficulty for the authenticity of the Oral Torah: although, as Goodman states, "it was axiomatic for the Rabbis that their own teachings bore the authority of divine inspiration since they had been passed on by word of mouth from one generation to the next . . . no compilation of rabbinic dicta was ever said to 'defile the hands.'"[39] This concern might be allayed if one considers the "compilation of rabbinic dicta" to reside within the Rabbis' bodies rather than through their written records. For a Jewish human corpse, even that of a Rabbi, conveys the "father of the fathers of uncleanliness," the highest degree of ritual impurity. Moreover, as demonstrated below, Rabbis likened their own bodies to scrolls rather than other bodies.

This One Observed What Is Written in That One

Rabbinic texts described the peculiar practice of placing a Torah scroll on the bier of a deceased sage and reciting the phrase "this one observed what is written in that one."[40] Material evidence also testifies to the practice of burying a Torah scroll with an important intellectual even though it "seems to run counter to the tendency to distance the corpse from the realm of the sacred."[41] Adiel Kadari has documented several theories for instigating this burial tradition:[42] perhaps it was done to ensure a scroll accompanied the sage to the afterlife so he could continue his studies. Or it may have simply been a mark of honor. It may have had a didactic purpose, pointing to the connection between Torah study and eternal life. It also may have emphasized that the sages were the authority on Torah, and without the sage to interpret, the book should be taken out of circulation.[43]

It is worth noting that Plutarch, the Greek contemporary of the *tannaim*, recalled that Romulus's successor and second king of Rome, Numa (753–673 B.C.E.) wrote twelve books of Roman priestly lore and twelve of Greek wisdom that he removed from circulation for similar reasons. Numa possessed the only copies and insisted that his priest commit them to memory. Numa decreed that he should buried with his books and that their contents be perpetuated only by memory.[44] Two coffins were buried at his funeral: one contained the body of King Numa, the other contained his books. When a storm uncovered the two coffins four hundred years later, Numa's coffin was found empty, but the other contained the perfectly preserved books. The rhetoric of the literary evidence presented below reflects similar rabbinic efforts to substitute certain people as law by placing them in physical proximity to the written version.

A passage from the *Mekhilta de Rabbi Ishmael*, a *tannaitic* midrash on the book of Exodus, described a version of this practice:

> Moreover, the coffin of Joseph would travel alongside the ark of everlasting life. And the nations of the world would say to the Israelites: 'what is the significance of these two chests?' And the Israelites would say to them: This one is the ark of everlasting life and the other is a coffin of a dead man. Then the nations of the world would say: What is the significance of this coffin that it should go alongside of the ark of everlasting life? And the Israelites would say to them: The one resting in this coffin has observed that which is written on the item resting in this ark.[45]

In part, this passage aimed to reconcile the end of the book of Genesis with the events of the Exodus. On his deathbed, Joseph asked that his body be buried in the land of Abraham, yet the last line of Genesis recorded was: "he was embalmed and placed in a coffin (ארון) in Egypt."[46] Exodus 13:19 reported that Moses "took with him the bones of Joseph" when the Israelites left Egypt, so rabbinic hermeneutical methods connected the coffin of Joseph with the ark (ארון) that Moses built, concluding that Israelites sojourned through the desert with two arks. Thus, Joseph's bones made it out of Egypt.

Yet this passage also worked to present oral and written law side by side and posited a relationship between them. The narrative seemed to defy chronology—Joseph kept the commandments in Egypt before they were given to Moses on Sinai?! The Rabbis continued the idea documented in other Jewish texts such as *Jubilees* and the works of Philo; righteous individuals observed the law even before it was given to Moses. By placing Joseph's coffin in parallel to the ark, the Rabbis supported Philo's perspective, which presented the Patriarchs as living laws. However, differences in their priorities are evident. Philo, intent on demonstrating that the written Torah perfectly compounded a universal natural law, pointed to the patriarchs as living laws to demonstrate the veracity of the textual version. The rabbinic outlook did not harbor the same embarrassment about a written Torah; their agenda lay in authorizing an oral version. In this midrash, Joseph was ratified as embodied law by the written contents of the ark and by the explicit statement, "this one observed what is written in that one." The passage perhaps also hinted—through the nations and their puzzled questions—that only outsiders did not know this. The Oral Torah, then, an invention of marginal Jewish scholars who are now called "the Rabbis," was presented in this midrash as an authentically ancient Jewish tradition.

This reading is supported by variations of this passage found in two other rabbinic texts that repeated the ritualized phrase, "this one observed what is written in that one." In these instances, "that one" no longer designated the ark of the covenant but a Torah scroll. *Lamentations Rabbah*, another early midrash, documented this phrase in describing the respects paid to Hezekiah, the eighth-century king of Judah who did "what was pleasing in the eyes of God," through his reforms. These reforms included centralizing the worship of the deity Yahweh and prohibiting the worship of other deities in the temple. *Lamentations Rabbah* honored Hezekiah's reforms of the temple by turning him into a Rabbi. The text reads: "R. Judah bar Simon said: 'they built a college over Hezekiah's tomb and when they went there they would say to him, "teach us."' R. Hanina said: 'they placed a Torah scroll over Hezekiah's tomb and said, "the one who lies in this coffin observed what is written in this."'"[47]

Hezekiah had restored the Temple as the central place of worship and destroyed the altars of other gods. In the logic of this passage, these temple reforms merited his esteem as a teacher. Hezekiah's transformation is emblematic of the larger pattern of late antique religious transformation Guy Stroumsa observed in *The End of Sacrifice*—the shift from a sacrificial system and worship in the temple to book central worship.[48] Hezekiah, the seventh century B.C.E. restorer of the temple, becomes, in the late antique *Lamentations Rabbah*, the restorer of the Torah. The Rabbis turned his tomb into a place of study, featuring Hezekiah as the expert scholar. Moreover, they uttered the same aphorism over Hezekiah used to honor the patriarch Joseph as pre-Sinai law. By turning Hezekiah into a scholar, the passage implied that those who restored obedience to the Torah became honorary Rabbis, perhaps embodying the law to the extent of Joseph. While the Rabbis may have been concerned with honoring Hezekiah, this discussion also served the emerging rabbinic program. The passage recognized ones who restored proper religious observance as Rabbis. By doing so, it implicitly compared the rabbinic concept of Oral Torah, which "reestablished" Jewish law after the destruction of the temple, with the religious reforms of Hezekiah that reestablished proper temple worship.

A Talmudic description connected the honor accorded to Hezekiah to rituals of rabbinic burial practice: "Our Rabbis taught: They honored him when he died—this is Hezekiah King of Judah—by bringing out thirty-six thousand pallbearers before him, so said Rabbi Judah; Rabbi Nehemiah said to him: did they not do so before Ahab? Rather, they placed a Torah scroll on his bier and they said to him, 'this one observed what is written in that one.' Do we not do likewise?"[49] The response "do we not do likewise" indicates that placing a Torah scroll on the coffin of an esteemed individual was part of ancient Jewish burial customs. The Talmud also mentioned two Babylonian sages, Rabbi Huna and Rabbi Chisda, who objected to this practice.[50] Their objections, however, indicate that sages were, on occasion, buried with Torah scrolls.

Other funerary customs drew explicit comparisons between sages as law and Torah scrolls. For instance, the stipulations for mourning a Torah scholar were informed by the customs for mourning a damaged Torah scroll. How does one properly mourn a sage? The Talmud stipulated that one must tear his garments, then cited an earlier ruling of Rabbi Simeon ben Eleazar, who claimed, "One who stands near the dying, at the time when he breathes his last, he is duty bound to rend his clothes." This situation was declared analogous to the destruction of a Torah scroll: "To what is this like? To a scroll of law that is burnt, when one is duty bound to rend his clothes."[51] In addition to reflecting an outlook in which Torah scrolls and scholars were interchangeable, the idea that a damaged Torah scroll could "die" suggested that the scroll itself was thought of in similar terms to a living body.[52]

The Talmud also developed a legal equivalence of the Torah scroll and Torah scholar by demanding equal obeisance; one should behave the same way toward a Torah scholar as a Torah scroll. Torah scrolls were to be treated like sages (and vice versa) both when living and deceased. For example, the question was posed, "must one stand up before a Torah scroll?" The legal ruling was derived from a comparison between scroll and scholar: "*A minore ad maius*, since we rise before those who study Torah, how much more so should we rise before the Torah itself!"[53] If a scroll should be honored like a body, conversely, the desecration of one deserved the desecration of the other: "Rabbi Parnach said in the name of Rabbi Yohanan, whoever holds a Torah scroll naked will be buried naked."[54] In a more overt transposition between scroll and scholar, Yerushalmi Berakhot permitted a Torah scroll to complete the number necessary for a quorum of ten if only nine adults were present.[55] These stipulations cohered into a tradition in which the sacred book comprised both the body and scroll.

The Parchment Burns but Writing Flies in the Air

An Oral Torah could circumvent the problems with the written word that Plato had pointed out: written documents lacked the ability to explain themselves and therefore left themselves open to misinterpretation. On the other hand, Oral Torah came from the mouth of a living teacher, and books of the heart came from Valentinus's followers, at hand to clarify and explain. However, the canonization oral and living books opened up new problems. Both Valentinus and Jewish sages, locating sparks of the Logos in living teachers as well as texts, confronted similar challenges to this dual format. Written texts could be copied; oral texts were at the mercy of a good memory. Disagreement between written texts could be mediated by the reader. But living sparks could clash. What happens when the authorities offer diverging opinions? What happens when one leading Rabbi forbids teaching Torah in public and another claims it is a divine imperative? Or a group of Rabbis declare an oven unclean but one Rabbi declares it clean? What happens when living books disagree?

Irenaeus had argued that disagreement implied inauthenticity. Although extant Valentinian sources did not defend themselves against such a charge, rabbinic sources did. BT Avodah Zara 17b–18a and BT Sanhedrin 65a presented an insider perspective on the problem of disagreeing living books. The dispute is a distinctive feature of rabbinic discussion, but the idea that certain teachers were living repositories of Torah altered the stakes of these disagreements—can sacred books contradict one another? These two rabbinic narratives confronted this difficulty and shared some distinctive traits. Both stories featured a halachic dispute between leading *tannaim*. In both narratives, the judgment of a sage was challenged and the sage died with the matter unresolved. In both cases, a voice from heaven attempted to intercede on behalf of the sage. Both narratives also included the striking detail of Rabbis mutating into Torah scrolls at the moment of death. These bibliomorphoses indirectly addressed the problem of disagreeing books. Just as the *Gospel of Truth*'s depiction of Jesus crucified as a scroll described the nature of the Valentinian sacred book, the dying-scholar-as-scroll motif in the rabbinic narrative context illustrated a dual Torah, canonizing the oral version at the very moment its authoritative status was in doubt.

A compelling illustration of this principle is found in BT Avodah Zara 17b–18a.[56] This narrative shares a distinctive feature with the *Gospel of Truth*: both texts described teachers executed in own their books—Jesus was rolled up in a book and nailed to the cross and Rabbi Hanina was wrapped in his Torah scroll and burned. Although these killings reflected contemporary Roman practice,[57] both texts relied on this detail to turn a story of a criminal execution into a narrative about the nature of the sacred book. The death of the living book in the *Gospel of Truth* showcased Valentinus's idea of an oral and written sacred text; the dying book in BT Avodah Zara 17b–18a visually represented the rabbinic idea of a dual Torah.

In the rabbinic narrative, Rabbi Jose ben Kisma and Rabbi Hanina disagreed about teaching Torah in public, an act of sedition under Roman law. Rabbi Jose ben Kisma argued that because Roman rule was ordained by God, the Roman legislation prohibiting teaching Torah in public should be obeyed. Rabbi Hanina disagreed; the Lord had commanded him to teach Torah; surely God would absolve him for disobeying this Roman law, whatever the civil consequences.[58] He answered Rabbi Jose's accusations simply: "heaven will have mercy on us," and continued to teach Torah in public. Jose ben Kisma predicted, "I would be astonished if they do not burn you and the Torah scroll in the fire." It turns out, Rabbi Jose ben Kisma was correct—on the day of Jose ben Kisma's own funeral, attended by the "great men of Rome," Rabbi Hanina was discovered

> sitting, engaged in Torah and preaching to the masses with a Torah scroll resting on his chest. They seized him, wrapped him in the Torah scroll and heaped green vines upon him and set them on fire. They brought tufts of wool, soaked them in water and laid them on his heart so his soul would not depart quickly. His daughter said to him, "Father, must I see you in such a state?" He said to her, "If I were being burned alone, this situation would be difficult for me. Now that I am burned with a Torah scroll, the ones who resent the insult to the Torah scroll will resent the insult to me." His students said to him, "Rabbi, what do you see?" He said to them, "the scroll burns but the letters are flying away." "You too open your mouth and let the fire enter you." He said to them, "it is better that the one who gives takes than for one to do violence against himself." The executioner said to him, "Rabbi, If I make the flame bigger and remove the tufts of wool from your heart will you bring me to life in the world to come?" He said to him, "yes." "Promise me?" He promised him. So the executioner made the flame bigger and removed the tufts of wool from his heart and his soul departed quickly. Then the executioner leapt and fell into the middle of the fire. And a *Bat Kol* came forth and said: "Rabbi ben Teradion and the executioner

> have been invited to life in the world to come." When Rebbi heard it he wept and said: "one may acquire eternal life in a single hour, another in so many years."[59]

Rabbi Hanina's execution under Roman authority brought into focus the issue of his own authority as teacher and embodiment of Torah. Despite the disagreement between the two sages, the narrative pointed out that *both* were correct. Although Rabbi Hanina was admonished for teaching publicly and perished just as Rabbi Jose ben Kisma predicted, heaven did have mercy on him—the executioner spontaneously offered to make the fire hotter and remove the wet bandages to limit his suffering. In case there was any doubt on heaven's verdict, the *Bat Kol* concluded, "Rabbi Hanina ben Teradion and the executioner are summoned for life in the world to come."

Yet the story insinuated that there *was* doubt about Rabbi Hanina's provoking of Romans. Both the *Gospel of Truth*'s Jesus and Hanina had attracted large audiences with their public lessons. Yet when Jesus the book "came into the midst" the majority of his audience mocked him; only the little children paid attention. Rabbi Hanina's public Torah teaching similarly attracted "the masses," and although the text did not specify whether his audience was hostile, friendly, or simply curious, Rabbi Hanina hoped that the presence of a burning Torah scroll might incite outrage over his death. The Talmud hints disapproval of his actions—not teaching Torah, but teaching Torah *publicly* to incite unrest.[60] And yet, consistent with other rabbinic discourse about honoring sages, here the written Torah lent symbolic validity to the dubious judgement of the Oral Torah embodied in Rabbi Hanina.

As the *Gospel of Truth* did with Jesus's execution, the rabbinic authors capitalized on the opportunity to turn Hanina's grim historical end into a didactic moment. Valentinus eulogized Jesus's crucifixion as a "great teaching," representing "knowledge and completion" as he "read out the contents of his heart" on the cross. Rabbi Hanina similarly used his death pedagogically, imparting new lessons even as he died. As students congregated at the base of the cross to receive the book to be inscribed on their own hearts, so were Hanina's own students present to receive revelation from the martyr, perhaps hoping to learn what happens at death.[61] Although they attempted to comfort their teacher, advising him on a method to make his own death easier, Rabbi Hanina remained the authority. He left them with a final Torah lesson: "It is better that he who give take than for one to do violence against himself," indicating he could not take any part in bringing about his own death, even to the extent of removing the wet rags causing his body to burn slowly, or opening his mouth to burn quickly. Rabbi Hanina's lesson even convinced the executioner, who comprehended his own role in reconciling Hanina's prediction of heaven's mercy with the reality of his slow, torturous death.

Hanina's death, also like Jesus's in the *Gospel of Truth*, associated the physical Torah scroll with the body of the teacher. His deathbed vision of "scroll burning but letters flying away" described a destructible scroll with indestructible contents, comparable to his own body, smoldering under slow-burning green vines, while his soul awaited transport to the afterlife. His students further drew comparison between the written and oral versions of Torah as they encouraged their teacher to do as the scroll did: "You too open your mouth and the fire will enter you." The comparison to the written Torah pointed to his role as Oral Torah. While other versions of the narrative claimed Rabbi Hanina's death was punishment for mixing charity funds with the general collection,[62] here his death fulfilled the predictions of Rabbi Jose ben Kisma.

The Bavli narrative expressed little unease about the disagreement between the two Rabbis. Instead it seemed to neutralize the conflict and display an ambivalence about the position of both Rabbis. In the end, both living books had valid points: As Rabbi Jose ben Kisma predicted, Rabbi Hanina and his scroll were burned. The narrative acknowledges the seditious nature of Rabbi Hanina's actions, and does not necessarily endorse them. Yet, if avoiding death was the chief concern, Rabbi Jose ben Kisma was not rewarded for cooperating with the Romans—he died anyway. Rabbi Hanina's martyrdom occurred on the day of Rabbi Jose ben Kisma's own funeral. As Rabbi Hanina hoped, at the moment of death, heaven was merciful, and he died quickly. Valentinus's writings conveyed a similar unconcern with disagreement. He ignored conflicting passages, as he located books of the heart in the "shared matter" between books of various orientations. Consequently, *contra* Irenaeus, the right question to be asking about living books was not whether they disagree, but *how* they should disagree.

Arms Like Torah Scrolls

The circumstances surrounding the demise of Rabbi Eliezer ben Hyrcanus addressed this question. Like Rabbi Hanina, Rabbi Eliezer died while engaged in a legal dispute with leading sages of his generation and the dispute itself contributed to his demise. Yet unlike the circumstances of Rabbi Hanina's death, where the original disagreement was smoothed over by the fact that both sages were correct, in the case of Rabbi Eliezer, the issue of disagreement itself was at stake.

The account of Rabbi Eliezer's death was redacted in BT Sanhedrin 65a–b, but the story presumed the circumstances of his excommunication, narrated in BT Baba Metzia 59a–b—popularly dubbed the "Oven of Akhnai" and probably one of the most commented-on stories in the Talmud. I offer another discussion of the story below, not as a new contribution to the discussion within the field of rabbinic literature, but for what light it can shed on Valentinian scriptural practice.

The Oven of Akhnai story has been identified as one of the "poster children for the celebration of rabbinic polysemy and pluralism."[63] The multilayered narrative considered questions relating to divine and human authority, and also explored the limits of disagreement between living sources of divine law. Just as Irenaeus invented Valentinian heresy, in the tale of the Oven of Akhnai, as the narrative considered what it meant for Rabbis—living versions of the Torah—to engage in legal debate, a heretic was made. The two main characters, *tannaim* R. Eliezer and R. Joshua, lived in the same century as Valentinus. They displayed competing views about what constitutes a convincing argument. Rabbi Eliezer built his defense on sensational, supernatural means of argumentation (such as flying trees), while Rabbi Joshua countered the supernatural with scholarly rebuke and citations of authoritative texts. The Talmudic narrative critiqued both methods—in disagreements, the scholarly majority is not always right; on the other hand, showy miracles required the cooperation of heaven, undermining the theology that the Torah was "no longer in heaven." Thus, the Talmud aimed to establish an etiquette for disputes between sages.[64]

The way the Babylonian editors positioned the Oven of Akhnai narrative indicates as much. They interpreted the story as an opinion piece on the right protocol for debate. The story followed a Mishnaic law about verbal wrongdoing. The law reads: "Just as there is wrongdoing in buying and selling, also there is wrongdoing with words. One may not say to another, 'How much is that item?' if he does not want to buy it. If someone has repented, one may not say to him, 'remember your former deeds.' If someone is a foreigner, one may not say to him, 'Remember the deeds of your ancestors.' As it is said, 'Now a stranger you shall neither taunt nor oppress.'"[65]

The ensuing Talmudic narrative begins in typical rabbinic fashion with a legal question: was a segmented oven (an Akhnai oven) clean or unclean? The initial disagreement, preserved in M Kelim 5:10, centered on the mundane matter of whether an oven composed of many tiles separated with sand was to be considered clean. Yet the narrative quickly moves away from this halachic issue, focusing instead on the right and wrong words of argument.

> We learned there: If someone cuts sections and puts sand between the sections Rabbi Eliezer declares it pure, but the Sages impure. And this is the Oven of Akhnai. What is Akhnai? Rav Yehuda said Shmuel said, "Because they surrounded him with words like a snake making him susceptible to impurity." It was taught: On that day Rabbi Eliezer brought forth all the arguments in the world, but they did not accept them. He said to them, "If the halakha agrees with me, let the carob tree prove it." The carob tree was uprooted from its place one hundred cubits—and some say four hundred cubits. They said to him "No proof is brought from a carob tree." He said to them, "If the halakha agrees with me, let the walls of the study house prove it." The walls of the study house began to fall. Rabbi Yehoshua shouted at them. He said to them, "When Sages conquer one other in halakha, what right do you have?" They did not fall in honor of Rabbi Yehoshua, and they did not stand in honor of Rabbi Eliezer, and they still stand leaning. He said to them, "If halakha agrees with me, let it be proved from heaven." A heavenly voice came forth and said, "What is it for you with Rabbi Eliezer, since the halakha agrees with him in every way?" Rabbi Yehoshua stood on his feet and said, "It is not in heaven." What is "It is not in heaven"? R. Yirmiah said, "Because the Torah was already given on Mount Sinai. We do not consider a heavenly voice because you already wrote in the Torah on Mount Sinai, 'Incline after the majority.'" Rabbi Natan came upon Elijah. He said to him, "What was the holy one doing at that moment?" He said to him, "He was laughing and said 'My sons have defeated me, My sons have defeated me.'" And they said, "At that time, they brought all the objects which Rabbi Eliezer had ruled were pure and burned them with fire. They voted about it and excommunicated him. They said, 'who will go tell him?' Rabbi Akiba said to them, 'I will go inform him in case a person who is not fit goes and informs him and brings about the destruction of the whole world.' What did he do? He wore black and covered himself in black and sat in front of him a distance of four cubits away and his eyes streamed with tears. Rabbi Eliezer said to him, 'Akiva, why is this day different from other days?' He said to him, 'My teacher, it

seems to me that your colleagues are shunning you.' He also tore his garments and removed his shoes."

No clear protagonist or villain emerges in this story. Both sides were guilty of verbal wrongdoing—the sages in their eventual excommunication of Rabbi Eliezer, and Rabbi Eliezer in that he abandoned the use of words completely. In his zealous defense of the cleanliness of an oven, he brought forth "all the arguments in the world," and, when these failed, pulled out some supernatural tricks. In old-fashioned Mosaic style, Rabbi Eliezer drew carob trees out of the earth, made water flow uphill, and tilted walls of stone to testify in his defense. His argument might be summarized as "I am right because Heaven says so." His arguments were not verbal but physical—a carob tree uprooted, rolling across the ground, and a stream of water reversing its direction testified to the fact that, legally speaking, R. Eliezer was correct: the oven should be considered clean. However, the other *tannaim* remained unconvinced by these arguments, and each time they responded "no proof is brought from . . ." the operative word being "proof." The *tannaitic* rejection of R. Eliezer's arguments was a rejection of his methodology of miracle.[66]

The narrative appeared to be concerned with establishing the right versus wrong ways for books of the mouth to disagree. The Oven of Akhnai tale reveals that when it came to sources' authority on sacred matters, Rabbis expected their sources to clash. By focusing on developing proper protocol, they avoided criticisms similar to the charge Irenaeus had directed at Valentinus—utter chaos results from each preaching his own opinion. In essence, by appealing to heaven, rather than the apostolic-like chain of transmission of the Oral Torah, the heresy of Rabbi Eliezer, was to, in Rebecca Scharbach Wollenberg's words, "scorn the modes of cultural transmission"[67] that defined the rabbinic program.

The narrative also provided support for the authenticity authority of the Oral Torah. Despite a rare appearance of the *Bat Kol*, the heavenly voice, who explicitly stated, "the law agrees with him in every way," Rabbi Joshua won the argument by turning to the written Torah, using the deity's own words against him: he constructed his argument, "it is not in heaven," from Deuteronomy 30:11–14: "For this commandment I give to you today is not too difficult for you, nor is it distant. It is not in heaven so one may say, 'who will go up for us to the heavens and take it for us so we may hear it and do it?' Nor is it beyond the sea so one may say 'who will venture beyond the sea and take it for us so we may hear it and do it?' *For the word is very near to you, in your mouths and in your hearts*, so you may do it."

Appealing to the written law, claiming "it is not in heaven," Rabbi Joshua located the law in the collective mouth (and heart) of the Rabbis.[68] Rabbi Joshua spoke forth the law residing in his own mouth, despite the fact that it conflicted with the claims of another living book and even with the judgment of the deity itself, who confirmed that the Akhnai oven was clean. Irenaeus would have found the very exchange heretical—in his logic, texts of the body were supposed to corroborate their written versions, not conflict with them. Irenaeus expected perfect consistency among books of the heart and the four Gospels.

There is consistency between the way the rabbinic narrative and the Valentinian sources regarded the relationship between the oral utterances of select individuals and sacred writings. As Susan Handelman observed about the Oven of Akhnai tale, it asserts "even though revelation was given at Sinai, revelation is ongoing and mediated by interpreters."[69] Moreover, as Richard Hidary has demonstrated, the rabbinic project viewed the interpretation of scripture as endless, and, moreover, the interpreters themselves became scripture.[70] The same can be said for Valentinian scriptural practice. Just as the *Gospel of Truth* urged individuals to "speak the truth because you are a form of it," Rabbi Joshua spoke forth the text that he insisted resided within his own mouth. He did not focus on the inconsistency between his internal text and the legal ruling of the deity. Valentinus also ignored conflicting matter and was more concerned with the "shared material" among books of the heart. As fragment 6 asserted, Valentinus accepted wisdom from many sources, oral or written, ignoring their contradictions. This rabbinic narrative suggested a deep indifference to perfect consistency, evident by the deity's own response to his living books' conflict over an oven—rather than expressing Irenaeus's doctrinal outrage over diverging texts and teachers, God laughed.[71]

The sages' excommunication of Rabbi Eliezer provoked more questions about the nature of Oral Torah. If Oral Torah was to be esteemed equally to written Torah, his excommunication implied that he was ejected from an oral canon of living books. What happens to Oral Torah when it is excommunicated? Does it become profane, incapable of making judgments or unqualified as a source of authority or wisdom? BT Sanhedrin 68a took up these questions, exploring the fate of decanonized Oral Torah through the death of Rabbi Eliezer. At the very moment the value of Rabbi Eliezer's legal opinions was questioned, the story reinstated Rabbi Eliezer's authority as Torah without resolving his disagreement with other sages. It did so by relying on the scholar-as-scroll motif that had canonized the *Gospel of Truth*'s Jesus and Rabbi Hanina as living books.

BT Sanhedrin 68a observed that excommunicated Oral Torah was still capable of sound legal judgment, despite expectations to the contrary. As Rabbi

Eliezer lay dying, he was tended to by his wife and daughter, then visited by former students. In his final hour, he transformed into a Torah scroll, and he reclaimed his position as living (albeit dying) law. The Talmud reports:

> He moved his two arms and rested them upon his heart and said, "woe is you. My two arms are like two Torah scrolls that have been rolled up. Much Torah have I learned but I did not diminish my teachers even as much as a dog laps from the sea. Much Torah have I taught, but my students did not diminish me as much as an eyeshadow brush in its tube. Moreover, I studied three hundred laws about leprosy but no person ever came to ask me about them. Furthermore, I studied three hundred, some say three thousand laws, about the planting of cucumbers but no person ever asked me about them except Akiva ben Joseph. Once, when he and I were walking down a road, he said to me, 'Rabbi, teach me about the planting of cucumbers.' I said a single word and the whole field filled with cucumbers. He said to me, 'Rabbi, you have taught me their planting. Teach me their uprooting.' I said a single word and all of them were gathered to one place." They said to him, "a globe, a shoemaker's last, a jeweled amulet and small weight–what are they?" He said to them, "they are impure and their purification lies in what they are." "A sandal upon a raised shoemaker's last–what is it?" He said to them, "it is pure," and his soul departed in purity. Rabbi Johannan stood upon his feet and said, "the vow is void, the vow is void."[72]

In this passage, Rabbi Eliezer lamented the opportunities lost for Torah study resulting from his excommunication. He knew laws concerning leprosy and the planting of cucumbers that almost no one learned. In the tradition of deathbed wisdom, the other sages tried to scramble for a last-minute lesson, ironically about purity—the very issue at stake in the Akhnai oven affair. They returned to a disagreement catalogued by the Mishnah: is a shoe still on its last considered susceptible to uncleanliness?[73] In the Mishnah, Rabbi Eliezer disagreed with the sages and his answer was no. Revisiting the question here, his answer was still no. Pronouncing "הוא טהור," he died with the word "pure" on his lips, a legal ruling about a shoe on its last to be sure, but also a general pronouncement—Rabbi Eliezer maintained his disagreement, yet his soul departed in purity. His excommunication was annulled upon his death, and the disagreement never satisfactorily resolved. On one hand, the rabbis won—Rabbi Eliezer accepted their methodology, participating in debate rather than calling on heaven for sensational miracles.[74] At the same time, it was Rabbi Eliezer who literally had the last word on the matter.

The dying Torah scroll signaled Rabbi Eliezer's undiminished capacity as Oral Torah; his body described as two Torah scrolls took him from a position of pedagogical notoriety to piety.[75] This bibliomorphosis reinforced his elite status at the very moment it was in question. Despite being excommunicated and ending his life exiled from his intellectual circle, Rabbi Eliezer was not excluded from the Oral Torah. The Rabbi-as-book motif included Rabbi Eliezer and Rabbi Hanina in the select class of teachers whose words counted as Torah even as one was excommunicated and the other executed as a criminal.

The death scenes of both Rabbis addressed the question: what did it mean for versions of Oral Torah to disagree? The answers provided in both narratives indicate that disagreement was expected and variation normal. In the context of rabbinic thought, this seems obvious, but when compared to the expectations of Christian theologians such as Irenaeus, the contrast is striking. Irenaeus's Gospel concept demanded perfect consistency; the rabbinic dual Torah expected conflict. As Daniel Boyarin reads the Oven of Akhnai narrative, the sin of Rabbi Eliezer was to embrace Irenaeus's position, the creedal discourse of nascent orthodoxy, with its appeal to faith and miracles, rather than conform to the theological disputation that became the hallmark of Rabbinic Judaism.[76] Valentinus's sin, then, might be thought of in similar terms. His exclusion, and ultimate demonization, in early Christian circles stemmed from an ideology of revelation that resembled the rabbinic dual Torah more than a fourfold Gospel.

Gospel of the Heart and Torah of the Mouth

As concepts and not simply descriptive terms for a genre, both Torah and Gospel encompass a wide semantic range.[77] As one could hear the gospel (good news) or read a Gospel, one could obey the Torah (law), read Torah, or embody Torah. With the Gospel of the heart and Torah of the mouth, Valentinus and the Rabbis proposed similar definitions of the sacred book in an age when the definition was not so obvious. Consequently, to understand Valentinian books of the heart it is useful to consider rabbinic parallels. Like other religious circles, they had to draw lines between the texts that are sacred and those that are not. And, as traditions that accept living canons, they also had to explore where the sage ends and the text begins. Both traditions put forward a sacred book that existed in written and corporeal form. In the *Gospel of Truth*, the book could reside in the heart of the elect; in the rabbinic tradition, it was found in the mouth of an elite class of teachers. Living books possessed revelatory authority, adding the advantage that the book was always present to explain and expound. To be sure, other groups (such as the Montanists) maintained traditions about living authorities on divine matters, but these leaders were regarded as prophets, not books.

Both Valentinus and the Rabbis also shared a significant degree of tolerance for disagreement among their sacred books. Valentinus expressed no interest in resolving inconsistencies between books of the church and books of Greek wisdom; disagreement was a cornerstone of rabbinic discourse. From the perspective of other ancient writers, such as Irenaeus and Epiphanius, who criticized groups lacking coherent and consistent collections of texts, this was troubling. They were particularly suspicious of groups who displayed variety in their teaching. How does one persuade people to accept the authority of teachers as living books? Valentinus and the Rabbis both resorted to the scroll, calling upon the written document to ratify the oral text. They depicted their esteemed teachers dying, wrapped in their own books—a gruesome lesson about the nature of sacred text.

If literary descriptions of the form and function of books reveal anything about the way authors regarded their literary endeavors, the shared scholar-as-scroll motif indicates that the concept of Oral Torah enhances our own understanding of Valentinus's book of the heart. Both groups proposed that the sacred book included written and oral permutations: just as the Rabbis had the idea of an Oral Torah, transmitted orally from Moses through certain teachers, Valentinus similarly posited a bodily Gospel, transmitted both in writing and orally, originating with Jesus on the cross. The concept of the book of the heart was represented in the *Gospel of Truth* by the way the author chose to describe the physical book—Jesus, a crucified book, replicated the contents of his heart onto the hearts of his followers. The teacher-as-text motif in the *Gospel of Truth* reflected Valentinus's idea of what a sacred book was, and the bibliomorphoses in the Talmud functioned in a similar way. Rabbis as books, a visual demonstration of a Torah comprising both written and oral formats, pointed to their concept of sacred book. However, the Valentinian record is not nearly as complete as the rabbinic record. The *Gospel of Truth* revealed limited information about the book of the heart: it was preexistent, resided in the body of Jesus, and could copy itself onto pure human hearts. Fragment 6 demonstrated that Valentinus was not simply being poetic when he described a book of the heart, because he found evidence for it in written texts published for a variety of audiences. But evidence ends there.

What does it mean to endorse books in oral form? To the modern reader, a text such as the *Gospel of Truth*, which resembles oral discourse more than a formal literary composition, is homily. To the ancient critic, a text such as the *Gospel of Truth*, bearing no resemblance to other Jesus-centric compositions, was nonsense. Yet the more detailed rabbinic record pointed to one way that a tradition of living, conflicting books could function as a meaningful category. The Talmud treated the oral and written versions of the Torah identically in many activities—studying, handling, and burial practices. The living book could be studied as well as the written one; a dynamic corpus is no less serious than a static one. Written documents can appear contradictory, and scholars can disagree without losing authority. A Torah scholar must be accorded the same honors as a Torah scroll, in life, and upon deterioration and death. Thus, the concept of living books allows the scroll and scholar to elevate one another, and blurs the line between sacred text, author, and reader. The idea of a living book could be taken as seriously as its written counterpart, even as the sacred text grew beyond the bounds of contents. It is an attested tradition, fragmentary in Valentinian sources, and developed with the emerging Rabbinic movement.

A shared tradition of human, sacred books does not indicate dependence, influence, or awareness of one group by the other. There are significant differences that make this clear. The book of the heart was self-replicating; the book of the mouth took years to acquire. The book of the heart subsumed both written and oral formats; the book of the mouth did not describe the written Torah. Rabbinic sages from all generations placed restrictions on the number of written authoritative texts; fragment 6 indicates Valentinus did not. Furthermore, Valentinus's writings suggest that his idea about what a sacred text was supposed to be was organic. The term "Gospel" originally connoted oral discourse; its application to written texts was secondary. There is no indication that Valentinus struggled with the term Gospel, and even Irenaeus relied on both meanings. Because Gospel could designate written or oral information, the writings of the church, writings of Greek philosophers, and the verbal proclamations of leaders all fell naturally under the rubric of sacred book. In contrast, the Rabbis fought hard for the dual Torah. Put another way, as the terms "Gospel" and "Torah" developed in opposite directions, so did the two ideas of living books. The idea of oral texts faded quietly from the Gospel tradition as the authority of Oral Torah gained momentum under an increasingly organized rabbinic community.[78]

These differences do not make comparison a futile exercise in "parallelomania."[79] Instead, the similarities between the corpora of living books demonstrate how two groups confronted challenges stemming from the empire-wide "struggle over the relative value of the sacred book in antiquity."[80] As various groups debated the significance and function of the book in a religious context, oral books allowed both Valentinus and the Rabbis to continue composing even as this activity was being reigned in. If Christians insisted the Logos resided only in the body of Jesus and Jews claimed the Logos belonged only to the Torah, both Valentinus and the Rabbis redefined these terms. Through the shared image of the teacher as book, the *Gospel of Truth* was able to claim that Gospel was both body and book and the Rabbis could insist that Torah designated both a scroll and a scholar.

CONCLUSION

The Iconic Book

The Crucified Book has identified questions that arise in the development of "book religions." What is a sacred book? In what form does it exist? From what people or spirits does it arise? What authority and what power does it possess? Is it living, and can it die? Unencumbered by later canonicity, we find a varied landscape.[1] Valentinus envisioned a sacred book that resided fragmentarily in books and in the hearts of certain Christians. While Marcion confined the source of divine knowledge to one text, Montanus and his New Prophets channeled the divine spirit to speak through them. Justin's spermatic word permitted divine truths in works of multiple authors, even Greek philosophers, while his student Tatian streamlined several Gospel accounts into one text. Irenaeus defended a fourfold written Gospel amid these other ideas of embodied and spoken texts.

But Irenaeus's position focuses our view of the past onto the end product. According to Irenaeus, a sacred book is written, it has boundaries, is immutable and unchanging. His sacred book has become a major identifying feature, even a shorthand, for an entire religious tradition. Max Müller, when introducing book religion as an academic category, was aware of the category's shortcomings, warning: "To the student of religion canonical books are, no doubt, of the utmost importance, but he ought never to forget that canonical books too give the reflected image only of the real doctrines of the founder of a new religion, an image always blurred and distorted by the medium through which it had to pass."[2]

In this passage, Müller echoed Plato's assertion that written words are imperfect records of the past, in this case the teachings of the original founder. This book has not been interested in whether the *Gospel of Truth* represents the teachings of the historical Jesus. Implied above, though, the very presence of *canonical* books distorts the full historical picture. A closed set of scriptures, a Bible with ends, obscures other scriptural practices of antiquity, Valentinian included. But if we heed Müller's caution, we can accept that the canon itself is a distortion. Then we can find other scriptural traditions, other "shapes of scriptures,"[3] in Eva Mroczek's words, blurred and distorted by the canonical books that eventually prevailed.

One of these shapes takes form in the *Gospel of Truth*. At one time, the *Gospel of Truth* exemplified a revelatory text and envisioned a revelatory text. The *Gospel of Truth* is so unusual, not just for its radical storytelling, but for offering so many answers to questions about sacred books in such short space. It offers answers to one question after another:

> *What is a sacred book?* It is a preexistent, heavenly book, a text "written in the thought and mind of the Father," and existed "before the foundation of the All."
>
> *In what form does it exist?* The book is equated with the body of Jesus, and appears on the "hearts of the little children," and is published by "reading out the contents of the heart."
>
> *From what people or spirits does it arise?* The book is "written in the thought and mind of the Father," published by the Son on the cross, and distributed as individuals "speak the truth."
>
> *What authority and what power does it possess?* The book constitutes "knowledge of the Father" and has the capacity to kill even as it promises eternal life for those who are written in it.
>
> *Is it living, and can it die?* The book is called the "living book of the living" even as it dies. The book promises eternal life for those who become written in it, even as it predicts that the "one who takes up the book will be slaughtered."

The body-as-book, then, signaled a mode of holy book that resisted Irenaeus's call for a fixed collection of written texts.

Christian orthodoxy did not mark the end to these questions—they shifted but did not resolve. In the fourth century, by the time Christian orthodoxy found its center, new debates about the role of sacred writing arose. Ecclesiastical writers no longer focused their attention solely on distinguishing right books from wrong books; they also addressed the proper format and use of sacred texts. They expressed concerns about the popular talismanic use of Gospel books and debated the extent to which a Gospel could function as a magical object.[4] For instance, the use of miniature Gospel codices as apotropaic devices is well attested by the fourth century. Christian monks were known to hang small Gospel books around their necks when traveling.[5] Euplus, a Christian martyred in Sicily in 304 C.E., brought a Gospel book to his trial and performed bibliomancy to argue his case.[6] At the time of his execution the book was hung around his neck, simultaneously a marker of his crime from the perspective of his captors, and a symbol of his righteousness for Euplus and the Christian audiences of his martyrdom.

John Chrysostom also bore witness to the practice of wearing Gospel books, although his opinion of the practice was less favorable. He complained, "Do you not see how women and little children suspend Gospels from their necks as powerful amulets, and carry them about in all places wherever they go?"[7] John did not approve of the practice, likening miniature Gospel codices to magical amulets: "And what are these amulets (φυλακτήρια) and borders? Since they were continually forgetting God's benefits, he commanded that his wonders be inscribed on little books and that these should be suspended from their hands . . . which they call phylacteries (φυλακτήρια), as now many of our women have Gospels hanging from their necks."[8]

John Chrysostom observed that it had become popular—too popular for his taste—for women to wear Gospels as necklaces. In part, Chrysostom's objections to this practice stemmed from his larger agenda to eradicate "Judaizing" influences from Christianity.[9] He thought the wearing of Gospel books was influenced by the Jewish practice of wearing phylacteries, which in his logic was sufficient reason to condemn the practice.

Yet his contemporary Augustine presented a different perspective. He too frowned upon Christians wearing amulets, but he did see a difference between an amulet which might contain portions of Christian scripture, and Gospel books, which would contain the text in its entirety: "When you have a headache, we commend you if you put the Gospel by your head and do not hurry to an amulet. For human frailty has come to this, and men who hurry to amulets must be so lamented that we rejoice when we see that a man, confined to his bed, is tossed by fever and pain and yet has placed no hope anywhere else except that he put the Gospel by his head, not because the Gospel was made for this, but because it has been preferred to amulets."[10]

It is not clear whether Augustine fully approved of using Gospel books for healing purposes, but in his mind, it was preferable to the use of amulets.[11] While John Chrysostom saw no distinction between amulet and Gospel codex for magical purposes, Augustine placed the two in separate categories. These debates ran concurrent to Rabbinic discussions about what constitutes a Torah scroll. Many Christian amulets quoted portions of Gospel, yet Augustine, at least, was convinced that was not the same thing as a Gospel book. In this way, questions about the form of the sacred book, its authority and powers, continued as two church fathers wrestled with questions of materiality.

John Chrysostom and Augustine were contemporaries in disagreement. We must acknowledge, then, that the material sacred book of today does not necessarily match those of antiquity. Today, sacred books are considered extraordinary objects worthy of extraordinary treatment. Torah scrolls, swaddled in bejeweled velvet, reside behind ornate curtains in a synagogue. In a Catholic Mass, the priest kisses the golden covers of the Gospel before opening it and reading aloud.[12] These methods of handling reflect a sanctity of texts that extends beyond their contents—a mode of holiness that has been termed "iconic."[13] But this was not the universal experience of the early Christian. If the manner in which a book is destroyed makes a statement about its value, AnneMarie Luijendijk's observation, that "the majority of biblical manuscripts we have today were found in garbage dumps,"[14] reminds us not to take the sacred materiality of the book for granted.

Luijendijk also urges us to find meaning in a book's destruction. In the *Gospel of Truth*, the crucified book is a revelatory act, a way of publishing divine knowledge. The idea that the heavenly book could be represented in writing and in body, and thus "die," can be found in a broader push to equate holy body and holy book. Several recent studies have examined the sacred book as a signifying, material object, particularly at the moment of its "death." The practices of holding funerals for books and burying them, attested across traditions both east and west, provide culturally specific examples of the symbolic bodily significance of books. As books have become cheaper to produce, the proliferation of holy books has forced traditions to reflect on the significance of their written documents, particularly as they deteriorate. While the Jewish practice of depositing decaying texts into a *genizah* is very ancient, elaborate funerary rites have developed to honor a deceased Torah scroll.[15] In Bengal, one might find a body or a book floating down the Ganges, a Hindu burial for pure individuals.[16] An old Qur'an might be buried in a Muslim cemetery or soaked in water until the ink drifts off the pages.[17] Ritual burials of sacred texts are also found across Sikh, Christian, Jain, and Buddhist traditions, incited by a seemingly universal human discomfort about throwing away holy books, especially as they represent the body of a holy person or contain a divine presence.[18]

Müller's convenient category "people of the book" implicitly places people and books in separate ontological categories. But the boundaries between speaking bodies and written texts are never clear. The Lotus Sutra, self-identifying as dying words of Buddha, for example, is said to contain the whole body of the Buddha.[19] Rabbinic literature, too, leveraged the symbolic capital of the scroll to ratify the oral lessons of dying rabbis. In the writings of Valentinus, we find similar efforts to join holy person and holy book. As Roman jurists legally defined a book, and Roman authors considered their writing as progeny, they spoke of the written word in terms of the human body. Valentinus utilized the metaphorical language of his time as he joined holy book and holy person as sources of revelatory authority. When book and body are tied together, in metaphor and in law, oral texts and their speakers achieve parallel authority and power to written texts.

Why was there so much debate, especially beginning in the second century, about whether certain sources were authoritative? It is not just that Christianity and Rabbinic Judaism, two new religious movements, were coming into their own. The questions did not just ask which books were in or out, but sought a fundamental reexamination of textual authority. Second-century scholars found their ecosystem of texts complicated by the convenience of the codex and the ensuing proliferation of new texts and wider circulation, prompting the question, "what is a sacred book?" The rapidly changing format and wider availability of texts prompted ancient scholars to scrutinize the workings of the divine book, as empire-wide discussions addressed the role of books as sources of information, avatars for people, or both.

Moreover, just as new technology incited funerary practices for books, the very recent scholarly interest in these topics might be explained by our own technological advances. Rapidly changing formats complicate our definitions of books and their attendant textual authority, but also inspire scholars across disciplines to scrutinize their research subjects' representations of the written word. Currently, categories that seem clear—book, article, lecture—have been upended by the changing, multiple formats of the written word and force us to consider the significance of our own writings, especially as these writings confer authority. Which new forms are "publications" for tenure or valid for scholarly conferences?[20] Might a digital humanities project replace a traditional dissertation? How long before a priest reads scripture from an electronic book? How much longer before the physical presence of such a device inspires reverence from the congregation? To answer these questions, we are forced to consider the same questions about older texts: what gave the printed "hard copy" book authority in the first place that the electronic "soft copy" is doubted? Whenever new formats of text arise, whether the codex of antiquity or the e-text of today, close examinations of the written word and its authority follow.

This book has also complicated the traditional boundaries between texts. The fixation and fixity of a Bible cannot be presumed, certainly not in second temple Jewish literature, as Eva Mroczek has demonstrated, nor for rabbinic Jews and the first Christians, as scholars such as Azzan Yadin and David Brakke have argued. The *Gospel of Truth* sits amid nascent Christianity and second temple Judaism. It also resides in a broader Greco-Roman textual community, and, as Duncan MacRae has shown us, this context did embrace a complex theory of sacred book. So if we accept current models about the parting of the ways, we have to hold up Nag Hammadi texts to all of these contexts. This book has attempted to do that. Focusing on "the book" puts aside the identities of religious groups that scholars have located in antiquity, and instead asks the question: for these readers, what makes a text sacred and from where does it get its authority? Some of those we call "Christian" created their identity around the person of Jesus as some of those we call "Jewish" did with Torah. Valentinus presented an option in which divine authority was tied up in both the book and body; moreover, many books and many bodies. Valentinus sanctioned all formats of sacred "book," written on papyrus or written in the heart of the speaker. This theory of sacred book places him not at the periphery of a crystallizing Christianity, but at the center.

NOTES

INTRODUCTION

1. Dionysius of Halicarnassus, *Roman Antiquities* 7.69.2; Josephus, *Antiquities* 7.69.2.

2. Robin Jensen, *The Cross: History, Art, and Controversy* (Cambridge, MA: Harvard University Press, 2017), 221.

3. The elements of Valentinian spirituality are comprehensively described in Einar Thomassen, *The Spiritual Seed: The Church of the "Valentinians,"* NHMS 60 (Leiden: Brill, 2006), 133–93. For Valentinus's authorship, see H. C. Puech and G. Quispel, "Les écrits gnostiques du Codex Jung," *VC* 8, no. 1 (1954): 22–38. For arguments against Valentinus's authorship: Christoph Markschies, *Valentinus Gnosticus? Untersuchungen zur valentinianischen Gnosis mit einem Kommentar zu den Fragmenten Valentins*, WUNT 65 (Tübingen: Mohr Siebeck, 1992), 339–65.

4. *Gos. Truth* 20.24–39. ⲉⲧⲃⲉ ⲡⲉⲓ ⲁϥⲟⲩⲁⲛϩ̄ ⲁⲃⲁⲗ ⲛ̄ϭⲓ ⲓⲏⲥⲟⲩⲥ ⲁϥϭⲁⲗⲉϥ ⲙ̄ⲡⲓϫⲱⲙⲉ ⲉⲧⲙ̄ⲙⲉⲩ ⲁⲩⲁϥⲧϥ̄ ⲁⲩϣⲉ ⲁϥⲧⲱϭⲉ ⲙ̄ⲡⲇⲓⲁⲧⲁⲅⲙⲁ ⲁⲃⲁⲗ ⲛ̄ⲧⲉ ⲡⲓⲱⲧ ϩⲓ ⲡⲉⲥⲧⲁⲩⲣⲟⲥ ⲱ̂ ⲙⲛ̄ϯⲛⲁϭ ⲛ̄ⲥⲃⲱ ⲛ̄ⲧⲉⲉⲓϭⲁⲧ ⲉϥⲥⲱⲕ ⲙ̄ⲙⲁϥ ⲁⲡⲓⲧⲛ̄ ⲁⲡⲙⲟⲩ ⲉⲣⲉⲡⲓⲱⲛϩ̄ ⲛ̄ⲁⲛⲏϩⲉ ⲧⲟ ϩⲓⲱⲱϥ ⲉⲁϥⲃⲱϣ ⲙ̄ⲙⲁϥ ⲛ̄ⲛⲓⲡⲗ̄ϭⲉ ⲉⲧⲧⲉⲕⲁⲓ̈ⲧ ⲁϥϯ ϩⲓ̈ⲱⲱϥ ⲛ̄ⲧⲙⲛ̄ⲧⲁⲧ ⲧⲉⲕⲟ ⲡⲉⲉⲓ ⲉⲧⲉ ⲙⲛ̄ ϣϭⲁⲙ ⲛ̄ⲗⲁⲩⲉ ⲁϣ ϥⲓⲧϥ̄ ⲛ̄ⲧⲟⲟⲧϥ̄ ⲉⲁϥϣⲉ ⲁϩⲟⲩⲛ ⲁⲛⲓⲙⲁⲉⲓⲧ ⲉⲧϣⲟⲩⲉⲓⲧ ⲛ̄ⲧⲉ ⲛⲓϩⲣ̄ⲧⲉ ⲁϥⲥⲓⲛⲉ ⲁⲃⲁⲗ ϩⲓ̈ⲧⲟⲟⲧⲟⲩ ⲛ̄ⲛⲉⲉⲓ ⲉⲧⲃⲏϣ ⲁⲃⲁⲗ ⲛ̄ⲧⲟⲟⲧⲥ̄ ⲛ̄ⲧⲃ̄ϣⲉ ⲉϥⲟⲉⲓ ⲛ̄ⲛⲟⲩⲥⲁⲩⲛⲉ ⲙⲛ̄ ⲟⲩϫⲱⲕ ⲉϥⲱϣ ⲛ̄ⲛⲉⲧⲛ̄ϩⲏⲧ [Attridge and MacRae, 86]. This book consults the Coptic critical edition of Harold Attridge and George W. MacRae, S.J., "The *Gospel of Truth*," in *Nag Hammadi Codex I (The Jung Codex) Nag Hammadi Studies Series XXII* (Leiden: Brill, 1985).

5. Guy Stroumsa, *The Scriptural Universe of Ancient Christianity* (Cambridge, MA: Harvard University Press, 2016), 10–28.

6. On the intellectual world of Fredrich Max Müller, see N. J. Girardot, "Max Müller's Sacred Books and the Nineteenth-Century Production of the Comparative Science of Religions," *History of Religions* 41, no. 3 (2002): 213–50.

7. F. Max Müller, *Introduction to the Science of Religion: Four Lectures Delivered at the Royal Institution, in February and May 1870* (London: Longmans, Green, and Co., 1882), 53.

8. *Div. inst.* 5.1.26–27. Cf. Claudio Moreschini and Enrico Norelli, *Early Christian Greek and Latin Literature*, trans. Matthew J. O'Connell (Peabody, MA: Hendrickson Publishers, 2005), 324.

9. C. F. Evans, "Tradition and Scripture," *Religious Studies* 3, no. 1 (1967): 324.

10. Harry Gamble, *Books and Readers in the Early Church* (New Haven: Yale University Press, 1995), 11.

11. Ignatius, *Phld.* 8.2. See Daniel Boyarin, "Why Ignatius Invented Judaism," in *The Ways that Often Parted: Essays in Honor of Joel Marcus*, ed. Lori Baron, Jill Hicks-Keeton, and Matthew Thiessen, 319 (Atlanta: SBL Press, 2018).

12. Eusebius, *Historia Ecclesia* 3.39.4. οὐ γὰρ τὰ ἐκ τῶν βιβλίων τοσοῦτόν με ὠφελεῖν ὑπελάμβανον ὅσον τὰ παρὰ ζώσης φωνῆς καὶ μενούσης. Eusebius. *Ecclesiastical History, Volume I: Books 1-5,* Translated by Kirsopp Lake, LCL 153 (Cambridge, MA: Harvard University Press, 1926), 292.

13. William V. Harris, *Ancient Literacy* (Cambridge, MA: Harvard University Press, 1989), 22.

14. Irenaeus, *Ad. haer.* 3.8.11.

15. The presumed oral origins of biblical texts have driven the methods of modern biblical studies. Form criticism—works of scholars from Hermann Gunkel to Rudolf Bultmann—sought an oral *ur*-tradition, reconstructing the spoken words by locating commonalities and variations in the Hebrew Bible and written Gospels. But these methods of textual analysis seem powerless to retrieve the oral past, or to distinguish this past from contemporary community. Later work was not so ambitious as to attempt reconstruction of an earlier oral text. Rather, it focused on the oral features of Early Christian literature, no longer pitting the oral against the written. Works of William Graham, Pieter Botha, Werner Kelber, and Birger Gerhardsson, among others, drew scholarly attention to oral markers in the Gospels. Pieter Botha, *Orality and Literary in Early Christianity*, Biblical Performance Criticism 5 (Eugene, OR: Cascade Books, 2012); Birger Gerhardsson, *Memory and Manuscript: Oral Tradition and Written Transmission in Rabbinic Judaism and Early Christianity* (Lund and Copenhagen: C.W.K. Gleerup and Ejnar Munksgaard, 1961); William A. Graham, *Beyond the Written Word: Oral Aspects of Scripture in the History of Religion* (Cambridge, UK: Cambridge University Press, 1993), 45–57; Werner H. Kelber, *The Oral and the Written Gospel* (Philadelphia: Fortress Press, 1983).

16. Attridge and MacRae categorize the text as "homiletic reflections." Attridge and MacRae, "Gospel of Truth," 67. For a useful discussion on the performative aspects of the *Gospel of Truth*, see Katrine Brix, "The Gospel of Truth," in *Die Nag Hammadi Schriften in der Literatur und Theologiegeschichte des frühen Christentums*, ed. Jens Schröter and Konrad Schwarz, 233–47 (Mohr Siebeck, 2017).

17. L. W. Hurtado, "Oral Fixation and New Testament Studies? 'Orality,' 'Performance' and Reading Texts in Early Christianity," *NTS* 60 (2014): 321–40.

18. Gamble, *Books and Readers in the Early Church*, 11.

19. Most recently, Chris Keith, *The Gospel as Manuscript: An Early History of the Jesus Tradition as Material Artifact* (New York: Oxford University Press, 2020). Also Chris Keith, "Early Christian Book Culture and the Emergence of the First Written Gospel," in *Mark, Manuscripts, and Monotheism: Essays in Honor of Larry W. Hurtado*, ed. Chris Keith and Dieter T. Roth, 22–39, Library of New Testament Studies 528 (London: Bloomsbury T&T Clark, 2014); William E. Klingshirn and Linda Safran, *The Early Christian Book*, CUA Studies in Early Christianity (Washington, DC: Catholic University of America Press, 2007).

20. Chris Keith, "Prolegomena on the Textualization of Mark's Gospel: Manuscript Culture, the Extended Situation, and the Emergence of Written Gospels," in *Memory and Identity in Ancient Judaism and Early Christianity: A Conversation with Barry Schwartz*, ed. Tom Thatcher, 171, Semeia Studies 78 (Atlanta: SBL, 2014).

21. Guy Stroumsa, *The End of Sacrifice: Religious Transformations of Late Antiquity*, translated by Susan Emanuel (Chicago: University of Chicago Press, 2009).

22. Eva Mroczek, *The Literary Imagination in Jewish Antiquity* (New York: Oxford University Press, 2016), 5.

23. Annette Reed, "Ευαγγελιον: Orality, Textuality and the Christian Truth in Irenaeus' *Adversus Haereses*." *VC* 56, no. 1 (2002): 22. Also Guy Stroumsa, *Hidden Wisdom: Esoteric Traditions and the Roots of Christian Mysticism* (Leiden: Brill), 85–86.

24. *Adv. haer.* 3.11.8. Επεὶ γὰρ τέσσαρα κλίματα τοῦ κόσμου ἐν ῷ ἐσμὲν καὶ τέσσαρα καθολικὰ πνεύματα κατέσπαρται δὲ ἡ ἐκκλησία ἐπι πάσης τῆς γῆς στῦλος δὲ καὶ στήριγμα ἐκκλησίας τὸ εὐαγγέλιον

καὶ Πνεῦμα ζωῆς εἰκότως τέσσαρας ἔχειν αὐτὴν στλύλους πανταχόθεν πνέοντας τὴν ἀφθαρσίαν καὶ ἀναζωπυροῦντας τοὺς ἀνθροπους [SC 211: 168–71].

25. *Adv. haer.* 3.4.2.

26. Adolf von Harnack, *Das Neue Testament um das Jahr 200: Theodor Zahn's Geschichte des neutestamentlichen Kanons* (Freiburg: Mohr Siebeck, 1889), 110.

27. Hans von Campenhausen, *The Formation of the Christian Bible*, trans. J.A. Baker (Philadelphia: Fortress Press, 1972), 20–42.

28. David Brakke, "Scriptural Practices in Early Christianity," in *Invention, Rewriting, Usurpation: Discursive Fights over Religious Traditions in Antiquity*, Early Christianity in the Context of Antiquity 11 (Frankfurt: Peter Lang, 2012), 265.

29. Matthew Larsen, *Gospels Before the Book* (New York: Oxford University Press, 2018), 1–10.

30. Origen, *Comm. Jn*, 1.5. Cécile Blanc, ed., *Commentaire sur saint Jean*, Sources Chrétiennes 120 (Paris: Les Éditions du Cerf, 1966), 66–68.

31. For discussion of the academic custom of dating *Against Heresies* to c. 180 C.E., see Giulo Chiapparini, "Irenaeus and the Gnostic Valentinus: Orthodoxy and Heresy in the Church of Rome around the Middle of the Second Century," *ZAC* 18 (2014): 95–119.

32. David Brakke, "Scriptural Practices in Early Christianity," in *Invention, Rewriting, Usurpation: Discursive Fights over Religious Traditions in Antiquity*, Early Christianity in the Context of Antiquity 11 (Frankfurt: Peter Lang, 2012), 265. A similar argument is articulated by Robert Kraft, "Para-mania: Beside, Before and Beyond Bible Studies," *JBL* 126, no. 1 (2007): 5–27. For a compelling example, Blossom Stefaniw, *Mind, Text, and Commentary: Noetic Exegesis in Origen of Alexandria, Didymus the Blind, and Evagrius Ponticus* (Frankfurt am Main: Peter Lang Verlag, 2010).

33. Stroumsa, *The Scriptural Universe of Ancient Christianity*, 10–28. Christoph Markschies, "The Canon of the New Testament in Antiquity," in *Homer, the Bible and Beyond*, ed. M. Finkelberg and G. G. Stroumsa, 175–94 (Leiden: Brill, 2003).

34. Kraft, "Para-mania," 5.

35. Pheme Perkins, "Gnosticism and the Christian Bible," in *The Canon Debate*, ed. Lee Martin McDonald and James A. Sanders, 1355–71 (Peabody, MA: Hendrickson, 2002).

36. This approach has proved fruitful for the study of other early Christian texts: Derek Kruger, *Writing and Holiness: The Practice of Authorship in the Christian East* (Philadelphia: University of Pennsylvania Press, 2004); Blossom Stefaniw, *Mind, Text, Commentary*. For this approach as it relates to Nag Hammadi texts, see Simon Gathercole, "The Nag Hammadi Gospels," in *Die Nag Hammadi Schriften in der Literatur und Theologiegeschichte des frühen Christentums*, ed. Jens Schröter and Konrad Schwarz, 199–218 (Tübingen: Mohr Siebeck, 2017).

37. *Torah in the Mouth: Writing and Oral Tradition in Palestinian Judaism 200 BCE–400 CE* (New York: Oxford University Press, 2001), 7.

38. On the book trade in the Greco-Roman world, see Gamble, *Books and Readers in the Early Church*, 83–92. For estimations of book prices, Roger S. Bagnall, *Early Christian Books in Egypt* (Princeton and Oxford: Princeton University Press, 2009), 50–69.

39. Alan Watson, trans., *Digest of Justinian*, 4 vols. (Philadelphia: University of Pennsylvania Press, 1985), 1:88–89. Watson originally translated *volumina* as "volumes" which does not necessarily convey that these units were rolled.

40. Plato, *Phaedrus*, 275e–276b. Ταὐτὸν δὲ καὶ οἱ λόγοι. δόξαις μὲν ἂν ὥς τι φρονοῦντας αὐτοὺς λέγειν, ἐὰν δέ τι ἔρῃ τῶν λεγομένων βουλόμενος μαθεῖν, ἕν τι σημαίνει μόνον ταὐτὸν ἀεί. C.J. Rowe, trans., Plato: *Phaedrus*, 2nd ed. (Wiltshire, UK: Aris & Phillips, 1988), 124.

41. On the revival of Greek culture and literature, see P. E. Easterling, "Books and Readers in the Greek World: The Hellenistic and Imperial Periods" in *The Cambridge History of Classical*

Literature, ed. P. E. Easterling and B. M. W. Knox, 38–39 (Cambridge, UK: Cambridge University Press, 1985).

42. On the Greek nature of Imperial Rome's literary culture, see G. W. Bowersock, D. C. Innes, and E. L. Bowie, "The Literature of the Empire," in *The Cambridge History of Classical Literature*, ed. P. E. Easterling and B. M. W. Knox, 642–714, esp. 655–58 (Cambridge, UK: Cambridge University Press, 1985).

43. Marcus Aurelius compared books to breath, or "air and not even that always the same, but every minute belched forth and again gulped down." Θέασαι δὲ καὶ τὸ πνεῦμα, ὁποῖόν τί ἐστιν ἄνεμος οὐδε ἀεὶ τὸ αὐτο, ἀλλὰ πάσης ὥρας ἐξεμούμενον καὶ πάλιν ῥοφούμενον [Haines, 28].

44. Larry W. Hurtado, *Destroyer of the Gods: Early Christian Distinctiveness in the Roman Empire* (Waco, TX: Baylor University Press, 2016), 105. Also see Bernhard Lang, "The Writings: A Hellenistic Literary Canon in the Hebrew Bible," in *Canonization and Decanonization*, ed. Arie van der Kooij, K. van der Toorn, and Joannes Augustinus Maria Snoek (Leiden: Brill, 1998), 55.

45. Dionysus, *Ant. rom.* 4.62.4. συνελόντι δ' εἰπεῖν οὐδὲν οὕτω Ρωμαῖοι φυλάττουσιν οὔθ' ὅσιον κτῆμα οὔθ' ἱερὸν ὡς τὰ Σιβύλλεια θέσφατα. Dionysius of Halicarnassus, *Roman Antiquities, Volume II: Books 3-4*, trans. Earnest Cary, LCL 347 (Cambridge, MA: Harvard University Press, 1939), 466.

46. Three major studies include: Sean Alexandre Gurd, *Work in Progress: Literary Revision as Social Performance in Rome* (Oxford: Oxford University Press, 2012); William Johnson, *Readers and Reading Culture in the High Roman Empire* (Oxford and New York: Oxford University Press, 2010); William A. Johnson and Holt N. Parker, eds., *Ancient Literacies: The Culture of Reading in Greece and Rome* (Oxford and New York: Oxford University Press, 2009). Most significantly, Duncan MacRae, *Legible Religion: Books, Gods, and Rituals in Roman Culture* (Cambridge, MA: Harvard University Press, 2016).

47. Mroczek, *The Jewish Literary Imagination*; Jacqueline Vayntraub: *Beyond Orality: Biblical Poetry on Its Own Terms* (New York: Routledge, 2019); Rebecca Scharbach Wollenberg, "The Book That Changed: Tales of Ezran Authorship as a Form of Late Antique Biblical Criticism," *JBL* 138, no. 1 (2019), 143–60; "The Dangers of Reading as We Know It: Sight Reading as a Source of Heresy in Classical Rabbinic Literature," *JAAR* 85, no. 3 (2017), 709–45.

48. Brakke, "Scriptural Practices in Early Christianity"; Chris Keith, "Early Christian Book Culture and the Emergence of the First Written Gospel," in *Mark, Manuscripts, and Monotheism: Essays in Honor of Larry W. Hurtado*, ed. Chris Keith and Dieter T. Roth, 22–39, Library of New Testament Studies 528 (London: Bloomsbury T&T Clark, 2014); "Prolegomena on the Textualization of Mark's Gospel: Manuscript Culture, the Extended Situation, and the Emergence of Written Gospels," in *Memory and Identity in Ancient Judaism and Early Christianity: A Conversation with Barry Schwartz*, ed. Tom Thatcher, 161–86, Semeia Studies 78 (Atlanta: SBL, 2014).

49. For instance, Hans Jonas, *The Gnostic Religion: The Message of the Alien God and the Beginning of Christianity* (Boston: Beacon Press, 1958; 2nd ed., 1963), 310.

50. Origen, *Comm. Jn*, 1.5

51. Ismo Dunderberg, *Beyond Gnosticism: Myth, Lifestyle and Society in the School of Valentinus* (New York: Columbia University Press, 2008), 1.

52. To use the term coined by Brian Stock, *The Implications of Literacy: Written Language and Models of Interpretation in the Eleventh and Twelfth Centuries* (Princeton: Princeton University Press, 1983).

53. Daniel Boyarin, *Dying for God: Martyrdom and the Making of Christianity and Judaism* (Stanford, CA: Stanford University Press, 1999), 126.

54. On this point, see David Brakke, *The Gnostics: Myth, Ritual and Diversity in Early Christianity* (Cambridge, MA: Harvard University Press, 2010), 112–37.

55. Daniel Boyarin, *Borderlines* (Philadelphia: University of Pennsylvania Press, 2004), 128–30.

56. Stroumsa, *Hidden Wisdom*, 79–91. Harris, *Ancient Literacy*, 22.

57. Colin H. Roberts and T. C. Skeat, *The Birth of the Codex* (London: Oxford University Press, 1983), 45–57. Roger Bagnall's recent study calls into question whether Christians really did prefer the codex. See Bagnall, *Early Christian Books in Egypt*, 70–90.

CHAPTER 1

1. Barbara Aland et al., *The Greek New Testament*, 4th rev. ed. (New York: United Bible Societies, 1983). On these verses and Johannine ideas of scripture, see Julia D. Lindenlaub, "The Beloved Disciple as Interpreted and Author of Scripture in the Gospel of John" (PhD diss., University of Edinburgh, 2020).

2. Jn 20:30–31. In the vast corpus of early Christian hermeneutics, ancient biblical interpreters have not mentioned these verses, either finding them unworthy of comment or too problematic to consider. On the role of these verses in the formation of scripture, see Chris Keith, "The Competitive Textualization of the Jesus Tradition in John 20:30–31 and 21:24–25," *CBQ* 78. no. 2 (2016): 321–37.

3. Campenhausen, *Formation of the Christian Bible*, 92.

4. Justin Martyr, *1 Apol.* 5.

5. Mark Edwards, "Justin's Logos and the Word of God," *JECS* 3, no. 3 (Fall 1995): 278.

6. Irenaeus, *Adv. Haer.* III 11.19. "*Sidquidem in tantum processerunt audaciae uti quod ab his non olim conscriptum est Veritatis Evangelium titulent*" [SC 210:17274].

7. The elements of Valentinian spirituality are comprehensively described in Einar Thomassen, *The Spiritual Seed: The Church of the "Valentinians,"* NHMS 60 (Leiden: Brill, 2006), 133–93. Salvific ritual is also a prominent feature of many Valentinian texts, but overt references to baptisms and bridal chambers are absent in the *Gospel of Truth*. Consequently, Thomassen considers it likely that the text is Valentinian: Thomassen, "Notes pour la délimitation d'un corpus valentinien à Nag Hammadi," in *Les textes de Nag Hammadi et la problème de leur classification*, ed. Louis Painchaud and Anne Pasquier, 242–60 (Quebec: Les Presses de l'Université Laval, 1995).

8. Thomassen, *Spiritual Seed*, 147.

9. For Valentinus's authorship, see H. C. Puech and G. Quispel, "Les écrits gnostiques du Codex Jung," *VC* 8, no. 1 (1954): 22–38. For arguments against Valentinus's authorship: Christoph Markschies, *Valentinus Gnosticus? Untersuchungen zur valentinianischen Gnosis mit einem Kommentar zu den Fragmenten Valentins*, WUNT 65 (Tübingen: Mohr Siebeck, 1992), 339–65.

10. Portions of section II, and section III are adapted from a previously published article: A. Kreps, "The Passion of the Book: The *Gospel of Truth* as Valentinian Scriptural Practice," *JECS* 24, no. 3 (2016): 311–35.

11. Bentley Layton has translated the opening line: "The proclamation of the Truth is a joy for those who have received grace from the Father of truth." On the use of the term euaggelion, he remarked, "proclamation" (Gk. euaggelion): the Greek word can be translated also "Gospel." The title plays on this double meaning. Bentley Layton, *The Gnostic Scriptures: A New Translation with Annotations and Introductions* (Garden City, NY: Doubleday, 1987), 253. Katrine Brix has provided a useful summary of the debates over the Gospel's genre, noting that most see the text as a sort of homily. See Brix, "The Gospel of Truth," in *Die Nag Hammadi Schriften in der Literatur und Theologiegeschichte des frühen Christentums*, ed. Jens Schröter and Konrad Schwarz, 234 (Tübingen: Mohr Siebeck, 2017).

12. Layton, *Gnostic Scriptures*, 251.

13. Harold W. Attridge, *Nag Hammadi Codex I (the Jung codex)*, Nag Hammadi Studies, 22–23 (Leiden: Brill, 1985), 106.

14. Pheme Perkins, "What Is a Gnostic Gospel?," *CBQ* 71, no. 1 (January 2009): 106.

15. For example, Justin Martyr, *1 Apol.* 66:3.

16. For his use of the term to designate written documents, see *Smyrn.* 5 and 7.

17. For Ignatius's use of the term to designate oral teachings, see *Phil.* 5, *Tral.* 10, and *Eph.* 12.

18. *Phld* 8.2. ἐπεὶ ἤκουσά τινων λεγόντων ὅτι, ἐὰν μὴ ἐν τοῖς ἀρχείοις εὕρω, ἐν τῷ εὐαγγελίῳ οὐ πιστεύω. *The Apostolic Fathers, Volume I: I Clement. II Clement. Ignatius. Polycarp. Didache*, ed. and trans. Bart D. Ehrman, LCL 24 (Cambridge, MA: Harvard University Press, 2003), 290.

19. See *Phld.* 8. ἐμοὶ δὲ ἀρχεῖά ἐστιν Ιησοῦς Χριστός, τὰ ἄθικτα ἀρχεῖα, ὁ σταυρὸς αὐτοῦ καὶ ὁ θάνατος καὶ ἡ ἀνάστασις αὐτοῦ [Ehrman, 290].

William R. Schoedel argues persuasively that the term "archive" in this context refers to the writings we now call the Old Testament. William R. Schoedel, "Ignatius and the Archives," *HTR* 71, no. 1/2 (1978): 97–106. For a discussion on the history of interpretation of this intriguing passage in Ignatius, see Jonathon Lookadoo, "Ignatius of Antioch and Scripture" *Zeitschrift Für Antikes Christentum* 23, no. 2 (2019): 201–27. Also see Daniel Boyarin, "Why Ignatius Invented Judaism," in *The Ways that Often Parted: Essays in Honor of Joel Marcus*, ed. Lori Baron, Jill Hicks-Keeton, and Matthew Thiessen, 309–24 (Atlanta: SBL Press, 2018).

20. See Lookadoo, "Ignatius of Antioch and Scripture," 201–27.

21. Annette Yoshiko Reed notes that even Irenaeus used the term both ways. See Annette Yoshiko Reed, "Ευαγγελιον: Orality, Textuality and the Christian Truthin Irenaeus' Adversus Haereses," *VC* 56, no. 1 (2002): 11–46.

22. See Origen, *Comm. Jn* 1.5.

23. As claims Jn 21:25.

24. Rudolf Kittel, *Biblia Hebraica Stuttgartensia: Editio funditus renovata adjuvantibus,* H. Bardtke [et al.] cooperantibus, H. P. Rüger et J. Ziegler ediderunt, K. Elliger et W. Rudolph. Textum Masoreticum curavit H. P. Rüger. Masoram elaboravit G. E. Weil (Stuttgart: Deutsche Bibelstiftung, 1977).

25. *Gos. Truth* 16:31–17:4. The English text of the *Gospel of Truth* in this chapter is my translation of the critical edition by Harold Attridge and George W. MacRae, S.J., "The *Gospel of Truth*," in *Nag Hammadi Codex I (the Jung Codex) Nag Hammadi Studies Series XXII* (Leiden: Brill, 1985), 55–122. ⲡⲉⲩⲁⲅⲅⲉⲗⲓⲟⲛ ⲛ̄ⲧⲙⲉ ⲟⲩⲧⲉⲗⲏⲗ ⲡⲉ ⲛ̄ⲛⲉⲉⲓ ⲛ̄ⲧⲁϩϫⲓ ⲡⲓϩⲙⲁⲧ ⲁⲃⲁⲗ ϩⲓ̈ⲧⲟⲟⲧϥ̄ ⲙ̄ⲡⲓⲱⲧ ⲛ̄ⲧⲉ ⲧⲙⲏⲉ ⲁⲧⲣⲟⲩⲥⲟⲩⲱⲛϥ̄ ϩⲛ̄ ⲧϭⲁⲙ ⲙ̄ⲡⲓϣⲉϫⲉ ⲛ̄ⲧⲁϩⲓ̈ ⲉⲃⲁⲗ ϩⲛ̄ ⲡⲓⲡⲗⲏⲣⲱⲙⲁ ⲡⲉⲉⲓ ⲉⲧϩⲛ̄ ⲡⲓⲙⲉⲉⲩⲉ ⲟⲩⲁϩⲁ ⲡⲓⲛⲟⲩⲥ ⲛ̄ⲧⲉ ⲡⲓⲱⲧ ⲉⲧⲉ ⲡⲉⲓ ⲡⲉ ⲉⲧⲟⲩϣⲉϫⲉ ⲁⲣⲁϥ ϫⲉ ⲡⲥⲱⲧⲏⲣ ⲉⲡⲣⲉⲛ ⲙ̄ⲫⲱⲃ ⲉⲧϥ̄ⲛⲁⲉⲉⲓϥ ⲡⲉ ⲁⲡⲥⲱⲧⲉ ⲛ̄ⲛⲉⲉⲓ ⲛ̄ⲧⲁϩⲣ̄ ⲁⲧⲥⲟⲩⲱⲛ ⲡⲓⲱⲧ ⲉⲡⲓⲣⲉⲛ ⲇ̣ⲉ̣ [ⲙ]ⲡⲉⲩⲁⲅⲅⲉⲗⲓⲟⲛ ⲡⲉ ⲡⲟⲩⲱⲛϩ̄ ⲁⲃⲁⲗ ⲛ̄ⲧⲉ ϯϩⲉⲗⲡⲓⲥ ⲉⲡϭⲓⲛⲉ ⲡⲉ ⲛ̄ⲛⲉⲉⲓ ⲉⲧⲕⲱⲧⲉ ⲛ̄ⲥⲱϥ.

26. Geoffrey S. Smith, "Constructing a Christian Universe: Mythological Exegesis of Ben Sira 24 and John's Prologue in the *Gospel of Truth*," in *Jewish and Christian Cosmogony in Late Antiquity*, ed. Lance Jenott and Sarit Kattan Gribetz, 67 (Tübingen : Mohr Siebeck, 2013). See Harold Attridge, ed., "The Gospel of Truth as an Exoteric Text," in *Nag Hammadi, Gnosticism, & Early Christianity*, 239–55 (Peabody, MA: Hendrickson Publishers, 1986. Also Jacqueline A. Williams, *Biblical Interpretation in the Gnostic Gospel of Truth from Nag Hammadi*. Society of Biblical Literature Dissertation (Decatur, GA: Scholars Press, 1988).

27. Hans-Martin Schenke, *Die Herkunft des sogenannten Evangelium Veritatis* (Göttingen: Vandenhoeck & Ruprecht, 1959), 33. See Odes of Solomon 7.

28. Geoffrey S. Smith, "Constructing a Christian Universe: Mythological Exegesis of Ben Sira 24 and John's Prologue in the *Gospel of Truth*," 64–84.

29. See Prov 8:30–31.

30. Crum, s.v. ⲧⲏⲗⲏⲗ.

31. Attridge and MacRae, *Nag Hammadi Codex* I, 42.

32. *Gos. Truth* 16.31–17.2.

33. Valentinus liked ambiguous language and perhaps purposefully obscured his pronouns. Benoït Standaert, "L'Evangile d'Verité: Critique et Lecture," *NTS* 22, no. 3 (1976): 265.

34. The retroversion into Greek makes the interpretive decision that the both verses referred to the Father. Jacques E. Ménard, *L'Évangile de Vérité. Rétroversion Grecque et commentaire* (Paris, Letouzey et Ané, 1962), 31–33.

35. Anne McGuire, "Conversion and Gnosis in the *Gospel of Truth*," *NT* 28, no. 4 (1986): 350.

36. Judith Hoch Wray, *Rest as a Theological Metaphor in the Epistle to the Hebrews and the Gospel of Truth: Early Christian Homiletics of Rest*, SBL.DS 166 (Atlanta, GA: Scholars Press, 1998), 21.

37. Prov 8:25.

38. *Gos. Truth* 20:1.

39. *Gos. Truth* 23:30–24 :1.

40. Grobel, *A Valentinian Mediation*, 61.

41. *Gos. Truth* 19:36. Jacques Menard has argued that this line demonstrates a melding of Semitic and Hellenistic thought. See *L'Evangile de Verite* (Leiden: Brill, 1972), 89.

42. Kendrick Grobel, *The Gospel of Truth: A Valentinian Mediation on the Gospel* (New York: Abignton Press, 1965), 61.

43. *Gos. Truth*, 24:13–14.

44. Jn 1:18.

45. Eliot Wolfson, "Inscribed in the Book of the Living," *JSJ* 38, no. 2 (2007): 266.

46. For an introduction to the history of Bereshit Rabbah, see Sarit Kattan Gribetz and David Grossberg, "Introduction: Genesis Rabbah, a Great Beginning," in *Genesis Rabbah in Text and Context*, 1–21 (Tübingen: Mohr Siebeck, 2016).

47. *GenR* 1:2. J. Theodor and Ch Albeck, *Midrash Bereshit Rabbah: Critical Edition with Notes and Commentary*, 3 vols., 2nd ed. (Jerusalem: Wahrmann 1965).

48. Peter Schafer, "Bereshit Bara Elohim: Bereshit Rabba, Parasha 1, Reconsidered," *in Empsychoi Logoi: Religious Innovations in Antiquity*, Studies in Honour of Pieter Willem van der Horst, ed. Alberdina Houtman et. al., 288 (Leiden: Brill, 2008).

49. As argues Burton L. Visotzky, "Genesis Rabbah 1:1—Mosaic Torah as the Blueprint of the Universe—Insights from the Roman World," in *Talmuda de-Eretz Israel: Archaeology and the Rabbis in Late Antique Palestine*, Studia Judaica 73, ed. Steven Fine and Aaron Koller, 127–40 (Boston: De Gruyter, 2014).

50. *Opif.* 19.

51. *Opif.* 17–19.

52. *Opif.* 18–19.

53. David Runia argues that this verb invokes the image of statues in temples or being carried in processions. Plato used this verb to describe Socrates carrying divine statues within himself (Symposium 215b). See Runia, *On the Creation*, 141.

54. Aaron P. Johnson, "Ancestors as Icons: The Lives of the Hebrew Saints in Eusebius' *Praeparatio Evangelica*," *GRBS* 44, no. 3 (2004): 258.

55. *Abr.* 5. οἱ γὰρ ἔμψυχοι καὶ λογικοὶ νόμοι ἄνδρες ἐκεῖνοι γεγόνασιν [Colson 6:7].

56. *Prob.* 62–63.

57. *Mos.* 2.11.

58. Burton L. Visotzky, "Genesis Rabbah 1:1—Mosaic Torah as the Blueprint of the Universe—Insights from the Roman World," 127–40.

59. On the manuscript history of Ben Sira, see Benjamin Wright's introduction in his translation of Sirach for NETS: "The Wisdom of Ben Sira or Sirach," in the *New Interpreter's Bible One Volume Commentary*, ed. David L.Petersen and Beverly R. Gaventa, 715–17 (Nashville: Abingdon, 2014). Also Pancratius C. Beentjes, *The Book of Ben Sira in Hebrew: A Text Edition of All Extant Hebrew Manuscripts and a Synopsis of All Parallel Hebrew Ben Sira Texts*, 13–21 (Leiden: Brill, 1997).

60. Sir 2:2.

61. Sir 24:3. Alfred Rahlfs, ed., *Septuaginta, editio altera* (Stuttgart: Deutsche Bibelgesellschaft, 2006), 2:337–471.

62. Boccaccini, *Middle Judaism*, 82–84.

63. Sir 24:12.

64. Sir 24:21.

65. Sir 24:23–29. ταῦτα πάντα βίβλος διαθήκης Θεοῦ ʽΥψίστου νόμον ὃν ἐνετείλατο ἡμῖν Μωυσῆς κληρονομίαν συναγωγαῖς ʼΙακώβ. ὁ πιμπλῶν ὡς Φισὼν σοφίαν καὶ ὡς Τίγρις ἐν ἡμέραις νέων, ὁ ἀναπληρῶν ὡς Εὐφράτης σύνεσιν καὶ ὡς ʼΙορδάνης ἐν ἡμέραις θερισμοῦ ὁ ἐκφαίνων ὡς φῶς παιδείαν ὡς Γηὼν ἐν ἡμέραις τρυγήτου. οὐ συνετέλεσεν ὁ πρῶτος γνῶναι αὐτήν καὶ οὕτως ὁ ἔσχατος οὐκ ἐξιχνίασεν αὐτήν· ἀπὸ γὰρ θαλάσσης ἐπληθύνθη διανόημα αὐτῆς καὶ ἡ βουλὴ αὐτῆς ἀπὸ ἀβύσσου μεγάλης [Rahlfs, 2:418–19].

66. Sir 24:31.

67. Eric D. Reymond, "Wordplay in the Hebrew to Ben Sira," *The Texts and Versions of the Book of Ben Sira: Transmission and Interpretation*, ed. Jean-Sébastien Rey and Jan Joosten, 38 (Leiden: Brill, 2011).

68. Sir 24:28. ὀυ συνετέλεσεν ὁ πρῶτος γνῶναι αὐτήν, καὶ οὕτως ὁ ἔσχατος οὐκ ἐξιχνίασεν αὐτῆς [Rahlfs, 419].

69. *Gos. Truth*, 17:5–20.

70. Smith, "Constructing a Christian Universe," 10.

71. Sir. prologue [Rahlfs, 378].

72. Sir. prologue. ὅπως οἱ φιλομαθεῖς καὶ τούτων ἔνοχοι γενόμενοι πολλῷ μᾶλλον ἐπιπροσθῶσιν διὰ τῆς ἐννόμου βιώσεως [Rahlfs, 2:377].

73. Francis Borchardt, "The Prologue of Sirach (Ben Sira) and the Question of Canon," in *Sacra Scriptura: How "Non-Canonical" Texts Functioned in Early Judaism and Early Christianity*, ed. J. H. Charlesworth and L. M. McDonald with B. A. Jurgens, 71. T&T Clark Jewish and Christian Text Series (London: Bloomsbury T&T Clark, 2014).

74. Sir. prologue. οὐ γὰρ ἰσοδυναμεῖ αὐτὰ ἐν ἑαυτοῖς Εβραϊστὶ λεγόμενα καὶ ὅταν μεταχθῇ εἰς ἑτέραν γλῶσσαν. οὐ μόνον δὲ ταῦτα ἀλλὰ καὶ αὐτος ὁ νόμος καὶ αἱ προφητεῖαι καὶ τὰ λοιπὰ τῶν βιβλίων οὐ μικρὰν ἔχει τὴν διαφορὰν ἐν ἑαυτοῖς λεγόμενα [Rahlfs, 2:378].

75. On this point, see Benjamin G. Wright III, "Translation Greek in Sirach in Light of the Grandson's Prologue," in *The Texts and Versions of the Book of Ben Sira: Transmission and Interpretation*, ed. Jean-Sébastien Rey and Jan Joosten, 78–84 (Leiden: Brill, 2011).

76. Ibid, 79.

77. Benjamin G. Wright III, "Translation Greek in Sirach in Light of the Grandson's Prologue," 75–94.

78. J. K. Aiken, The Literary Attainment of the Translator of Greek Sirach," in *The Texts and Versions of the Book of Ben Sira: Transmission and Interpretation*, ed. by Jean-Sébastien Rey and Jan Joosten, 107 (Leiden: Brill, 2011).

79. Mroczek, 91.

80. The idea of language, and moreover the book, as a mechanism for creation can also be found in the second century mystical work, Sefer Yetsirah. Thanks to Daniel Boyarin for bringing this parallel to my attention.

81. *Gos. Truth*, 26:35–27:1.

82. *Gos. Truth,* 19:19.

83. These are features some look for when trying to pinpoint Gospel "genre." See Helmut Koester, *From Jesus to the Gospels* (Minneapolis: Fortress Press, 2007), 38.

84. *Gos. Truth,* 20:28. ⲱ ⲙⲛ̄ϯⲛⲁϭ ⲛ̄ⲥⲃⲱ ⲛ̄ⲧⲉⲉⲓϭⲁⲧ [Attridge and MacRae, 86].

85. *Gos. Truth,* 18:21–31; 20:10–38.

86. See for example, *On First Principles*, preface 1 and *Homily on Numbers* 25.3 Cf. Karen Jo Torjesen, *Hermeneutical Procedure and Theological Method in Origen's Exegesis* (Berlin: De Gruyter, 1986), 215–19.

87. Karen Jo Torjesen, *Hermeneutical Procedure and Theological Method in Origen's Exegesis* (Berlin and Boston: De Gruyter, Inc., 1986), 108–47.

88. *Gos. Truth* 21:23. ⲁⲥⲃⲱⲗⲕ̄ ⲁⲣⲁϥ ⲛ̄ϭⲓ ϯⲡⲗⲁⲛⲏ ⲁⲥⲡⲱⲧ ⲛ̄ⲥⲱϥ ⲁⲥϩⲱϣ ⲛ̄ϩⲏⲧϥ̄ ⲁⲥⲟⲩⲱⲥϥ [Attridge and MacRae, 88].

89. *Gos. Truth,* 18:24. ⲁⲩⲁϥⲧϥ̄ ⲁⲩϣⲉ [Attridge and MacRae, 84].

90. For example, Galatians 3:13.

91. *Gos. Truth,* 18:25. ⲁϥϣⲱⲡⲉ ⲛ̄ⲛⲟⲩⲧⲁϩ ⲙ̄ⲡⲓⲥⲁⲩⲛⲉ ⲛ̄ⲧⲉ ⲡⲓⲱⲧ [Attridge and MacRae, 84].

92. *Gos. Truth,* 18:26. ⲛⲧⲁϥⲧⲉⲕⲟ ϭⲉ ⲉⲛ ϫⲉ ⲁϩⲟⲩⲁⲙϥ̄ [Attridge and MacRae, 84].

93. *Gos. Truth,* 18:27–31. ⲛⲉⲛⲧⲁϩⲟⲩⲁⲙϥ ⲇⲉ ⲁϥϯ ⲛⲉⲩ ⲁⲧⲣⲟⲩϣⲱⲡⲉ ⲁⲩⲣⲉϣⲉ ⲛϩⲣⲏⲓ ⲛϩⲛ̄ⲡⲓϭⲓⲛⲉ ⲛ̄ⲧⲁϥ ⲛ̄ϫⲉ ⲛⲉⲉⲓ ⲛ̄ⲧⲁϥϭⲛ̄ⲧⲟⲩ ⲛ̄ϩⲏⲧϥ̄ ⲁⲩⲱ ⲛ̄ⲧⲁϥ ⲁⲩϭⲛⲧϥ̄ ⲛ̄ϩⲏⲧⲟⲩ [Attridge and MacRae, 84].

94. See, for example, Philo, *Abr.* 5–6. Johnson, "Ancestors as Icons," 258.

95. *Gos. Truth,* 18:30–31 [Attridge and MacRae, 84].

96. Attridge and MacRae, *Nag Hammadi Codex I*, 50.

97. Kendrick Grobel, *The Gospel of Truth: A Valentinian Meditation on the Gospel* (New York, Abingdon Press, 1960), 53.

98. Bentley Layton, *The Gnostic Scriptures*, 251.

99. *Gos. Truth,* 19:21–25.

100. *Gos. Truth*19.28-30.

101. *Gos. Truth,* 19:32–33. Einar Thomassen identifies this as part of the "dialectics of mutual participation," in the text. This is a concept prevalent in Valentinian literature that requires divinity and humanity to uphold one another. Thomassen, *The Spiritual Seed*, 52.

102. *Gos. Truth,* 19:34–35. ⲉⲁⲩ ⲁϥⲟⲩⲱⲛϩ̄ ⲁⲃⲁⲗ ϩⲙ̄ ⲡⲟⲩϩⲏⲧ ⲛ̄ϭⲓ ⲡⲓϫⲱⲱⲙⲉ ⲉⲧⲁⲛϩ̄ ⲛ̄ⲧⲉ ⲛⲉⲧⲁⲛϩ [Attridge and MacRae, 86].

103. *Gos. Truth,* 20:6–14. ⲉⲙⲡⲉⲗⲁⲩⲉ ϣⲟⲩⲁⲛϩ̄ ⲁⲃⲁⲗ ϩⲛ̄ ⲛⲉⲉⲓ ⲛ̄ⲧⲁⲩⲛ̄ϩⲟⲩⲧⲟⲩ ⲁⲡⲓⲟⲩϫⲉⲉⲓ ⲉⲛⲉⲙ̄ⲡⲉϥⲉⲓ ⲉⲧⲙⲏⲧⲉ ⲛ̄ϭⲓ ⲡⲓϫⲱⲱⲙⲉ ⲉⲧⲙ̄ⲙⲉⲩ. ⲉⲧⲃⲉ ⲡⲉⲉⲓ . . . ϩⲁⲛ̄ⲧⲉϥϥⲓ ⲙ̄ⲡⲓϫⲱⲱⲙⲉ ⲉⲧⲙ̄ⲙⲉⲩ ⲉⲡⲓⲇⲏ ϥⲥⲁⲩⲛⲉ ϫⲉ ⲡⲓⲙⲟⲩ ⲛ̄ⲧⲟⲟⲧϥ̄ ⲟⲩⲱⲛϩ ⲛ̄ϩⲁϩ ⲡⲉ [Attridge and MacRae, 86].

104. It is unclear whether this should be "his own agency" or "his agency" (that of the Father). This is representative of the ambiguity of pronouns in this text that Standaert observed in "L'Evangile d'Verité," 265.

105. *Gos. Truth,* 20:21–39. ⲉⲧⲃⲉ ⲡⲉⲓ ⲁϥⲟⲩⲁⲛϩ̄ ⲛ̄ϭⲓ ⲓⲏⲥⲟⲩⲥ ⲁϥϭⲁⲗⲉϥ ⲙ̄ⲡⲓϫⲱⲙⲉ ⲉⲧⲙ̄ⲙⲉⲩ ⲁⲩⲁϥⲧϥ̄ ⲁⲩϣⲉ ⲁϥⲧⲱϭⲉ ⲙ̄ⲡⲇⲓⲁⲧⲁⲅⲙⲁ ⲁⲃⲁⲗ ⲛ̄ⲧⲉ ⲡⲓⲱⲧ ϩⲓ ⲡⲉⲥⲧⲁⲩⲣⲟⲥ ⲱ ⲙⲛ̄ϯⲛⲁϭ ⲛ̄ⲥⲃⲱ ⲛ̄ⲧⲉⲉⲓϭⲁⲧ ⲉϥⲥⲱⲕ ⲙ̄ⲙⲁϥ ⲁⲡⲓⲧⲛ̄ ⲁⲡⲙⲟⲩ ⲉⲣⲉⲡⲓⲱⲛϩ̄ ⲛ̄ⲁⲛⲏϩⲉ ⲧⲟ ϩⲓⲱⲱϥ ⲉⲁϥⲃⲱϣ ⲙ̄ⲙⲁϥ ⲛ̄ⲛⲓⲡⲗ̄ϭⲉ ⲉⲧⲧⲉⲕⲁⲓⲧ ⲁϥϯ ϩⲓⲱⲱϥ ⲛ̄ⲧⲙⲛ̄ⲧⲁⲧⲧⲉⲕⲟ ⲡⲉⲉⲓ ⲉⲧⲉ ⲙⲛ̄ ϣϭⲁⲙ ⲛ̄ⲗⲁⲩⲉ ⲁϣ ϥⲓⲧϥ̄ ⲛ̄ⲧⲟⲟⲧϥ̄ ⲉⲁϥϣⲉ ⲁϩⲟⲩⲛ ⲁⲛⲓⲙⲁⲉⲓⲧ ⲉⲧϣⲟⲩⲉⲓⲧ ⲛ̄ⲧⲉ ⲛⲓϩⲣⲏⲧⲉ ⲁϥⲥⲓⲛⲉ ⲁⲃⲁⲗ ϩⲓⲧⲟⲟⲧⲟⲩ ⲛ̄ⲛⲉⲉⲓ ⲉⲧⲃⲏϣ ⲁⲃⲁⲗ ⲛ̄ⲧⲟⲟⲧⲥ̄ ⲛ̄ⲧⲃ̄ϣⲉ ⲉϥⲟⲉⲓ ⲛ̄ⲛⲟⲩⲥⲁⲩⲛⲉ ⲙⲛ̄ ⲟⲩϫⲱⲕ ⲉϥⲱϣ ⲛ̄ⲛⲉⲧⲛ̄ϩⲏⲧ [Attridge and MacRae, 86].

106. *Gos. Truth,* 20:24–26 [Attridge and MacRae, 86].

107. So suggests Grobel, *The Gospel of Truth,* 64–65.

108. The *Concordance Des Testes De Nag Hammadi* treats it as a form of ϭⲱⲗ. If the Coptic translator made this verb choice, it indicates that the author of the text, in the second century, presumed a scroll, not a codex, format for his sacred book. This complicated claims that from its inception, "Christianity was a religion of the paperback." Guy Stroumsa, *The End of Sacrifice: Religious Transformations of Late Antiquity,* trans. by Susan Emanuel (Chicago: University of Chicago Press), 43.

109. *Gos. Truth,* 20:32 [Attridge and MacRae, 88].

110. The solution of Attridge and Mac Rae, *Nag Hammadi Codex I,* 59.

111. *Gos. Truth,* 20:39. ⲉϥⲱϣ ⲛ̄ ⲛⲉⲧⲛ̄ϩⲏⲧ [Attridge and MacRae, 88].

112. *Phdr.* 275e–276b. C. J. Rowe, *Plato: Phaedrus,* 2nd ed. (Wiltshire, UK: Aris & Phillips, 1988), 124.

113. 2 Cor 3:7. Bruce Metzger et al., eds., *The Greek New Testament,* 4th ed. (Stuttgart: Deutsche Bibelgesellschaft, 1998), 616.

114. Col 2:14–15. [Metzger, 690]

115. Jacqueline Williams, *Biblical Interpretation in the Gnostic Gospel of Truth,* 53.

116. For discussions on the symbolic capital of writing in other contexts of late antiquity, see Sara Rappe, *Reading Neoplatonism: Non-Discursive Thinking in the Texts of Plotinus, Proclus and Damascius* (Cambridge: Cambridge University Press 2000), xi. Also David Frankfurter, *Religion in Roman Egypt: Assimilation and Resistance* (Princeton: Princeton University Press, 1998), 240.

117. Alexander Gurd has examined what it meant for Roman authors to revise their work. He demonstrated that some authors viewed this communal publishing process as fundamentally republican in its opportunity for the entire community to participate in the composition. In contrast, some poets of the empire used this process to produce their own perfect text. See Alexander Gurd, *Work in Progress,* 1–22. Peter White observes that during these readings the author was observing the audience's reaction. White, 283.

118. Rex Windsury, *The Roman Book: Books, Publishing and Performance in Classical Rome* (London: Duckworth, 2009), 102. For the Greek counterparts to Latin publishing terms, see B. A. van Groningen, "ΕΚΔΟΣΙΣ," *Mnemosyne,* Fourth Series, 16 (1963): 1–17.

119. In this respect, a book was fundamentally different from orality, not a shadow of it. Published books were meant for anonymous audiences. On this point, see Joseph Farrell, "The Impermanent Text in Catullus and Other Roman Poets," in *Ancient Literacies,* 212.

120. Meyer, *Legitimacy and Law,* 21–43.

121. Elizabeth A. Meyer, *Legitimacy and Law in the Roman World* (Cambridge: Cambridge University Press, 2004), 216. More recently, David Petrain, *Homer in Stone: The Tabulae Iliaca in their Roman Context* (Cambridge, UK: Cambridge University Press, 2014).

122. *Gos. Truth,* 20:26–27. ⲁϥⲧⲱϭⲉ ⲙ̄ⲇⲓⲁⲧⲁⲅⲙⲁ ⲁⲃⲁⲗ ⲛ̄ⲧⲉ ⲡⲓⲱⲧ ϩⲓ̈ ⲡⲉⲥⲧⲁⲩⲣⲟⲥ [Attridge and MacRae, 86].

123. Karen King, *What Is Gnosticism* (Cambridge, MA: Harvard University Press, 2005), 155.

124. E. A. Meyer, *Legitimacy and Law in the Roman World: Tabulae in Roman Belief and Practice* (Cambridge: Cambridge University Press, 2004), 101.

125. For example, Justinian *D* 2.1.7.2

126. *Gos. Truth,* 20:15–17. ⲙ̄ⲡⲣⲏⲧⲉ ⲛ̄ⲛⲟⲩⲇⲓⲁⲑⲏⲕⲏ ⲉⲙ̄ⲡⲁⲧⲟⲩⲏⲛ ⲁⲣⲁⲥ ⲉⲥϩⲏⲡ ⲛ̄ϭⲓ ϯⲟⲩⲥⲓⲁ ⲙ̄ⲡⲛⲉⲡ ⲙ̄ⲡⲏⲉⲓ ⲉⲛⲧⲁϩⲙⲟⲩ [Attridge and MacRae, 86].

127. Edward Champlin, *Final Judgments Duty and Emotion in Roman Wills, 200 B.C.–A.D. 250* (Berkeley: University of California Press, 1991), 10.

128. On the challenges of protecting intellectual property in the Roman literary world, see Kenny, "Books and Readers in the Roman World," in *The Cambridge History of Classical Literature*, 1–32. In particular, in the first centuries of the common era a new, anonymous "reading public" emerged that made publication riskier as it was no longer bound by personal ties. Fitzgerald, "The World of the Book," 140.

129. Plato, *Phaedrus* 276e–277a.

130. And not a Kanonisierungsformel as claims F. Hahn, "Die Sendscheiben der Johannesapokalypse: Ein Beitrag zur Bestimmung prophetischer Redeformen," in *Tradition und Glaube: Das fruehe Christentum in seiner Umwelt*, ed. G. Jeremias, H. W. Kuhn, and H. Stegemann, 361 (Gottingen: Vandenhoeck und Ruprecht, 1971).

131. Martial, *Epi.* 1.66. Martial points out that it is difficult to steal published works, but unpublished poems, "if its face is not yet pumiced, nor decorated with knobs and without a cover, buy it: such books I have; nobody will know a thing." *Sed pumicata fronte si quis est nondum/nec umbilicis cultus atque membrana mercare: tales habeo; nec sciet quisquam.*

132. *Gos. Truth.* 23:8–9. ⲟⲩⲉⲉⲧⲟⲩ ⲉⲟⲩⲙⲉⲉⲩⲉ ⲉϥϫⲏⲕ ⲡⲉ ⲡⲥϩⲉⲉⲓ ⲡⲥϩⲉⲉⲓ ⲙ̄ⲡⲣⲏⲧⲉ ⲛ̄ⲛⲟⲩϫⲱⲱⲙⲉ ⲉϥϫⲏⲕ ⲁⲃⲁⲗ [Attridge and MacRae, 90].

133. *Gos. Truth*, 23:4–7. ⲉϩⲛ̄ⲧⲟⲡⲟⲥ ⲉⲛ ⲛⲉ ⲛ̄ⲧⲉ ϩⲛ̄ⲥⲙⲏ ⲟⲩⲇⲉ ϩⲛ̄ⲥϩⲉⲉⲓ ⲉⲛ ⲛⲉ ⲉⲩϣⲁⲁⲧ ⲛ̄ⲛⲟⲩϩⲣⲁⲩ ϣⲓⲛⲁ ⲛⲧⲉⲟⲩⲉⲉⲓ ⲁϣⲟⲩ ⲛ̄ϥⲙⲉⲩⲉ ⲁⲩⲡⲉⲧϣⲟⲩⲉⲓⲧ [Attridge and MacRae, 90]. There are two possible meanings for my rendering of the Coptic ϩⲛ ⲥⲙϩ . . . ⲉⲩϣⲁⲁⲧ ⲛⲛⲟⲩϩⲣⲁⲩ: "with voice . . . or mute," referring to reading aloud or silently or "vowels and consonants." For these options, see Layton, *The Gnostic Scriptures*, 256; and Grobel, *The Gospel of Truth*, 82.

134. *Gos. Truth*, 23:8. ϩⲛ̄ⲥϩⲉⲉⲓ ⲛⲉ ⲛ̄ⲧⲉ ϯⲙⲛ̄ⲧⲙⲏⲉ [Attridge and MacRae, 90].

135. *Gos. Truth*, 23:14–18. ⲉϩⲛ̄ⲥϩⲉⲉⲓ ⲛⲉ ⲁⲩⲥⲁϩⲟⲩ ⲁⲃⲁⲗ ϩⲓ̈ⲧⲟⲟⲧⲥ ⲛ̄ϯⲙⲛ̄ⲧⲟⲩⲉⲉⲓ ⲉⲁϩⲁⲡⲓⲱⲧ ⲥⲁϩⲟⲩ ⲛ̄ⲛⲓⲁⲓⲱⲛ ϣⲓⲛⲁ ⲁⲃⲁⲗ ϩⲓ̈ⲧⲟⲟⲧⲟⲩ ⲛ̄ⲛⲓⲥϩⲉⲉⲓ ⲛ̄ⲧⲟⲟⲧϥ ⲉⲩⲁⲥⲟⲩⲱⲛ ⲡⲓⲱⲧ [Attridge and MacRae, 90].

136. *Gos. Truth*, 21:4.

137. Thomassen, *Spiritual Seed*, 153–54.

138. *Gos. Truth*, 18:30.

139. *Gos. Truth*, 19:32–34.

140. *Gos. Truth*, 20:39.

141. To borrow a term from Bill Schniedewind, *How the Bible Became a Book* (Cambridge: Cambridge University Press, 2004), 195.

142. For a survey of the use of the image of a book of the heart in late antiquity, see Eric Jager, *The Book of the Heart* (Chicago and London: Chicago University Press, 2000), 2–15.

143. *Gos. Truth*, 19:21–22. ⲛ̄ⲥⲟⲫⲟⲥ ⲛ̄ϩⲣⲏⲓ̈ ϩ̄ⲙ ⲡⲟⲩϩⲏⲧ ⲟⲩⲁⲉⲉⲧⲟⲩ [Attridge and MacRae, 86].

144. *Gos. Truth*, 19:35–37. ⲁϥⲟⲩⲱⲛϩ̄ ⲁⲃⲁⲗ ϩⲙ̄ ⲡⲟⲩϩⲏⲧ ⲛ̄ϭⲓ ⲡⲓϫⲱⲱⲙⲉ ⲉⲧⲁⲛϩ̄ ⲛ̄ⲧⲉ ⲛⲉⲧⲁⲛϩ̄ ⲡⲉⲉⲓ ⲉⲧⲥⲏϩ ϩⲣⲏⲉⲓ ϩⲙ̄ ⲡⲓⲙⲉⲉⲩⲉ ⲟⲩⲁϩⲙ̄ ⲡⲓⲛⲟⲩⲥ ⲛ̄ⲧⲉ ⲡⲓⲱⲧ [Attridge and MacRae, 86].

145. Clement, *Strom.* 1.

146. As Mira Seo has observed, Martial was the first author to use the term plagiarism to refer to stealing literary works, but in its legal context, the word means to kidnap. Seo, "Plagiarism and Poetic Identity in Martial," *American Journal of Philology* 130, no. 4 (2009): 567.

147. On the dismal existence of foundlings and orphans in the Roman home, see Paul Veyne, *A History of Private Life: From Pagan Rome to Byzantium*, trans. Arthur Goldhammer, 79 (Cambridge, MA: Harvard University Press, 1992). Victoria Rimell has observed, "books are often pictured as slaves, a class of people who conceptually didn't have any physical boundaries, and could legally be used, beaten, penetrated or killed by their masters." Victoria Rimell, *Martial's Rome: Empire and Ideology of Epigram* (Cambridge: Cambridge University Press, 2008), 25.

148. While Martial will express a wry ambivalence about the fate of his poetry, Horace's concern seemed to be geared to convincing his readers that his books were "more than the sum of its physical parts." Roman, "Literary Materiality in Martial," 121. Horace's revision process also seemed geared to maintaining authorial control, as he suggested that writers keep their complete work for nine years for revision before allowing it to circulate widely. Kenny, "Books and Readers in the Roman World," 11.

149. Horace, *Epist.* 1.20. H. Rushton Fairclough, *Horace: Satires. Epistles; The Art of Poetry,* LCL 194 (Cambridge, MA: Harvard University Press, 1926), 388.

150. Martial wrote several of what D. P. Fowler calls "talking to the book" epigrams. Fowler, "Martial and the Book," in *Roman Literature and Ideology: Ramus Essays for J.P. Sullivan,* 31 (Bendigo, Australia: Aureal Publications, 1995). See epigrams 1.3, 1.70, 3.2, 3.5, 4.86, 4.89, 7.84, 7.97, 8.1, 8.72, 9.99, 10.104, 11.1, 12.2, 12.5.

151. Martial, *Epi.* 11.1. Walter C. A. Ker, *Martial: Epigrams,* rev. ed. LCL (London: William Heinemann LTD, 1968), 2:236.

152. This is also one example of Martial alluding to a new reading public, which, for the first time, is anonymous—a remarkable shift from Horace, who preferred his works to circulate among acquaintances. William Fitzgerald, "World of the Book," 140. Also, Fitzgerald, *Martial: The World of the Epigram* (Chicago: University of Chicago Press, 2007), 16.

153. *Epi.* 11.15 [Ker, 2:248].

154. When Martial spoke to his books, he "engages in an informal dialogue with the Roman reading public about itself, a dialogue in which he directly reflects the feelings and views of his audience." Thus, when Martial addresses his books, he is really giving instructions to the reader. See A. Spisak, "Martial's Special Relationship to the Reader," 362.

155. Matthew Larsen has demonstrated how this treatise provides insight into Roman publication practices, and a window into how the Gospels were first composed as unfinished notes before developing into literary texts. Larsen, 29.

156. These include *On the Bringing Up of Blood, On the Motion of the Chest and Lungs, and his commentary on* Chrysipus*'s Book of Syllogistic.* Galen, *Lib.Prop.* prologue. For the Greek edition, see C. G. Kühn, ed., *Claudii Galeni opera omnia* (1830; repr., Hildesheim: Georg Olms Verlagsbuchhandlung), 19:9.

157. *Epi.* 7.51. *non lector meus hic . . . sed liber est* [Ker, 1:458]. On Martial's idea of books living on the tongues of readers, Remell, *Martial's Rome,* 26–28.

CHAPTER 2

1. Origen, *Comm. Jo.* 32:44–45.

2. Origen, *Cels.* 6 :10.

3. Corine B. Milad, "Incarnation and Transfiguration," *Journal of Theological Interpretation* 12, no. 2 (2018): 211.

4. See Blossom Stefaniw, *Mind, Text, and Commentary: Noetic Exegesis in Origen of Alexandria, Didymus the Blind, and Evagrius Ponticus* (Frankfurt am Main: Peter Lang, 2010).

5. Karen Jo Torjesen, *Hermeneutical Procedure and Theological Method in Origen's Exegesis* (Berlin and Boston: De Gruyter, Inc., 1986), 129.

6. Origen, *Comm. Matt.* 12:38.

7. Brakke, "Scriptural Practices in Early Christianity," 248.

8. Plutarch, *Is.Os.* 3.

9. *Gos. Truth*, 32:31–35. ϣⲉϫⲉ ϭⲉ ⲁⲃⲁⲗ ϩⲛ̄ ⲫⲏⲧ . . . ϣⲉϫⲉ ⲁⲧⲙⲏⲉ [Attridge and MacRae, 102].

10. Clement *Strom.* 2.114:3–6. P.-T. Camelot, C. Mondésert, et al, eds., *Clément D'Alexandrie: Stromate*, SC 30, 38, 278, 279, 428, 446, 463 (Paris: Les Éditions du Cerf, 1951–2001), 38:120–22. Εἶς δὲ ἐστιν ἀγαθος οὗ παρρησία ἡ διὰ τοῦ υἱοῦ φανέρωσις. Καὶ δι᾽ αὐτοῦ μόνου δύναιτο ἂν ἡ καρδία καθαρὰ γενέσθαι, παντὸς πονηροῦ πνεύματος ἐξωθουμένου τῆς καρδίας. Πολλὰ γὰρ ἐνοικοῦντα αὐτῇ πνεύματα οὐκ ἐᾷ καθαρεύειν, ἕκαστον δὲ αὐτῶν τὰ ἴδια ἐκτελεῖ ἔργα πολλαχῶς ἐνυβριζόντων ἐπιθυμίας οὐ προσηκούσαις. . . . Τὸν τρόπον τοῦτον καὶ ἡ καρδία, μέχρι μὴ προνοίας τυγχάνει, ἀκάθαρτος [οὖσα], πολλῶν οὖσα δαιμόνιων οἰκητήριον ἐπειδὰν δὲ ἐπισκέψηται αὐτὴν ὁ μόνος ἀγαθὸς πατήρ. ἡγίασται καὶ φωτὶ διαλάμπει, καὶ οὕτω μακαρίζεται ὁ ἔχων τὴν τοιαύτην καρδίαν, ὅτι ὄψεται τὸν θεόν.

11. *Gos. Truth*, 21:5–6 [Attridge and MacRae, 88].

12. See *Gos. Truth*, 19:19–20:1.

13. Christoph Markschies, *Valentinus Gnosticus?: Untersuchungen Zur Valentinianischen Gnosis; Mit Einem Kommentar Zu Den Fragmenten Valentins* (Tübingen: Mohr, 1992), 66. In the recurrent discussion of predeterminism in Valentinian thought, this passage is quoted to explain all sides of the debate. Einar Thomassen's position was essentially a compromise; "the empirical distinction between the various groups can be made only on the basis of their reactions to the revelation, which in itself is a universal event. In frg. 2, Valentinus does not imply either that all human hearts will be cleansed from the demons cf. the optative δύναιτο ἄν." Thomassen, *Spiritual Seed*, 453 n. 62.

14. Valentinian Fragment 6 = Clement *Strom.* 4.52:3–53:1 [SC 446:166-68]. Πολλὰ τῶν γεγραμμένων ἐν ταῖς δημοσίαις βίβλοις εὑρίσκεται γεγραμμένα ἐν τῇ ἐκκλησίᾳ τοῦ θεοῦ τὰ γὰρ κοινὰ ταῦτά ἐστι τὰ ἀπὸ καρδίας ῥήματα,νόμος ὁ γραπτὸς ἐν καρδίᾳ οὗτος ἐστιν ὁ λαὸς ὁ τοῦ ἠγαπημένου, ὁ φιλούμενος καὶ φιλῶν αὐτόν. Emphasis supplied.

15. Josephus *Ap.* 2.40.

16. For a survey of the history of scholarship, see Thomassen, *Spiritual Seed*, 474–78. The most comprehensive study of the fragments remains Elaine Pagels, *The Johannine Gospel in Gnostic Exegesis: Heracleon's Commentary on John* (Nashville: Abingdon Press, 1973).

17. As suggests Christoph Markschies, *Valentinus Gnosticus?*, 66.

18. Yehoshua Amir, "Authority and Interpretation of Scripture in the Writings of Philo," in *Mikra: Text, Translation, Reading and Interpretation of the Hebrew Bible in Ancient Judaism and Early Christianity*, ed. Martin Jan Mulder and Harry Sysling, 422–23 (Peabody, MA: Hendrickson Publishers, 2004).

19. See *Leg.* 1.19; *Abr.* 11.

20. Gerhard von Rad, *Genesis: A Commentary*, trans. J. H. Marks, 68 (Philadelphia: Westminster Press, 1961). Cf. Edgard W. Conrad, "Heard but Not Seen: The Representation of 'Books' in the Old Testament," *JSOT*, no. 54 (1992): 47–48.

21. *Leg.* I.19 'Αὕτη ἡ βίβλος γενέσεως οὐρανοῦ καὶ γῆς ὅτε ἐγένετο' οὗτος ὁ κατὰ ἑβδομάδα κινούμενος τέλειος λόγος ἀρχὴ γενέσεως τοῦ τε κατὰ τὰς ἰδέας νοῦ τεταγμένου καὶ τῆς κατὰ τὰς ἰδέας τεταγμένης νοητῆς εἰ οἷόν τε τοῦτο εἰπεῖν αἰσθήσεως. βιβλίον δὲ εἴρηκε τὸν τοῦ θεοῦ λόγον, ᾧ συμβέβηκεν ἐγγράφεσθαι καὶ ἐγχαράττεσθαι τὰς τῶν ἄλλων συστάσεις [Colson and Whitaker, 1:156–58].

22. *Abr.* 1.

23. *Abr.* 2. εὖ μέντοι καὶ τὴν βίβλον γενέσεως τοῦ πρὸς ἀλήθειαν ἀνθρώπου προσεῖπεν, οὐκ ἀπὸ σκοποῦ, διότι γραφῆς καὶ μνήμης ἄξιος ὁ εὔελπις, οὐ τῆς ἐν χαρτιδίοις ὑπὸ σητῶν διαφθαρησομένοις, ἀλλὰ τῆς ἐν ἀθανάτῳ τῇ φύσει, παρ᾽ ᾗ τὰς σπουδαίας πράξεις ἀναγράπτους εἶναι συμβέβηκεν [Colson, 6:11].

24. *Legat.* 31. θεόχρηστα γὰρ λόγια τοὺς νόμους εἶναι ὑπολαμβάνοντες καὶ τοῦτο ἐκ πρώτης ἡλικίας τὸ μάθημα παιδευθέντες ἐν ταῖς ψυχαῖς ἀγαλματοφοροῦσι τὰς τῶν διατεταγμένων εἰκόνας [Colson and Barp, 10:108].

25. *Prob.* 62.

26. T. Engberg-Pedersen, "Philo's *De Vita Contemplativa*: A Philosopher's Dream," *JSJ* 30 (1999), 40–64.

27. *Contempl.* 25. ἀλλα νόμους καὶ λόγια θεσπισθέντα διὰ προφητῶν καὶ ὕμνους καὶ τὰ ἄλλα οἷς ἐπιστήμη καὶ εὐσέβεια συναύξονται καὶ τελειοῦνται [Colson, 9:126].

28. *Contempl.* 29.

29. *Contempl.* 78. ἅπασα γὰρ ἡ νομοθεσία δοκεῖ τοῖς ἀνδράσι τούτοις ἐοικέναι ζῴῳ καὶ σῶμα μὲν ἔχειν τὰς ῥητὰς διατάξεις, ψυχὴν δὲ τὸν ἐναποκείμενον ταῖς λέξεσιν ἀόρατον νοῦν [Colson 9:160].

30. Valentinian Fragment 6 = Clement *Strom.* 4.52:3–53:1 [SC 446:166–68].

31. On the manuscript history of *4 Ezra*, see Michael Stone and Matthias Henze, *4 Ezra and 2 Baruch: Translations, Introductions, and Notes* (Minneapolis: Fortress Press, 2013), 6–17.

32. Ezra 4:4–5, for example, recorded efforts of the natives to thwart the reconstruction process by intimidation and bribery.

33. NRSV 671.

34. *4 Ezra* 3:1. Proposed dates for the text range from 70–218 C.E. The reference to "the thirtieth year after the destruction of the city" works on a narrative level to set the story in the aftermath of the destruction of the first temple, but also suggests a context for the author writing thirty years after the destruction of the second temple.

35. *4 Ezra* 14:25.

36. *4 Ezra* 14:26.

37. For example, Jack N. Lighthouse, "The Rabbis' Bible: The Canon of the Hebrew Bible and the Early Rabbinic Guild," in *The Canon Debate*, ed. Lee Martin McDonald and James A. Sanders, 197 (Peabody, MA: Hendrickson Publishers, 2002). On *4 Ezra* and the problem of the canon, Mroczek 167–71.

38. On the history of interpretation of the books in *4 Ezra*, see Najman, *Losing the Temple and Recovering the Future*, 155–56.

39. Mroczek, *The Literary Imagination in Jewish Antiquity*, 161.

40. Najman, *Losing the Temple and Recovering the Future*, 92–94.

41. Najman, 157.

42. *4 Ezra* 14:45–46

43. Michael E Stone and Frank Moore Cross, *Fourth Ezra*. Hermeneia: A Critical and Historical Commentary on the Bible (Minneapolis: Augsburg Fortress Publishers, 1990), 428.

44. *4 Ezra* 4:20.

45. *4 Ezra* 14:21.

46. Mroczek, 171.

47. Christoph Markschies, *Valentinus Gnosticus? Untersuchungen zur valentinianischen Gnosis mit einem Kommentar zu den Fragmenten Valentins*, WUNT 65 (Tübingen: Mohr Siebeck, 1992), 339–65.

48. Clement, *Strm.*, 4.9.

49. Origen, *Comm. John* 2.14. C. Blanc, *Origène. Commentaire sur saint Jean, 5 vols. Sources chrétiennes* 120, 157, 222, 290, 385 (Paris: Éditions du Cerf, 1:1966; 2:1970; 3:1975; 4:1982; 5:1992), 157: 100.

50. Origen, *Comm. John* 6.92 [Blanc 222:92].

51. Origen, *Comm. John* 6.108. Ο λόγος μὲν ὁ σωτήρ ἐστιν φωνὴ δὲ ἡ ἐν τῇ ἐρήμῳ ἡ διὰ Ιωάννου διανοουμένη ἦχος δὲ πᾶσα προφητικὴ τάξις [Blanc, 108].

52. Origen, *Comm. John* 6.108.

53. Origen, *Comm. John* 6.111. Οὐκ οἶδα δ᾽ ὅπως χωρίς πάσης κατασκευῆς ἀποφαίνεται τὴν φωνὴν οἰκειοτέραν οὖσαν τῷ λόγῳ λόγον γίνεσθαι ὡς καὶ τὴν γυναῖκα εἰς ἄνδρα μετατίθεσθαι [Blanc, 111].

54. *Gos. Thomas* 114.

55. Origen, *Comm. John* 6.111. τῷ ἤχῳ φησὶν ἔσεσθαι τὴν εἰς φωνὴν μεταβολὴν μαθητοῦ μὲν χώραν διδοὺς τῇ μεταβαλλούσῃ εἰς λόγον φωνῇ δούλου δὲ τῇ ἀπὸ ἤχου εἰς φωνήν [Blanc, 111].

56. *GTr* 23:2–7.

57. Irenaeus, *Adv. haer.*, preface.

58. The two most current and comprehensive treatments of this letter include Christoph Markschies, "New Research on Ptolemaeus Gnosticus," *ZAC* 4, no. 2 (2000): 225–54; Einar Thomassen, *The Spiritual Seed: The Church of the 'Valentinians'* (Nag Hammadi and Manichaean Studies. Leiden: Brill, 2006), 119–32.

59. This chapter consults the critical edition of Gilles Quispel, *Ptolémée, Lettre à Flora, Analyse, texte critique, traduction, commentaire et index grec*, SC 24 (Paris, 1966). Epiphanius, *Panarion* 3,1. "Τὸν διὰ Μωσέως τεθέντα νόμον" [Quispel, 46].

60. William Schniedewind, *How the Bible Became a Book*, 195.

61. Ep. *Pan.*, 4.1. ὁ σύμπας ἐκεῖνος νόμος ὁ ἐμπεριεχόμενος τῇ Μωσέως πεντατεύχῳ . . . [Quispel, 50].

62. Ep. *Pan.*, 5.3. Καὶ ἔστι μὲν ὁ τοῦ θεοῦ νόμος, ὁ καθαρὸς καὶ ἀσύμπλοκος τῷ χείρονι [Quispel, 56].

63. Ep. *Pan.*, 5.4. ὁ δὲ ἐστιν συμπεπλεγμένος τῇ ἀδικίᾳ [Quispel, 58].

64. F. F. Fallon, "The Law in Philo and Ptolemy: A Note on the Letter to Flora," *VC* 30, no. 1 (1976): 45–51.

65. That is, pace Thomassen, it was not necessarily "written as an introduction to Valentinian Christianity for the uninitiated." Thomassen, *Spiritual Seed*, 119.

66. Ep. *Pan.*, 3.1. τὰς διαφωνούσας γνώμας περὶ αὐτοῦ [Quispel, 46].

67. Ep. *Pan.*, 3.1. οἱ μὲν γὰρ ὑπὸ τοῦ θεοῦ καὶπατρὸς νενομοθετῆσθαι τοῦτον λέγουσιν, ἕτεροι δὲ τούτοις τὴν ἐναντίαν ὁδὸν τραπέντες ὑπὸ τοῦ ἀντικειμένου φθοροποιοῦ διαβόλου τεθεῖσθαι τοῦτον ἰσχυρίζονται [Quispel, 46].

68. Ep. *Pan.*, 3.2. ὡς καὶ τὴν τοῦ κόσμου προσάπτουσιν αὐτῷ δημιουργίαν, πατέρα καὶ ποιητὴν τοῦτον λέγοντες εἶναι τοῦδε τοῦ παντός [Quispel, 46].

69. Cf. Markschies, "New Research on Ptolemaeus Gnosticus," 234. Quispel, *Ptolémée, Lettre à Flora*, 76. Campenhausen, *Formation of the Christian Bible*, 148.

70. For example, see Hippolytus, *Ref.* VI 35.1.

71. As suggests Harnack, *Der Brief des Ptolemäus an die Flora* (SPAW.PH 1902), 531. Cf. Markschies,"New Research," 28.

72. As argues Quispel, *Ptolémée, Lettre à Flora*, 76.

73. For an illuminating analysis of this tripartite structure of the letter, and its place in ancient rhetorical traditions, see Markschies, "New Research on Ptolemaeus Gnosticus," 228–33.

74. Unlike Philo, for instance, who saw the Mosaic hand as interpretive. See *De vita Mosis* 1.4. Also Fallon, "The Law in Philo and Ptolemy," 49–51.

75. Ep. *Pan* 4.11. ὅτι δὲ καὶ τῶν πρεσβυτέρων εἰσίν τινες συμπεπλεγμέναι παραδόσεις ἐν τῷ νόμῳ [Quispel, 54].

76. Markschies, "New Research on Ptolemaeus Gnosticus," 235.

77. Ep. *Pan.*, 7.3.

78. For the equation between the figures of the Savior and the Demiurge in Ptolemy's letter, see Markschies, "New Research on Ptolemaeus Gnosticus," 240–41. Also Thomassen, *Spiritual Seed*, 122–23.

79. Ep. *Pan.*, 4.5.

80. Ep. *Pan.*, 3.6.

81. Ep. *Pan.*, 5.15.

82. Ep. *Pan.*, 4.3.and 3.8.

83. Ep. *Pan.*, 3.8.

84. Rebecca Scharbach Wollenberg, "The Book That Changed: Narratives of Ezran Authorship as Late Antique Biblical Criticism," *JBL* 38, no. 1 (2019): 143–60.

85. Wollenberg, "The Book That Changed," 158.

86. Wollenberg, "The Book That Changed," 158.

87. Justin Martyr, *1 Apol.* 66.3; 67.3–4. Also *Dial.* 99–107.

88. For the use of the phrase "spiritual seed" to designate Valentinian Christians, see Thomassen, *Spiritual Seed*, 83–102.

89. Irenaeus, *Ad. haer.* 3.2.1.

90. Tertullian, *Val.* 4.13.

91. Ep. *Pan.*, 9.6.

92. *Phld.* 8.

CHAPTER 3

1. *haer.* 3.11.19 [SC 210:172–74]. *Sidquidem in tantum processerunt audaciae uti quod ab his non olim conscriptum est Veritatis Evangelium titulent . . .*

2. Andrew Jacobs, *Epiphanius of Cyprus: A Cultural Biography of Late Antiquity* (Oakland: University of California Press, 2016), 2.

3. Jackson Lashier, *Irenaeus on the Trinity*, Supplements to *Vigiliae Christianae* 147 (Leiden: Brill, 2014), 2.

4. There are several detailed histories of Gnosticism: Karen King, *What Is Gnosticism?* (Cambridge, MA: Harvard University Press, 2005); David Brakke, *The Gnostics: Myth, Ritual, and Diversity in Early Christianity* (Cambridge, MA: Harvard University Press, 2010).

5. As observes Nicola Denzey Lewis, *Cosmology and Fate in Gnosticism and Graeco-Roman Antiquity*, Nag Hammadi and Manichaean Studies 81 (Leiden: Brill, 2013), 13 n1.

6. See *Adv. haer.* 1.1.1. Also Attridge and MacRae, "The Gospel of Truth," in *Nag Hammadi Codex I (the Jung Codex)* Nag Hammadi Studies Series XXII (Leiden: Brill, 1985), 40.

7. This position is best represented by Philip L. Tite, *Valentinian Ethics and Paraenetic Discourse* (Leiden: Brill, 2009) and Adiel Schremer, *Brothers Estranged: Heresy, Christianity and Jewish Identity in Late Antiquity* (Oxford: Oxford University Press, 2009).

8. *Gospel of Truth*, 24:14.

9. Adelin Rousseau and Louis Doutreleau, *Irénée de Lyon: Contre Les Heresies,* Sources Chrétiennes 100–101, 210–211, 263–264, 293–294, 406 (Paris: Les Éditions du Cerf, 1965–1995). *Adv. haer.* 1.8.5.

10. Philip L. Tite, *Valentinian Ethics and Paraenetic Discourse* (Leiden: Brill, 2009), 218.

11. Kendrick Grobel, *The Gospel of Truth: A Valentinian Mediation on the Gospel* (New York: Abington Press, 1965), 62.

12. See Johanes Quasten, *Patrology* (Utrecht: Spectrum Press, 1950), 1:291.

13. Photius's *Bibl. Cod.* 121 mentions that Hippolytus claimed discipleship to Irenaeus.

14. It is also unclear why Irenaeus's claims that the *Gospel of Truth* was a new composition would exclude Valentinus as author. Their lives did overlap, and, at the time Irenaeus wrote *Against*

the Heresies in 180, the Gospel of Truth would have been only 20 to 40 years old, indeed "recent" in the scope of Irenaeus's holy literature.

15. Tite, *Valentinian Ethics*, 19.

16. This is the major distinction Adiel Schremer makes between Rabbinical efforts of standardization and unification of Judaism and the goals of the Church Fathers, whose interests in unification he attributes to academic theological speculation. Adiel Schremer, *Brothers Estranged: Heresy, Christianity and Jewish Identity in Late Antiquity* (Oxford: Oxford University Press, 2009).

17. Prudentius wrote a hymn on the martyr Hippolytus ("Peristephanon," hymn XI, in P.L., LX, 530 sqq.), in which he places the scene of the martyrdom at Ostia or Porto, and describes Hippolytus as being torn to pieces by wild horses. The chronographer of 354 reported that Hippolytus and Pontianus had been martyred on Sardinia.

18. *Ref.* IX, ii.

19. *Ref.* IX, ii.

20. *HE* VI.20.22.

21. See Jerome, *Illustrious Men*, 61.

22. Prudentius, "Peristephanon," hymn XI.

23. William Tabernee, *Prophets and Gravestones: An Imaginative History of Montanists and Other Early Christians* (Peabody, MA: Hendrickson Publishers, 2009), 128.

24. On this point, see Paul Parvis, "Who Was Irenaeus? An Introduction to the Man and His Work," in *Irenaeus: Life, Scripture, Legacy*, ed. Sara Parvis and Paul Foster, 19 (Minneapolis: Fortress Press, 2012).

25. Todd Berzon, *Classifying Christians: Ethnography, Heresiology, and the Limits of Knowledge in Late Antiquity* (Oakland: University of California Press, 2016), 7.

26. Michael Bérubé. "What's the Matter with Cultural Studies?" *Chronicle Review*, September 14, 2009. "In an especially rich essay, 'The Toad in the Garden: Thatcherism Among the Theorists'—in *Marxism and the Interpretation of Culture* (1988), edited by Cary Nelson and Lawrence Grossberg—Hall wrote: 'The first thing to ask about an "organic" ideology that, however unexpectedly, succeeds in organizing substantial sections of the masses and mobilizing them for political action, is not what is *false* about it but what is *true*.'"

27. Brakke, *The Gnostics*, 15.

28. Larsen, *Gospels Before the Book*, 79.

29. Gamble, *Books and Readers in the Early Church*, 124–125.

30. Donavan, *One Right Reading?*, 32. Also see *Adv. haer.* 1.3.6.

31. Pace Mark Edwards, I think these similarities suggest genuine intellectual kinship rather than intentional efforts on Irenaeus's part to "shadow" the rhetoric of Valentinus. Mark Edwards, *Catholicity and Heresy in the Early Church*, 11–35.

32. *Adv. haer.* 1 pr 2.33–34.

33. *Adv. haer.* 1.18.2.

34. See Annette Yoshiko Reed, "Ευαγγελιον: Orality, Textuality and the Christian Truth in Irenaeus' *Adversus Haereses*," *VC* 56, no. 1 (2002): 22. Also Benoit, "Ecriture et Tradition," 41–43; Stroumsa, *Hidden Wisdom: Esoteric Traditions and the Roots of Christian Mysticism* (Leiden: Brill), 30, 38, 85–86.

35. Irenaeus identified four covenants (καθολικαὶ διαθῆκαι) revealed to humanity—the single command to Adam, the Noahide covenant, the Mosaic covenant, and the Gospel. *Adv. haer.* 3.9.8.

36. *Adv. haer.* 3.11.8. Επεὶ γὰρ τέσσαρα κλίματα τοῦ κόσμου ἐν ῷ ἐσμὲν καὶ τέσσαρα καθολικὰ πνεύματα κατέσπαρται δὲ ἡ ἐκκλησία ἐπι πάσης τῆς γῆς στῦλος δὲ καὶ στήριγμα ἐκκλησίας τὸ εὐαγγέλιον

καὶ Πνεῦμα ζωῆς εἰκότως τέσσαρας ἔχειν αὐτὴν στλύλους πανταχόθεν πνέοντας τὴν ἀφθαρσίαν καὶ ἀναζωπυροῦντας τοὺς ἀνθροπους [SC 211: 168–71].

37. See Mark Edwards, *Catholicity and Heresy*, 35–57.

38. For example, *Adv. haer.* 2.24.3. Mark Edwards might mark this passage as an example of Irenaeus's "shadowing" the heretical writings and appropriating their rhetoric for orthodoxy. However, early authors, such as Philo, establish that this kind of numerological patterning of the divine was part of Irenaeus and Valentinus's shared heritage. See Edwards, *Catholicity and Heresy*, 35–57.

39. *Adv. haer.*, 2.25.1.

40. *Adv. haer.*, 2.25.1.

41. *Adv. haer.* 3.11.9.

42. William Tabbernee, "Perpetua, Montanism, and Christian Ministry in Carthage c. 203 C.E." *PRS* 32 (2005):435–38.

43. *Adv. haer.* 3.11.9. Καὶ γὰρ Μαρκίων ὅλον ἀποβάλλων τὸ εὐαγγέλιον, μᾶλλον δὲ τοῦ εὐαγγελίου ἑαυτὸν ἀποκόπτων μόριον καυχᾶται ἔχειν τοῦ εὐαγγελίου. . . . Οἱ δὲ ἀπὸ Οὐαλεντίνου πάλιν ἔξω παντὸς ὑπάρχονωτες φόβου ἴδια συγγράμματα ἐκφέροντες πλείονα ἔχειν καυχῶνται αὐτῶν τῶν εὐαγγελίων . . . [SC 211:171–75].

44. *Adv. haer.* 3.11.9. εἴπερ εἰς τοσοῦτον προεληλύθασι τόλμης ὥστε τὸ ὑπ᾽αὐτῶν οὐ πάλαι συντεταγμένον ἀληθείας εὐαγγέλιον ἐπιγράφειν, ἐν μηδενὶ συμφωνοῦν τοῖς τῶν ἀποστόλων εὐαγγελίοις, ἵνα μηδὲ τὸ εὐαγγέλιον ᾖ παρ᾽αὐτοῖς ἀβλασφήμητον. Εἰ γὰρ τὸ ὑπ᾽αὐτῶν ἐκφερόμενον ἀληθείας ἐστὶν εὐαγγέλιον . . . μηκέτι εἶναι τὸ ὑπὸ τῶν ἀποστόλων παραδεδομένον ἀληθείας εὐαγγέλιον [SC 211:175].

45. See Thomas C. K. Ferguson, "The Rule of Truth and Irenaean Rhetoric in Book 1 of 'Against Heresies,'" *VC* 55, no. 4 (2001): 356–75. *Adv. haer.* 1.20.1; 2.25.3.

46. *Adv. haer.* 3.11.9. μηκέτι εἶναι τὸ ὑπὸ τῶν ἀποστόλων παραδεδομένον ἀληθείας εὐαγγέλιον [SC 211:173].

47. *Adv. haer.* 3.1.1 τελείαν τὴν γνῶσιν [SC 211:21].

48. *Gos. Truth*, 18:25–31.

49. *Gos. Truth*, 36:35–37:6. ϥⲥⲁⲩⲛⲉ ⲛ̄ⲛⲓϫⲟ ⲛ̄ⲧⲟⲟⲧϥ̄ ϫⲉ ⲛ̄ⲧⲁϥ ⲡⲉ ⲛ̄ⲧⲁϥϫⲟ ⲙ̄ⲙⲁⲩ ϩⲛ̄ ⲡⲓⲡⲁⲣⲁⲇⲓⲥⲥⲟⲥ ⲛ̄ⲧⲟⲟⲧϥ̄ ⲡⲉϥⲡⲁⲣⲁⲇⲓⲥⲥⲟⲥ ⲇⲉ ⲡⲉ ⲡⲉϥⲙⲁ ⲛⲙ̄ⲧⲁⲛ ⲡⲉⲉⲓ ⲡⲉ ⲡⲓϫⲱⲕ ⲁⲃⲁⲗ ϩⲛ̄ ⲡⲓⲙⲉⲩⲉ ⲛ̄ⲧⲉ ⲡⲓⲱⲧ ⲟⲩⲉϩⲛ̄ ⲛⲉⲉⲓ ⲛⲉ ⲛ̄ϣⲉϫⲉ ⲡⲉ ⲡϩⲱϥ ⲛ̄ⲧⲉ ⲡⲉϥⲟⲩⲱϣⲉ ⲟⲩⲉⲉⲓ ϩⲙ̄ ⲡⲟⲩⲱⲛϩ̄ ⲁⲃⲁⲗ ⲛ̄ⲧⲉ ⲡⲉϥϣⲉϫⲉ [Attridge and MacRae, 108].

50. *Adv. haer.* 5.20.2. Πεφύτευται γὰρ ἡ ἐκκλησία παράδεισος ἐν τῷδε τῷ κοσμῳ. Απο παντὸς οὖν ξύλου τοῦ παραδείσου βρώσει φαγη φησὶ τὸ Πνεῦμα τοῦ θεοῦ τουτέστιν ἀπὸ πάσης κυριακῆς γραφῆς φάγε ἀπὸ δὲ τῆς ὑπερφρονήσεως μὴ φάγῃς μηδὲ ἅψῃ πάσης τῆς αἱρετικῆς διχοστασίας. Ομολογοῦσιν γὰρ αὐτοὶ ἑαυτοὺς γνῶσιν ἔχειν καλοῦ τε καὶ πονηροῦ καὶ ὑπὲρ τὸν πεποιηκότα αὐτοὺς θεὸν τείνονται τὰς διανοίας αὐτῶν [SC 153: 259].

51. Origen, *Hom. in Ex.* 1.1.1. For a discussion of Origen's metaphors for scripture, see Catherine Chin, *Grammar and Christianity in the Late Roman World* (Philadelphia: University of Pennsylvania Press, 2008), 74–76.

52. *Adv. haer.* 5.20.1.

53. We recall that Tertullian also knew of the Valentinian concept of the spiritual seed. He derisively had located this seed inside "every man." This seed manifested as heretical writings personified as a well-dressed prostitute. In this way, Tertullian insinuates that the Valentinians, the receivers of the "spiritual seed," were prostitutes.

54. Josephus, *Against Apion*, 1.3.15.

55. Eric Jager described the invention of the book of the heart within early Christianity as a development from Paul to Augustine. Paul's "book of the heart" was a universal Gospel that aimed

to replace the particular "letter of the law." Augustine's book of the heart was interior—an individual confessional record. Jager's work focuses primarily on the book of the heart's medieval developments, so in between Paul and Augustine, he claims, "Origen, a prolific Christian allegorist may have invented the book of the heart." The evidence the *Gospel of Truth* and Irenaeus offer indicates that this is incorrect. See Eric Jager, *The Book of the Heart*, 17–18.

56. On the concept of Paradosis, see Albert Baumgarten, "The Pharisaic *Paradosis*," *HTR* 80, no. 1 (1987): 63–77; Guy Stroumsa, *Hidden Wisdom*, 27–45.

57. *Adv. haer.* 3.4.2. Ηι τάξει πείθονται πολλὰ ἔθνη βαρβάρων τῶν εἰς Χριστὸν πεπιστευκότων ἄνευ χάρτου καὶ μέλανος ἐγγεγραμμένην ἐχόντων διὰ τοῦ Πνεύματος ἐν ταῖς καρδίαις αὐτῶν τὴν σωτηρίαν καὶ τὴν ἀρχαίαν παράδοσιν ἐπιμελῶς φυλασσόντων, εἰς ἕνα θεὸν πιστευόντων . . . Οἷς ἐάν τις ἀπαγγείλῃ τὰ ὑπὸ τῶν αἱρετικῶν παρεπινενοημένα τῇ ἰδίᾳ αὐτῶν διαλέκτῳ προσομιλήσας παραυτίκα ἀποκλείοντες τὰ ὦτα πόρρω που καὶ μακρὰν φεύξονται μηδὲ ἀκοῦσαι ὑπομένοντες τὴν βλάσφημον ὁμιλίαν. Οὕτως δι᾽ἐκείνης τῆς ἀρχαίας τῶν ἀποστόλων παραδόσεως οὐδὲ εἰς ἔννοιαν ἀποδέχονται ὅ τι τούτων τερατολογία ἐστίν [SC 211: 47–49].

58. Eusebius, *HE* 5.20.1.

59. Eusebius, *HE* 5.20.5–7.

60. A similar position was recorded in the Apocryphon of James, which depicted each of the apostles writing down revelation told uniquely to him. Consistent with Irenaeus's observations that Valentinians justified preaching "their own opinions" by claiming the apostles had not received the complete revelation, in the Apocryphon of James, not all the apostles were told everything. James received a special revelation, which he recorded in two books because he had "opened his heart." Ap.Jas. 14.27. ⲈϨⲀⲦⲈⲦⲚ̄ⲞⲨⲎⲚ ⲀⲠⲈⲦⲚ̄ϨⲎⲦ.

61. Eusebius provides an ecclesiastical history of Montanism in *Hist.eccl.* 5.16.1 and 5.18.1.

62. Christine Trevett, *Montanism: Gender, Authority, and the New Prophecy* (Cambridge, UK: Cambridge University Press, 1996), 1–3.

63. *Ad. Val.* 5.

64. William Tabbernee, *Fake Prophecy and Polluted Sacraments: Ecclesiastical and Imperial Reactions to Montanism* (Leiden: Brill, 2007), 16.

65. See Eusebius, *HE* 5.16–19.

66. Turid Karlsen Seim, *Johannine Echoes in Early Montanism* (Leiden: Brill, 2009), 347.

67. *Refut. omn. haer.* 8.19.

68. Laura Nasrallah, *An Ecstasy of Folly: Prophecy and Authority in Early Christianity, Harvard Theological Studies 52* (Cambridge, MA: Harvard University Press, 2003), 100.

69. On Tertullian's shift in rhetorical priorities, see L. WM. Countryman, "Tertullian and the Regula Fidei," *SecCen* 2, no. 4 (1982): 212–13.

70. Quasten, *Patrology*, 3:270.

71. *Praescr. Haer,* xv.

72. David Rankin, *Tertullian and the Church* (Cambridge, UK: Cambridge University Press, 1995), 47.

73. *Praescr. Haer.* xxxiix. Translations of Tertullian follow Peter Holmes, *The Writings of Quintus Sept. Flor. Tertullianus*, vol. 2, ed. Rev. Alexander Roberts and James Donaldson, *Ante-Nicene Christian Library: Translation of the Writings of the Fathers, Down to AD 325* (Edinburgh, UK: T&T Clark: 1870).

74. *Praescr. Haer.* xxxviii.

75. *Praescr. Haer.* xxxviii.

76. *Praescr. Haer.* xxxviii.

77. *Praescr. Haer.* xiv.

78. See *Praescr. Haer.* xxii. For a positive evaluation of plurality, see the *Prayer to the Apostle Paul* and *Apo. Jas.*

79. *Praescr. Haer.* xxix.

80. *Praescr. Haer* xxix. *Aliquos Marcionitas et Valentinianos liberanda veritas expectabat* [CSEL 1:209].

81. *Praescr. Haer.* xxx. *Item Valentinus aliter exponens et sine dubio emendans, hoc nomine quicquid emendat, ut mendosum retro, alterius fuisse demonstrat* [CSEL 1:211].

82. *Ad. Val.* iv.

83. Jerome, *De Ill,* 53.

84. *Ad. Val.* i.

85. *Ad Val.* iii.

86. *Adv. Val.* iv.

87. *Adv. Val.* xxxix.

88. *Adv. Val.* iv. *Alioquin tantum se huic haeresi suadere permissum est, quantum lupae feminae formam cotidie supparare sollemne est. Quidni, cum spiritale illus semen suum sic in unoquoque recenseant? Si aliquid noui adstruxerint, revelationem statim appellant praesumptionem et charisma ingenium, nec unitatem sed diversitatem* [CSEL 2:755].

89. *Praedestinatus,* xxvi. "Irenaeus' 'New Testament' is basically a collection of works conceived to be written by, or to report the teaching of, *apostles*; and while he differs radically from Valentinus about how such books should be read, he does not, save in the case of Acts, seem to differ with them about the books that constitute the core list. It is Marcion, not the Gnostics, whom he openly accuses of truncating the list of essential Christian Scriptures." Richard A. Norris, Jr. "Irenaeus of Lyon," in the *Cambridge History of Early Christian Literature,* 50.

90. Tabbernee, *Prophets and Gravestones,* 129. Also see *On Flight in Persecution* viii–ix: Tertullian argues that although apostles were nomadic to avoid martyrdom, his congregation's historical times were different and the spirit was telling him they should embrace it. On the authority of the New Testament for Tertullian, see H. Karpp, *Schrift und Geist bei Tertullian* (Gütersloh: C. Bertelsmann Verlag, 1955). Also John Jansen, "Tertullian and the New Testament," *SecCen* 2, no. 4 (1982): 191–207.

91. In the last year, three important monographs have appeared that treat the *Panarion* as a text in its own right, and not simply a source for the history of Gnosticism. These include: Andrew S. Jacobs, *Epiphanius of Cyprus: A Cultural Biography of Late Antiquity* (Oakland: University of California Press, 2016); Kim, *Epiphanius of Cyrus: Imagining an Orthodox World*; T. Scott Manor, *Epiphanius' Alogi and the Johnannine Controversy* (Leiden: Brill, 2016).

92. See Socrates, *HE* 2.46; Sozomen, *HE* 25.

93. *Encyclopedia Britannica,* 11th ed., s.v. "Epiphanius."

94. A full English translation of the *Panarion* became available only in the mid-1990s.

95. Jacobs, *Epiphanius of Cyprus,* 62.

96. Chin, *Grammar and Christianity,* 78.

97. Ibid., 6.

98. This recalls the model of history found in *Jubilees,* which Eva Mroczek has described as a "book history," of sorts. Mroczek, *The Literary Imagination in Jewish Antiquity,* 143–44. Also A. Kreps, "From Jewish Apocrypha to Christian Tradition: Citations of *Jubilees* in Epiphanius' Panarion," *Journal of Church History* 87, no. 2: (2018): 345–70.

99. On Epiphanius's ideology behind these heresiological classifications, see Kim, *Epiphanius of Cyprus,* 56–79.

100. *Pan.* 1.9.
101. Judges 21:25.
102. Kim, *Epiphanius of Cyprus*, 56.
103. See *Pan.* 2.4; cf. Kim, 60–61.
104. *Pan.* 2.3.
105. Kim, *Epiphanius of Cyprus*, 59–60.
106. *Pan.* 3.11.
107. *Pan.* 8.2.1.
108. *Pan.* 8.6.1–4 [GCS 1:190–1].
109. Mroczek, *The Jewish Literary Imagination*, 166.
110. Ibid.
111. *Pan.* 9.1.1 [GCS 1:197].
112. *Pan.* 15.2.1
113. *Pan.* 18.1.3
114. *Pan.* 19.3-4
115. *Pan.* 31.3.4.
116. See *Pan.* II 26.2.2–3.1. Ορμῶνται δὲ ἀπὸ μωρῶν ὀπτασιῶν καὶ μαρτυριῶν ἐν ᾧ εὐαγγελίῳ ἐπαγγέλλονται [GCS 10/1:278].
117. *Pan.* 26.3.1. ἔστην ἐπὶ ὄρους ὑψηλοῦ καὶ εἶδον ἄνθρωπον μακρὸν καὶ ἄλλον κολοβόν, καὶ ἤκουσα ὡσεὶ φωνὴν βροντῆς καὶ ἤγγισα τοῦ ἀκοῦσαι καὶ ἐλάλησε πρός με καὶ εἶπεν· ἐγὼ σὺ καὶ σὺ ἐγώ, καὶ ὅπου ἐὰν ᾗς, ἐγὼ ἐκεῖ εἰμι, καὶ ἐν ἅπασίν εἰμι ἐσπαρμένος [GCS 10/1:278].
118. *Pan.* 26.3.1. Ορμῶνται δὲ ἀπο μωρῶν ὀπτασιῶν καὶ μαρτυριῶν ἐν ᾧ εὐαγγελιῳ ἐπαγγέλλονται [GCS 10/1:278].
119. *Pan.* 31.36.4–5.
120. *Pan.* II 31.34.1.
121. Pan 31.34.1.
122. Pan 31.34.1. δεύτερον δὲ ὅτι ἀσύστατα τὰ παρ᾽αὐτοῖς μυθοποιήματα, οὔτε που γραφῆς εἰπούσης οὔτε τοῦ Μωυσέως νόμου οὔτε τινὸς προφήτου τῶν μετὰ Μωυσέα, ἀλλ᾽ οὔτε τοῦ σωτῆρος οὔτε τῶν αὐτοῦ εὐαγγελιστῶν, ἀλλ᾽ οὔτε μὴν τῶν ἀποστόλων [GCS 10/1:436].
123. For example, Hugo Lundhaug, "The Nag Hammadi Codies in the Complex World of Fourth and Fifth Century Egypt," in *Beyond Conflicts: Cultural and Religious Cohabitations in Alexandria and Egypt between the 1st and the 6th Century CE*, edited by Luca Acari, 339–58 (Tübingen: Mohr Siebeck, 2017). Also Lance Jenott and Elaine Pagels, "Antony's Letters and Nag Hammadi Codex I: Sources of Religious Conflict in Fourth Century Egypt," *JECS* 18, no. 4 (2010): 557–89.
124. As Michael Kaler notes, scribe A left too much room, evidenced by scribe B's writing becoming larger toward the end of the work, as he noticed he had more than enough room to fit the entire text. Michael Kaler, "The Prayer of the Apostle Paul in the Context of Nag Hammadi Codex I," *JECS* 16, no. 3 (2008): 319–39.
125. On the *Prayer* added secondarily, see Michael Williams, *Rethinking Gnosticism: An Argument for Dismantling a Dubious Category* (Princeton: Princeton University Press, 1996), 253: "Though the short, two-page Prayer of the Apostle Paul is presently the opening writing in Codex I, it was evidently copied onto what was originally a blank flyleaf of the book . . . its purpose was surely not merely to fill up blank pages with any esoterica that happened to be at hand. Rather, this little prayer was likely deemed appropriate as a brief invocation to open the volume."
126. Michael Williams, *Rethinking Gnosticism*, 250.
127. Ibid., 251.

128. Codex analysis indicates that these two texts were later copied on the first pages of the codex, perhaps left blank for this purpose.

129. As suggested by Michael Kaler, "The Prayer of the Apostle Paul in the Context of Nag Hammadi Codex I," 319–39.

130. Kaler, 332.

131. *Prayer of the Apostle Paul*, 20–30. Dieter Mueller, "Prayer of the Apostle Paul," in *Nag Hammadi Codex I (the Jung Codex)*, ed. Harold Attridge, 8. Nag Hammadi Studies XXII (Leiden: Brill, 1985).

132. *Ap. Jas.* 1.5–10. Francis E. Williams, "The Apocryphon of James," in *Nag Hammadi Codex I (the Jung Codex)*, ed. Harold Attridge, 28. Nag Hammadi Studies XXII (Leiden: Brill, 1985). ⲁⲧⲣⲁⲧⲛ̄ⲛⲁⲩ ⲛⲉⲕ ⲛ̄ⲟⲩⲁⲡⲟⲕⲣⲩⲫⲟⲛ ⲉⲁⲩϭⲁⲗⲡ̄ϥ ⲁⲃⲁⲗ ⲛ̄ⲛⲏⲉⲓ ⲙⲛ ⲡⲉⲧⲣⲟⲥ ϩⲓⲧⲙ̄ ⲡϫⲁⲓ̈ⲥ. . . . ϩⲛ̄ ϩⲉⲛⲥϩⲉⲉⲓ ⲙⲙⲛ̄ⲧϩⲉⲃⲣⲁⲓⲟⲓⲥ ⲁϩⲓ̈ⲧⲛ̄ⲛⲁⲟⲩϥ ⲛⲉⲕ ⲛⲉⲕ ⲙⲉⲛ ⲟⲩⲁⲉⲉⲧⲕ̄. . . . ⲛ̄ⲅⲁⲣⲏϩ ⲁⲧⲙ̄ϫⲟⲩ ⲙ̄ⲡⲓϫⲱⲙⲉ ⲁϩⲁϩ ⲡⲉⲉⲓ ⲉⲧⲉ ⲙ̄ⲡⲉⲡⲥⲱⲧⲏⲣ ⲟⲩⲱϣ [ⲁ]ϫⲟⲟϥ ⲁⲣⲁⲛ ⲧⲏⲣⲛ̄ ⲡϥⲙⲛ̄ⲧⲥⲛⲁⲩⲥ ⲙ̄ⲙⲁⲑⲏⲧⲏⲥ.

133. *Ap. Jas.* 2.10–15. ⲡⲙⲛ̄ⲧⲥⲛⲁⲟⲩⲥ ⲙ̄ⲙⲁⲑⲏⲧⲏⲥ ⲁⲩⲱ ⲉⲩⲉⲓⲣⲉ ⲙ̄ⲡⲙⲉⲉⲩⲉ ⲛ̄ⲛⲉⲛⲧⲁϩⲁⲡⲥⲱⲧⲏⲣ ϫⲟⲟⲩ ⲁⲡⲟⲩⲉⲉⲓ ⲡⲟⲩⲉⲉⲓ ⲙ̄ⲙⲁⲩ ⲉⲓⲧⲉ ⲙ̄ⲡⲉⲧⲑⲏⲡ ⲉⲓⲧⲉ ⲙ̄ⲡⲉⲧⲟⲩⲁⲛϩ̄ ⲁⲃⲁⲗ ⲁⲩⲱ ⲉⲩⲣ̄ ⲧⲁⲥⲥⲉ ⲙ̄ⲙⲁⲩ ⲁϩ̄ⲛ ϫⲱⲱⲙⲉ. [Attridge and Williams, 30].

134. *Ap. Jas.* 15.35–16.3.

135. *Ap. Jas.* 14.40–15.2.

136. *Ap. Jas.* 16.13–14, 26–30.

137. Francis Williams, "The Apocryphon of James," 37.

138. As suggested by Michael Kaler, "The Prayer of the Apostle Paul in the Context of Nag Hammadi Codex I," 319–39.

139. This fragment is published in Alla I. Elanskaya, "The Literary Coptic Manuscripts in the A.S. Pushkin State Fine Arts Museum in Moscow," in *Supplements to VC* 18 (Leiden: Brill, 1994), 379–80. For identification as the thirty-ninth *Festal Letter* and French translation, see Enzo Lucchesi, "Un nouveau complément aux *Lettres festales* d'Athanase," *AnBoll* 119 (2001): 255–60.

140. 1 Cor 2:9.

141. See David Brakke, "Canon Formation and Social Conflict in Fourth Century Egypt: Athanasius of Alexandria's Thirty-Ninth Festal Letter," *HTR* 87, no. 4 (1994): 395–419.

142. Athanasius, Thirty-Ninth *Festal Letter* 21.

143. Thirty-Ninth *Festal Letter* 26:42–53. ⲁⲗⲗⲁ ⲡⲉϫⲁϥ ϫⲉⲁⲡⲁⲩⲗⲟⲥ ϫⲓⲟⲩⲙⲛⲧⲙⲛⲧⲣⲉ ⲉⲃⲟⲗ ϩⲛⲛⲁⲡⲟⲕⲣⲩⲫⲟⲛ ⲉϥϫⲱ ⲙⲙⲟⲥ ϫⲉⲛⲉⲧⲉⲙⲡⲉⲃⲁⲗ ⲛⲁⲩ ⲉⲣⲟⲟⲩ ⲙⲡⲉⲙⲁⲁϫⲉ ϭⲟⲧⲙⲟⲩ ⲛⲉⲧⲉⲙⲡⲟⲩⲁⲗⲉ ⲉϩⲣⲁⲓ ⲉϫⲙⲡϩⲏⲧ ⲛⲣⲱⲙⲉ. ϯⲛⲁⲟⲩϣⲃ ⲛⲁϥ ϫⲉⲡⲉⲓϩⲱⲃ ⲡⲁϩⲉⲛⲣⲱⲙⲉ ⲡⲉ ⲛⲣⲉϥϯⲧⲱⲛ ⲉⲣⲉⲡⲁⲩⲗⲟⲥ ⲥⲩⲛϩⲓⲥⲧⲁ ⲁⲛ ⲛⲛⲉϥϣⲁϫⲉ ϩⲓⲧⲛϩⲉⲛϣⲁϫⲉ ⲁⲗⲗⲁ ⲛⲉⲧⲥⲏϩ ⲛⲉ ϩⲛⲛⲉ ϩⲛⲛⲉⲅⲣⲁⲫⲏ. My translation is based on David Brakke's revisions of Elanskaya's *Literary Coptic Manuscripts*, 379–80. See David Brakke, "A New Fragment of Athanasius's Thirty-Ninth *Festal Letter*," 64.

CHAPTER 4

1. Avot 1.1. The phrase Oral Torah (תורה שבעל פה) first appeared as a technical term in the Babylonian Talmud (see Git 60b), but the concept of two Torot is present in the *tannaitic* midrashim. See *SifreDeut* 306 and 351; *Sifra Behuqotai* 8.12. On these passages see Martin Jaffe, *Torah in the Mouth: Writing and Oral Tradition in Palestinian Judaism 200 BCE-400 CE* (New York: Oxford University Press, 2001), 91–95. Also Steven Fraade, "Literary Composition and Oral Performance in Early Midrashim," *Oral Tradition* 4, no. 1 (1999): 33–51.

2. *Sifre Deuteronomy* 351.

3. As Martin Jaffee has argued, "Rabbinic distinctions between the written and spoken media of Torah are intimately connected to the social dominance of the Rabbinic Sage as a symbolic representation of Torah." Martin Jaffee, "A Rabbinic Ontology of the Written and Spoken Word: On Discipleship, Transformative Knowledge and the Living Texts of Torah," *JAAR* 65, no. 3 (1997): 528.

4. Rabbinic references to "Torah of the mouth" in the second century are nearly as sparse as Valentinian mentions of books of the heart. Jaffee, *Torah in the Mouth*, 97–98.

5. According to talmudic tradition, the Rabbis were the repository of oral law and the authorities on the written law (Shab 31a). Despite the prohibition against writing down the Oral Torah (Tem 14b), it comprises the rabbinic writings from the Mishnah through the Talmud. The question of when the concept of Oral Torah emerged is a matter of debate. At the pessimistic end of the spectrum, the Oral Torah was not a fully developed concept until the redaction of the Babylonian Talmud. On this, see also Jacob Neusner, ed., "The Oral Torah and the Oral Tradition: Defining the Problematic," in *Method and Meaning in Ancient Judaism* (Missoula, MT: Scholars Press, 1979), 59–78. Saul Lieberman has argued that the features of an oral text were present at the beginning of the rabbinic movement and that there is evidence it was written down by the third century. Saul Lieberman, *Hellenism in Jewish Palestine*, 2nd ed. (New York: Jewish Theological Seminary of America, 1962), 97. Also, Martin Jaffee, *Torah in the Mouth*, 162n6.

6. Examples discussed in this chapter include Yad 4.6, Ber 18a, MQ 25a-b, BQ 17a, *LamR* Petihta 25.

7. AZ 18a; Sanh 68a.

8. Many authors in Late Antiquity, irrespective of religious and philosophical orientation, considered what the apophatic nature of divine discourse meant for their own works. For shift from Pagan to Christian modes of persuasion, see Peter Brown, *Power and Persuasion in Late Antiquity: Towards a Christian Empire* (Madison: University of Wisconsin Press, 1992). For the function of debate in philosophical circles, see Richard Lim, *Public Disputation, Power and Social Order in Late Antiquity* (Berkeley: University of California Press, 1995). For the circumscription of debate in rabbinic circles, see Daniel Boyarin, *Borderlines: The Partitioning of Judaeo-Christianity* (Philadelphia: University of Pennsylvania Press, 2004), 171–201. For the circumscription of debate in Christian circles, David Brakke, "Canon Formation and Social Conflict in Fourth-Century Egypt: Athanasius of Alexandria's Thirty-Ninth *Festal Letter*," *HTR* 84, no. 4 (1994): 395–419. On the ineffable neoplatonic and Gnostic language, see Patricia Cox Miller, "In Praise of Nonsense," in *Classical Mediterranean Spirituality*, ed. A.H. Armstrong, 481–505 (New York: Crossroads, 1986); also *The Poetry of Thought in Late Antiquity: Essays in Imagination and Religion* (Aldershot: Ashgate Publishers, 2001), 247–72.

9. Rodney Stark, *Cities of God: The Real Story of How Christianity Became an Urban Movement and Conquered Rome* (San Francisco: Harper San Francisco, 2006), 1–24.

10. Jaffee, *Torah in the Mouth*, 97–98.

11. I use Alan Watson's translation of this law but offer several modifications. Here, Watson has translated *volumina* as "volumes," which does not convey that these units were specifically rolled. Cf. Alan Watson, trans., *Digest of Justinian*, 4 vols. (Philadelphia: University of Pennsylvania Press, 1985), 1:88–89.

12. Watson's translation renders this: "if books are bound." Although I agree with Watson's insinuation that Ulpian is discussing book covers, I have modified the translation to make more clear that Ulpian has moved from rolls to codices.

13. Watson has translated this as bindings, but Gaius Cassius was probably talking about protective leather pouches used to store individual scrolls.

14. Justinian, *D* 32.50.

15. C. H. Roberts and T. C. Skeat, *The Birth of Codex* (London and New York: Oxford University Press, 1983), 30.

16. See *D.* 32.50.

17. In Shab 115a-b, the Sages debated whether it is permitted to save a Torah scroll from fire on the Sabbath. The answer depended upon in what language the scroll was written.

18. BB 13b ff.

19. Git 60a and Yoma 37b discuss rabbinic debates about copying part of a scroll.

20. Ulpian's edict continues: In a legacy of books, the bookcases are not included, as Sabinus writes. So does Cassius; for he says that parchments with writing on them are due, but added that neither boxes not cases nor other receptacles for the books are due. But what Cassius writes of blank parchments is true. For neither are blank papyri are due in a legacy of books, nor when papyri are bequeathed will be books be due, unless by any chance we should here be impelled by the testator's wishes, for instance, if someone should happen to have left papyri in these terms, "my entire papyri," when he had nothing other than books, as one scholar to another; for then nobody will doubt that books are due, because many people commonly call books papyri. What then if someone has bequeathed blank papyri? Parchments will not be included, nor any other writing material, nor yet books that have begun to be written. *D* 32.50.

21. t.Yad 2.12.

22. Eruv 10.3.

23. Jastrow, *Dictionary of the Targumim, Talmud Babli, Yerushalmi and Midrashic Literatures*, s.v. מטבחים.

24. Kel 15.6.

25. The phrase "defile the hands" predates the earliest rabbinic decrees that applied it to Torah scrolls. Therefore, the earlier meaning may have been lost and the rabbinic laws tried to make sense of the arcane phrase. Martin Goodman detected a "rabbinic embarrassment about a system which they endorse but do not understand." Goodman, "Sacred Scripture," 102. The Talmud proposed that people would store their holy items together, including Torah scrolls and terumah—the harvest offerings allocated to the Temple. The realities of daily life put the Torah scrolls at risk by being close to the food offerings and the rodents attracted to them. Because contact with an unclean object would render terumah unfit for priestly consumption, unclean was a useful classification for Torah scrolls to keep them away from edibles. See BT Shab 14b. Martin Goodman noted that "it might seem to outsiders that in practice the difference between Jews' reverence for the Torah scroll and that of pagans was negligible," and posited that the description may have been a way to explain why Jews treated Torah scrolls the way they did, venerating them the way a pagan might venerate an idol. The claim that they defiled the hands, Goodman suggested, guarded against accusations that Jews practiced idolatry. On scriptures defiling the hands, see: Solomon Zeitlin, "A Historical Study of the Canonization of the Hebrew Scriptures," *PAAJR* 3 (1931–1932): 121–58. S. Z. Leiman, *The Canonization of Hebrew Scripture: The Talmudic and Midrashic Evidence* (Hamden, CT: Archon Books, 1976), 102–20. James Barton, *Oracles of God: Perceptions of Ancient Prophecy After the Exile* (New York and Oxford: Oxford University Press, 1986), 55–74. Martin Goodman, "Sacred Scripture and 'Defiling the Hands,'" *JTS* 41, no. 1 (1990): 99–107. Shamma Friedman, "The Holy Scriptures Defile the Hands—The Transformation of a Biblical Concept in Rabbinic Theology," in *Minhah le-Nahum: Biblical and Other Studies Presented to Nahum M Sarna in Honour of his 70th Birthday*, ed. Mark Brettler and Michael Fishbane, 117–32 (Sheffield: Sheffield Academic Press, 1993). Menahem Haran, The Biblical Collection (Jerusalem: Bialik Institute, 1996), 201–76 [Hebrew]. Chaim Milikowsky, "Reflections on Hand-Washing, Hand Purity and Holy Scripture

in Rabbinic Literature," in *Purity and Holiness*, ed. M. J. H. M Poorthuis and J. Schwartz, 149–62 (Leiden: Brill, 2000). Yehuda Cohen, *Tangled Up in Text: Tefillin in the Ancient World* (Providence: Brown Judaic Studies, 2008), 139–41. Timothy H. Lim, "The Defilement of the Hands as a Principle Determining the Holiness of Scriptures," *JTS* 61, no. 2 (2010): 501–15.

26. See Friedman, "The Holy Scriptures Defile the Hands," 130–31. Also Lim, "The Defilement of the Hands as a Principle Determining the Holiness of Scriptures," 501–15. Cf. Milikowski, 158.

27. t.Yad 2.14.

28. This is also the suggestion of James Barton, *Oracles of God: Perceptions of Ancient Prophecy in Israel after the Exile* (London: Darnton, Longman and Todd, 1986), 68–72.

29. Yad 4.6.

30. Zeitlin has argued that the Pharisees used this decree to keep the people from reading the Scriptures without the proper rabbinic interpretive authority. Zeitlin, "Canonization," 139.

31. Ber 18a. See p.Ber 3.5 and Semahot 49b for parallels.

32. Jacob Milgrom, "The Priestly Laws of Santa Contamination," in *Sha'arei Talmon: Studies in the Bible, Qumran, and Ancient Near East Presented to Shemaryahu Talmon* (Winona Lake, IN: Eisenbrauns, 1992), 137–46. Cf. Lim, 511.

33. Exod 29:21; Cf. Lim 511.

34. See 2 Sam 6:7; Chron 13:10.

35. See Lim, 509.

36. Deut 10:1–5; Exod 25:10–22.

37. CD 5:2–3.

38. Yad 3.5.

39. Goodman, 107.

40. MQ 25a-25b. This practice has been analyzed in detail in Adiel Kadari, "'This One Fulfilled What Is Written in That One': On an Early Burial Practice in Its Literary and Artistic Contexts," *JSJ* 41, no. 2 (2010): 191–213. While his article focused on historical burial customs, here I explore the hermeneutical significance of the practice.

41. For the material evidence, see Kadari, "This One Fulfilled What Is Written in That One," 207–13.

42. As Kadari has observed, none of the following reasons excludes the others. Kadari, 191.

43. This suggestion is supported by nonrabbinic evidence. Romans shared a cultural memory of King Numa buried with sacred books to keep them from falling into the wrong hands.

44. Plutarch, *Num.* 22.2.

45. Lauterbach, Jacob Z. ed., *Mekilta de-Rabbi Ishmael: A Critical Edition on the Basis of the Manuscripts and Early Editions with an English Translation, Introduction, and Notes,* 1:177–78 (Philadelphia: Jewish Publication Society, 1933/1961; repr.1976).

46. NRSV Gen 50:26.

47. *LamR Petihta* 25.

48. Guy Stroumsa, *The End of Sacrifice: Religious Transformations in Late Antiquity*, trans. Susan Emanuel, 63–70 (Chicago and London: University of Chicago Press, 2009).

49. BQ 17a.

50. MQ 25a–25b.

51. MQ 25a. This is oddly phrased because the conventional mourning practice (renting clothes for the deceased) is based on the strange practice (rending clothes for a Torah scroll). C. Friedman, "Laws of Mourning: The Tractate of Moed Katan and its Parallels" (PhD diss., Hebrew University, 2008), 236 [Hebrew]. Cf. Adiel Kadari, 199.

52. See Marianne Schleicher, "The Many Faces of the Torah: Reception and Transformation of the Torah in Jewish Communities," in *Receptions and Transformations of the Bible,* ed. Kirsten Nielsen, 145 (Aarhus: University Press, 2009). In a second article, she argues that this practice demonstrated the Torah scroll's holiness as an artifact, constructed from the ruins of the temple. See Marianne Schleicher, "Accounts of a Dying Scroll," in *The Death of Sacred Texts*, ed. Kristina Myrvold, 11–30 (Surrey and Burlington: Ashgate Press, 2010). These articles provide a fascinating look at how the Torah scroll developed efficacy as a holy object from the Middle Ages through modern times; there is no evidence for accompanying practices, such as genizot or funerals for scrolls, before the Arab conquest.

53. Qid 33b.

54. Shab 14b. אמר רבי פרנך אמר רבי יוחנן האוחז ספר תורה ערום נקבר ערו.

55. p.Ber 7:2 53b.

56. Rabbi Hanina ben Teradion's martyrdom is recounted in several rabbinic sources. While the circumstances leading to his death vary, a consistent feature of each story was the method of execution. See *SifreDeut* 32.4 307, Semaḥot 8 and Kallah 23, and AZ 17b–18a. Richard Kalmin has studied the strata to this narrative, arguing that the Babylonian layers demonstrate that Babylonian Sages placed a higher premium on Torah study than their Palestinian counterparts. See Richard Kalmin, *Jewish Babylonia Between Persia and Palestine* (Oxford: Oxford University Press, 2006), 21–26.

57. While Arthur Marmorstein argued that the story was too dramatic to reflect reality, Saul Lieberman put forth the position that the level of detail and accuracy indicates that eyewitnesses produced the narrative. Arthur Marmorstein, *Studies in Jewish Theology* (Oxford: University Press, 1950), pp. 142, 167, 174. Also Saul Lieberman, ed., "On Persecution of the Jewish Religion," in *Jubilee Volume in Honor of Salo Baron on the Occasion of his Eightieth Birthday*, 213–54 (New York: Columbia University Press, 1975) [Hebrew]. Cf. Herbert W. Basser, "Hanina's Torah: A Case of Verse Production or of Historical Fact?" in *Approaches to Ancient Judaism*, New Series, ed. Jacob Neusner (Atlanta: Scholars Press, 1990), 1:68. Other works of scholarship to address this story include: Saul Lieberman, "The Martyrs of Caesarea," *Annuairv de l'Institut de Philologie et d'Histoire Orientales et Slaves* 1 (1939-44): 395–446. G. Blidstein, "Rabbis, Romans and Martyrdom—Three Views," *Tradition* 21 (1984): 54–62. Daniel Boyarin, *Dying for God: Martyrdom and the Making of Christianity and Judaism* (Stanford, CA: Stanford University Press, 1999), 56–58. Daniel Boyarin and Virginia Burrus, "Hybridity as Subversion of Orthodoxy? Jews and Christians in Late Antiquity," *Social Compass* 52, no. 4 (2005): 431–41. Jan Willem van Henten, "Jewish and Christian Martyrs," in *Saints and Role Models in Judaism and Christianity*, ed. Marcel Poorthuis and Joshua Schwartz, 163–82 (Leiden and Boston: Brill, 2004). Richard Kalmin, *Jewish Babylonian Between Persia and Roman Palestine* (Oxford: Oxford University Press, 2006), 23–26.

58. This declaration has been read as a deliberate provocation of martyrdom on Rabbi Hanina's part. See Boyarin, *Dying for God*, 56–57.

59. AZ 18a.

60. The punishment of Rabbi Hanina's daughter—to "sit in a prostitute's booth"—has been interpreted as a judgement by proxy of Rabbi Hanina's public teaching of the Torah. See Boyarin, *Dying for God*, 70–71.

61. As Jonathan Schofer has observed, the deathbed scene was the "ultimate moment for instruction." See Jonathan Schofer, *The Making of a Sage: A Study in Rabbinic Ethics* (Madison: University of Wisconsin Press, 2005), 52.

62. *SifreDeut* 307; Semaḥot 8.

63. Steven D. Fraade, "Rabbinic Polysemy and Pluralism Revisited: Between Praxis and Thematization," *AJS Review* 31, no. 1 (2007), 3.

64. On this point, see Menachem Fisch, *Rational Rabbis: Science and Talmudic Culture* (Bloomington: Indiana University Press, 1997), 81. Also, David Kramer, *Mind of the Talmud: An Intellectual History of the Bavli* (New York and Oxford: Oxford University Press), 122.

65. BM 4.10.

66. As Heger notes, the Akhnai story "confirms the supremacy of rabbinic decisions." Paul Heger, *The Pluralistic Halakhah: Legal Innovations in the Late Second Commonwealth and Rabbinic Periods, Series Judaica* 22 (Berlin and New York: De Gruyter, 2003), 63–64.

67. Rebecca Scharbach Wollenberg, "The Dangers of Reading as We Know It: Sight Reading as a Source of Heresy in Early Rabbinic Traditions," *JAAR* 85, no. 3 (2017), 722.

68. Despite this verse from Deuteronomy functioning as a proof text for the concept of Oral Torah, the rabbis focus on the mouth and ignore the heart. *Leviticus Rabbah*, another *tannaitic* midrash, suggests that heresy was located in the heart, especially one's "own heart." See *LevR* XVIII and Moshe Halbertal, *People of the Book*, 25–27.

69. Susan Handelman, *Slayers of Moses: The Emergence of Rabbinic Interpretation in Modern Literary Theory* (Albany: SUNY Press, 1983), 40–41.

70. Richard Hidary, *Dispute for the Sake of Heaven: Legal Pluralism in the Talmud, Brown Judaic Studies Series* 353 (Providence: Brown Judaic Studies, 2010), 369–93.

71. In this respect, the narrative functions as "canonization of dissent." See Schofer, *The Making of a Sage*, 55.

72. Sanh 68a.

73. See Kel 26.4.

74. As Boyarin reminds us, Rabbi Eliezer was only rehabilitated by finally agreeing that "the endless dispute takes place within the confines of the Bet haMidrash and its discursive rules." *Borderlines*, 178.

75. Rabbi Eliezer's bibliomorphosis is absent in the Yersushalmi version of this story (p.Shab 2:7, 20d), suggesting that this Bavli detail developed a firmer connection between Rabbi Eliezer's oral proclamations and a physical Torah scroll.

76. See Boyarin, Borderlines, 178.

77. The relationship between Gospel and Torah is a matter of much discussion. In the traditional historical model, the Christian Gospels were the answer to the Jewish Torah. This position is reflected in the terminology "Old Testament" and "New Testament." In another model, the rabbinic Oral Torah was the answer to the Christian Gospels. This position is the implication of the arguments of Seth Schwartz, *Imperialism and Jewish Society, 200 B.C.E. to 640 C.E.* (Princeton and Oxford: Princeton University Press, 2001). The existence of Gospel and Oral Torah may also be mutually dependent—the shift in emphasis in Judaism towards oral tradition has been explained by the increased emphasis Christians began to place on written revelation. For this argument, see Guy Stroumsa, "The Scriptural Movement of Late Antiquity and Christian Monasticism," in *JECS* 16, no. 1 (2008): 61–77.

78. See Guy Stroumsa, *The End of Sacrifice: Religious Transformation in Late Antiquity*, trans. Susan Emanuel, 28–55 (Chicago and London: University of Chicago Press, 2009); *Hidden Wisdom: Esoteric Traditions and the Roots of Christian Mysticism*, Studies in the History of Religions 70 (Leiden: Brill, 1996; repr. 2005), 109–131.

79. This term was introduced to biblical studies in Samuel Sandmel's 1961 SBL presidential address. For a transcription of the speech, see Samuel Sandmel, "Parallelomania," in *JBL* 81, no. 1 (1962): 1–13.

80. Martin S. Jaffee, *Torah in the Mouth*, 7.

CONCLUSION

1. Christoph Markschies, "The Canon of the New Testament in Antiquity," in *Homer, the Bible and Beyond*, ed. M. Finkelberg and G. G. Stroumsa, 175–94 (Leiden: Brill, 2003).

2. F. Max Müller, *Introduction to the Science of Religion: Four Lectures Delivered at the Royal Institution, in February and May 1870* (London: Longmans, Green, and Co., 1882), 53.

3. Mroczek, *The Literary Imagination in Jewish Antiquity*, 118.

4. AnneMarie Luijendijk, "A Gospel Amulet for Joannia (P.Oxy. VIII 1151), in *Daughters of Hecate Women and Magic in the Ancient World*, ed. Kimberly B. Stratton and Dayna S. Kalleres, 418–43 (New York: Oxford University Press, 2014). Also, Michael J. Krueger, "P.Oxy. 840 Amulet or Miniature Codex?" *JTS*, new series 53/1 (2002):81–94.

5. See, for example, Raymond Van Dam, trans., *Gregory of Tours: Glory of the Confessors* (Liverpool: Liverpool University Press, 1988), 37.

6. H. Musurillo, *Acts of the Christian Martyrs* (Oxford: Clarendon, 1972), 319.

7. *Stat.* 19.14. Translated by W. R. W. Stephens, From *Nicene and Post-Nicene Fathers, First Series*, Vol. 9, ed. Philip Schaff (Buffalo, NY: Christian Literature Publishing Co., 1889), 470. Cf. Luijendijk, "A Gospel Amulet for Joannia (P.Oxy. VIII 1151)," 431 n. 2.

8. *Hom. Matt.* 72. Translated by Luijendijk, "A Gospel Amulet for Joannia (P.Oxy. VIII 1151)," 419. The term "φυλακτήρια," translated both as "amulet" and then "phylacteries," can also designate other ritual protections that John Chysostom would have approved, including baptism and the eucharist.

9. Luijendijk, "A Gospel Amulet for Joannia," 418.

10. Aug. *In Evang. Iohan.* 7.12.1; Trans. Rettig, *Tractates on the Gospel of John*, 1–10. Cf. Luijendijk, "A Gospel Amulet for Joannia (P.Oxy. VIII 1151)," 443 n. 93.

11. Joseph E. Sanzo, "Magic and Communal Boundaries: The Problem with Amulets in Chrystostom, *Adv. Iud.* 8, and Augustine, *In Io. Tra.* 7," *Henoch* 39, no. 2 (2017): 238.

12. Jonas Svensson, "Relating, Revering, and Removing: Muslim Views on the Use, Power, and Disposal of Divine Words," in *The Death of Sacred Texts*, 31–54.

13. For example: K. van der Toorn, ed., *The Image and the Book: Iconic Cults, Aniconism and the Rise of Book Religion in Israel and the Ancient Near East* (Leuven: Peeters, 1997); Herbert L. Kessler, "The Book as Icon," in *In the Beginning: Bibles Before the Year 1000*, ed. Michelle P. Brown, 77–103, 222–44 (Washington, DC: Smithsonian, 2006); William Klingshirn and Linda Safra, eds., *The Early Christian Book* (Washington, DC: Catholic University of America Press, 2007); Vincent L. Wimbush, *Theorizing Scriptures: New Critical Orientations to a Cultural Phenomenon* (New Brunswick, NJ: Rutgers University Press, 2008); James Bielo, ed., *The Social Life of Scriptures*: Cross-Cultural Perspectives in Biblicism (New Brunswick, NJ: Rutgers University Press, 2009); Max D. Moerman, "The Materiality of the Lotus Sutra: Scripture, Relic, and Buried Treasure," in *Dharma World* 37 (July–September 2010): 15–22; Dorina Miller Parameter, Craig A. Evans, and H. Daniel Zacharias, eds., *Jewish and Christian Scripture as Artifact and Canon* (London: T. & T. Clark, 2009).

14. AnneMarie Luijendijk, "Sacred Scriptures as Trash: Biblical Papyri from Oxyrhynchus," *VC* 64, no. 3 (2010): 220.

15. See Marianne Schleicher, "Accounts of a Dying Scroll: On Jewish Handling of Sacred Texts in Need of Restoration or Disposal," in *The Death of Sacred Texts: Ritual Disposal and Renovation of Texts in World Religions*, ed. Kristina Myrvold, 11–30 (London: Ashgate, 2010).

16. Måns Broo, "Rites of Burial and Immersion: Hindu Ritual Practices on the Disposing of Sacred Texts in Vrindavan," in *The Death of Sacred Texts: Ritual Disposal and Renovation of Texts in World Religions*, 91–106.

17. Jonas Svensson, "Relating, Revering, and Removing: Muslim Views on the Use, Power, and Disposal of Divine Words, in *The Death of Sacred Texts*, 31–54.

18. See the other fascinating articles in Kristina Myrvold, ed., *The Death of Sacred Texts: Ritual Disposal and Renovation of Texts in World Religions* (London: Ashgate, 2010).

19. See "Beholding the Precious Stupa," in *The Threefold Lotus Sutra*, trans. Bunno Kato, Yoshiro Tomura, and Kojiro Miyasaka, 195–207 (Tokyo: Kosei Publishing Co., 1975; repr. 1992). Also Reginald A. Ray, "Buddhism: Sacred Text Written and Realized," in *The Holy Book in Comparative Perspective*, ed. Fredrick M. Denny and Rodney L. Taylor, 148–80 (Columbia: University of South Carolina Press, 1985).

20. Jennifer Howard, "New Forms of Scholarship in a Digital World Challenge the Humanities," *Chronicle of Higher Education*, April 4, 2010.

BIBLIOGRAPHY

Anonymous. *Historia Augusta*. Translated by David Magie. LCL 140. Cambridge, MA: Harvard University Press, 1921.

———. *The Threefold Lotus Sutra*. Translated by Bunno Kato, Yoshiro Tmaura, and Kojiro Miyasaka. Reprint. Tokyo: Kosei Publishing Co., 1992.

Adler, William. "Fallen Angels and the History of Judaism and Christianity: The Reception of Enochic Literature." *JR* 88, no. 2 (April 2008): 261–63.

———. "The Origins of the Proto-heresies: Fragments from a Chronicle in the First Book of Epiphanius' Panarion." *JTS* 41, no. 2 (October 1990): 472–501.

———. "The Pseudepigrapha in the Early Church." In *The Canon Debate*, edited by Lee Martin McDonald and James A. Sanders, 211–28. Peabody, MA: Hendrickson Publishers, 2002.

———. *Time Immemorial: Archaic History and Its Sources in Christian Chronography from Julius Africanus to George Syncellus*. Washington, DC: Dumbarton Oaks Research Library and Collection, 1989.

Aiken, J. K. "The Literary Attainment of the Translator of Greek Sirach." In *The Texts and Versions of the Book of Ben Sira: Transmission and Interpretation*, edited by Jean-Sébastien Rey and Jan Joosten, 95–126. Leiden: Brill, 2011.

Aland, Barbara, Kurt Aland, Johannes Karavidopoulos, Carlo M. Martini, and Bruce M. Metzger, eds. *Novum Testamentum Graece*. 27th ed. Stuttgart: Deutsche Bibelgesellschaft, 2001.

Albeck, Chanoch. *Shiha Sidre Mishnah*. 6 vols. Jerusalem: Bialik Institute, 1952–1959.

Alexander, P. S. "Pre-emptive Exegesis: Genesis Rabbah's Reading of the Story of Creation." *JJS* 43, no. 2 (1992): 230–45.

Amir, Yehoshua. "Authority and Interpretation of Scripture in the Writings of Philo." In *Mikra: Text, Translation, Reading and Interpretation of the Hebrew Bible in Ancient Judaism and Early Christianity*, edited by Martin Jan Mulder and Harry Sysling, 421–53. Peabody, MA: Hendrickson Publishers, 2004.

Arai, Sasagu. *Die Christologie Des Evangelium Veritatis, Eine Religionsgeschichtliche Untersuchung.* Leiden: Brill, 1964.

Athanassiadi, Polymnia. "Canonizing Platonism: The Fetters of Iamblichus." In *Canon and Canonicity: The Formation and Use of Scripture*, edited by Einar Thomassen, 129–41. Copenhagen: Museum Tusculanum Press, 2010.

Attridge, Harold, ed. "The Gospel of Truth as an Exoteric Text." In *Nag Hammadi, Gnosticism, & Early Christianity*, 239–55. Peabody, MA: Hendrickson Publishers, 1986.

Attridge, Harold, and George W. MacRae, S.J. "The Gospel of Truth." In *Nag Hammadi Codex I (the Jung Codex)*, edited by Harold Attridge, 55–121. Leiden: Brill, 1985.

Aurelius, Marcus. *Meditations*. Edited and translated by C.R. Haines. LCL 58. Reprint. Cambridge, MA: Harvard University Press, 1930.

Bagnall, Roger S. *Early Christian Books in Egypt*. Princeton: Princeton University Press, 2009.

Baines, John. *Visual and Written Culture in Ancient Egypt*. New York: Oxford University Press, 2007.

Barr, James. *Holy Scripture: Canon, Authority and Criticism*. Philadelphia: Westminster Press, 1983.

Barrett, Charles K. "Theological Vocabulary of the Fourth Gospel and of the Gospel of Truth." In *Current Issues in New Testament Interpretation*, edited by W. Klassen and G. F. Snyder, 210–23. New York: Harper & Row, 1962.

Barton, James. *Oracles of God: Perceptions of Ancient Prophecy After the Exile*. New York: Oxford University Press, 1986.

Basser, Herbert W. "Hanina's Torah: A Case of Verse Production or of Historical Fact?" In *Approaches to Ancient Judaism*, New Series, edited by Jacob Neusner, 141–53. Atlanta: Scholars Press, 1990.

Bauer, Walter. *Rechtgläubigkeit und Ketzerei in ältesten Christentum*. Tübingen: Mohr, 1934.

Baumgarten, Albert. "The Pharisaic Paradosis." *HTR* 80, no. 1 (January 1987): 63–77.

Baynes, Leslie. *The Heavenly Book Motif in Judeo-Christian Apocalypses, 200 B.C.E.-200 C.E.* Leiden: Brill, 2012.

Beard, Mary, et al., eds. *Literacy in the Roman World*. Journal of Roman Archaeology Supplementary Series 3. Ann Arbor: University of Michigan, 1991.

Beard, Mary, John North, and Simon Price. *Religions of Rome*. 1998; repr., Cambridge, UK: Cambridge University Press, 2000.

Bedenbender, Andreas. "The Place of the Torah in the Early Enoch Literature." In *The Early Enoch Literature*, edited by Gabriele Boccaccini and John J. Collins, 65–79. Leiden: Brill, 2007.

Beentjes, Pancratius C. *The Book of Ben Sira in Hebrew: A Text Edition of All Extant Hebrew Manuscripts and a Synopsis of All Parallel Hebrew Ben Sira Texts*. Leiden: Brill, 1997.

Behr, John. *Asceticism and Anthropology in Irenaeus and Clement*. Oxford Early Christian Studies. Oxford: Oxford University Press, 2000.

Bekken, Per Jarle. *The Word Is Near You: A Study of Deuteronomy 30: 12-14 in Paul's Letter to the Romans in a Jewish Context*. Berlin: Walter de Gruyter, 2007.

Ben-Dov, Jonathan. "Writing as Oracle and as Law: New Contexts for the Book-find of King Josiah." *JBL* 127, no. 2 (2008): 223–39.

Benoît, André. *Saint Irénée; Introduction à l'étude de sa théologie*. Paris: Presses universitaires de France, 1960.

Berzon, Todd. *Classifying Christians: Ethnography, Heresiology, and the Limits of Knowledge in Late Antiquity*. Oakland: University of California Press, 2016.

Bérubé, Michael. "What's the Matter with Cultural Studies?" *Chronicle Review*, September 14, 2009.

Bielo, James, ed. *The Social Life of Scriptures: Cross-Cultural Perspectives in Biblicism*. New Brunswick, NJ: Rutgers University Press, 2009.

Blidstein, Gerald J. "Rabbis, Romans, and Martyrdom: Three Views." *Tradition* 21, no. 3 (Fall 1984): 54–62.

Bobertz, Charles A., David Brakke, and Rowan A. Greer. *Reading in Christian Communities: Essays on Interpretation in the Early Church*. Christianity and Judaism in Antiquity Series. Notre Dame, IN: University of Notre Dame Press, 2002.

Boccacini, Gabriele. *Beyond the Essene Hypothesis*. Grand Rapids, MI: Eerdmans, 1998.

———. "From Movement of Dissent to a Distinct Form of Judaism: The Heavenly Tablets in Jubilees as the Foundation of a Competing Halakah." In *Enoch and the Mosaic Torah: The*

Evidence of Jubilees, edited by Gabriele Boccaccini and Giovanni Ibba, 193–210. Grand Rapids, MI: Eerdmans, 2009.

———. *Middle Judaism: Jewish Thought, 300 B.C.E. to 200 C.E.* Minneapolis: Fortress Press, 1991.

Borchardt, Francis. "The Prologue of Sirach (Ben Sira) and the Question of Canon." In *Sacra Scriptura: How "Non-Canonical" Texts Functioned in Early Judaism and Early Christianity*, edited by J. H. Charlesworth and L. M. McDonald with B. A. Jurgens, 64–71. T&T Clark Jewish and Christian Text Series. London: Bloomsbury T&T Clark, 2014.

———. "The LXX Myth and the Rise of Textual Fixity." *JSJ* 43 (2012), 1–21.

Boorstein, Michelle. "Koran Burning Drew Little Attention," *Washington Post*, April 2, 2011.

Botha, Pieter. *Orality and Literary in Early Christianity*. Biblical Performance Criticism 5. Eugene, OR: Cascade Books, 2012.

Bowersock, G. W. "The Literature of the Empire," in *The Cambridge History of Classical Literature*, edited by P. E. Easterling and B. M. W. Knox, 642–714. Cambridge, UK: Cambridge University Press, 1985.

Bowman, Alan K., and Greg Woolf. *Literacy and Power in the Ancient World*. Cambridge, UK: Cambridge University Press, 1994.

Boyarin, Daniel. *Borderlines: The Partition of Judaeo-Christianity*. Philadelphia: University of Pennsylvania Press, 2004.

———. *Sparks of the Logos: Essays in Rabbinic Hermeneutics*. Brill Reference Library of Judaism. Leiden: Brill, 2003.

———. *Dying for God: Martyrdom and the Making of Christianity and Judaism*. Stanford, CA: Stanford University Press, 1999.

———. "Why Ignatius Invented Judaism." In *The Ways that Often Parted: Essays in Honor of Joel Marcus*, edited by Lori Baron, Jill Hicks-Keeton, and Matthew Thiessen, 309–24. Atlanta: SBL Press, 2018.

Boyarin, Daniel, and Virginia Burrus. "Hybridity as Subversion of Orthodoxy? Jews and Christians in Late Antiquity." *Social Compass* 52, no. 4 (2005): 431–41.

Brakke, David. "Canon Formation and Social Conflict in Fourth-Century Egypt: Athanasius of Alexandria's Thirty-Ninth 'Festal Letter.'" *HTR* 87, no. 4 (October 1, 1994): 395–419.

———. *The Gnostics: Myth, Ritual, and Diversity in Early Christianity*. Cambridge, MA: Harvard University Press, 2010.

———. "A New Fragment of Athanasius's Thirty-Ninth Festal Letter: Heresy, Apocrypha, and the Canon." *HTR* 103, no. 1 (2010): 47–66.

———. "Scriptural Practices in Early Christianity: Towards a New History of the New Testament Canon." In *Invention, Rewriting, Usurpation: Discursive Fights over Religious Traditions in Antiquity*, edited by Jörg Ulrich, Anders-Christian Jacobsen and David Brakke, 263–280. Frankfurt am Main: Peter Lang, 2012.

Bregman, Marc. "The Parable of the Lame and the Blind: Epiphanius' Quotation from an Apocryphon of Ezekiel." *JTS* 42, no. 1 (April 1991): 125–38.

Brent, Allen. "Was Hippolytus a Schismatic?" *VC* 49, no. 3 (1995): 215–44.

Broo, Måns. "Rites of Burial and Immersion: Hindu Ritual Practices on the Disposing of Sacred Texts in Vrindavan." In *The Death of Sacred Texts: Ritual Disposal and Renovation of Texts in World Religions*, edited by Kristina Myrvold, 91–106. Surrey: Ashgate Publishers, 2010.

Brown, Jonathan. *The Canonization of al Bukhārī and Muslim: The Formation and Function of the Sunnī Ḥadīth Canon*. Leiden: Brill, 2007.

Brown, Peter. *Power and Persuasion in Late Antiquity: Towards a Christian Empire*. Madison: University of Wisconsin Press, 1992.

Brown, Schuyler. "The Scriptural Reading of Scripture and the Coptic Gospel of Truth." *Society of Biblical Literature Seminar Papers* no. 29 (1990): 637–644.

Bruce, F. F., and Gordon Rupp. *Holy Book and Holy Tradition.* Grand Rapids, MI: Eerdmans, 1968.

Burridge, Richard A. *What Are the Gospels?* Grand Rapids, MI: Eerdmans Publishing, 2004.

Callick, Rowan. "Malaysia OKs Call to Burn Bibles," *The Australian*, October 13, 2014.

Cambron-Goulet, Mathilde. "The Criticism—and the Practice—of Literacy." In *Orality, Literacy and Performance in the Ancient World*, edited by Elizabeth Minchin, 201–26. Leiden: Brill, 2011.

Camelot, P. "The Nature of Truth in The Gospel of Truth and in the Writings of Justin Martyr: A Study of the Pattern of Orthodoxy." *Revue d'histoire ecclésiastique* 67, no. 2 (1972): 460–61.

Campenhausen, Hans. *The Formation of the Christian Bible.* Minneapolis: Fortress Press, 1972.

Cassius Dio Cocceianus. *Roman History.* Edited by Earnest Cary and Herbert Baldwin Foster. LCL 32, 33, 53, 66, 82, 83, 175, 176, 177. London: W. Heinemann, 1914–1927.

Casson, Lionel. *Libraries in the Ancient World.* New Haven: Yale University Press, 2001.

Cavallo, Guglielmo. *A History of Reading in the West.* Oxford: Polity Press, 1999.

Champlin, Edward. *Final Judgments: Duty and Emotion in Roman Wills, 200 B.C.-A.D. 250.* Berkeley: University of California Press, 1991.

Chapman, Stephen. "Second Temple Jewish Hermeneutics: How Canon Is Not an Anachronism." In *Invention, Rewriting, Usurpation: Discursive Fights over Religious Traditions in Antiquity*, edited by Jörg Ulrich, Anders-Christian Jacobsen, and David Brakke, 281–96. Frankfurt am Main: Peter Lang Verlag, 2011.

Chiapparini, Giulo. "Irenaeus and the Gnostic Valentinus: Orthodoxy and Heresy in the Church of Rome around the Middle of the Second Century." ZAC 18 (2014): 95–119.

Chin, C. Michael. "Origen and Christian Naming: Textual Exhaustion and the Boundaries of Gentility in Commentary on John 1." *JECS* 14, no. 4 (2006): 407–36.

Clark, Elizabeth Ann. *Reading Renunciation: Asceticism and Scripture in Early Christianity.* Princeton: Princeton University Press, 1999.

Clenman, Laliv. "The Fire and the Flesh: Self-Destruction of the Male Rabbinic Body." In *The Body in Biblical, Christian and Jewish Texts*, edited by Joan E. Taylor, 210–25. London and New York: Bloomsbury T&T Clark, 2014.

Clines, David J. A., S. E. Fowl, and S. E. Porter. *The Bible in Three Dimensions: Essays in Celebration of Forty Years of Biblical Studies in the University of Sheffield.* Sheffield, UK: JSOT Press, 1990.

Coarelli, Filippo. *The Column of Trajan.* Preface by Paul Zanker. Translated by Cynthia Rockwell. Rome: Editore Colombo with the German Archaeological Institute, 2000.

Cohen, Yehuda. *Tangled Up in Text: Tefillin in the Ancient World.* Providence: Brown Judaic Studies, 2008.

Collins, John. *The Invention of Judaism: Torah and Jewish Identity from Deuteronomy to Paul.* Oakland: University of California Press, 2017.

———. *Between Athens and Jerusalem: Jewish Identity in the Hellenistic Diaspora.* Second Edition. Grand Rapids, MI: Eerdmans, 2000.

Conrad, Edgar W. "Heard but Not Seen: The Representation of 'Books' in the Old Testament." *JSOT* 17, no. 54 (1992): 45–59.

Countryman, L. W. "Tertullian and the Regula Fidei." *SecCen* 2, no. 4 (1982): 212–13.

Crum, W. E. *A Coptic Dictionary.* Oxford: Clarendon Press, 1939.

Davies, Stevan L. "Gnostic Idealism and the Gospel of Truth." In *Religious Writings and Religious Systems,* edited by Ernest S. Frerichs and Jacob Neusner, 83–94. Atlanta: Scholars Press, 1989.

Davison, James E. "Structural Similarities and Dissimilarities in the Thought of Clement of Alexandria and the Valentinians." *SecCen* 3, no. 4 (1983): 201–17.

Dawson, David. "The Gospel of Truth as Rhetorical Theology." *Studia Patristica* 18, no. 1 (1985): 241–45.

———. *Allegorical Readers and Cultural Revision in Ancient Alexandria*. Berkeley: University of California Press, 1992.

DeConick, April D. "Becoming God's Body: The Kavod in Valentinianism." *Society of Biblical Literature Seminar Papers* no. 34 (1995): 23–36.

De Crom, Dries."The Letter of Aristeas and the Authority of the Septuagint." *JSP* 17, no. 2 (2008): 141–60.

Del Monte, M, P. Ausset, and Ra Lefevre. "Traces of Ancient Colors on Trajan's Column." *Archaeometry* 40, no. 2 (1998): 403–12.

Dilke, Oswald Ashton Wentworth. *Roman Books and Their Impact*. Leeds: Elmete Press, 1977.

Dillon, John. *The Middle Platonists: 80 B.C. to A.D. 220*. Ithaca, NY: Cornell University Press, 1977.

Dix, T. Keith. "'Public Libraries' in Ancient Rome: Ideology and Reality." *Libraries & Culture* 29, no. 3 (July 1, 1994): 282–96.

———. "Public Libraries in the City of Rome: From the Augustan Age to the Time of Diocletian." *MEFRA* 118, no. 2 (2006): 671–717.

Donovan, Mary Ann. *One Right Reading? A Guide to Irenaeus*. Collegeville, MN: Liturgical Press, 1997.

Drinkwater, J. F. *Roman Gaul: The Three Provinces, 58 BC–AD 260*. London: Croom Helm, 1983.

Droge, A. J. "'The Lying Pen of the Scribes': Of Holy Books and Pious Frauds." *MTSR* 15, no. 2 (2003): 117–47.

Dubois, Jean-Daniel. "Remarques sur le texte de L'Evangile de Verite (CG I, 2)." *VC* 29, no. 2 (June 1975): 138–40.

Dunderberg, Ismo. *Beyond Gnosticism: Myth, Lifestyle, and Society in the School in the School of Valentinus*. New York: Columbia University Press, 2008.

Dupont, Florence. "The Corrupt Boy and the Crowned Poet: or, the Material Reality and the Symbolic Status of the Literary Book at Rome." In *Ancient Literacies, the Culture of Reading in Greece and Rome*, edited by William A. Johnson and Holt N. Parker, 143–63. Oxford: Oxford University Press, 2009.

Dunn, W. "What Does the 'Gospel of Truth' Mean." *VC* 15, no. 3 (1961): 160–64.

Easterling, P. E. "Books and Readers in the Greek World: The Hellenistic and Imperial Periods." In *The Cambridge History of Classical Literature*, edited by P. E. Easterling and B. M. W. Knox, 38–39. Cambridge, UK: Cambridge University Press, 1985.

Edwards, Mark J. *Catholicity and Heresy in the Early Church*. Surrey: Ashgate Publishing Ltd, 2009.

———. "Gnostics and Valentinians in the Church Fathers." *JTS* 40, no. 1 (April 1989): 26–47.

———. "Justin's Logos and the Word of God." *JECS* 3, no. 3 (1995): 261–80.

Elanskaya, Alla I. "The Literary Coptic Manuscripts in the A.S. Pushkin State Fine Arts Museum in Moscow." In *Supplements to VC* 18, 379–80. Leiden: Brill, 1994.

Eliav, Yaron Z., Elise A. Friedland, and Sharon Herbert, eds. *The Sculptural Environment of the Roman Near East: Reflections on Culture, Ideology, and Power*. Leuven: Peeters, 2008.

Elman, Yaakov. *Authority and Tradition: Toseftan Baraitot in Talmudic Babylonia*. New York and Hoboken, NJ: Michael Scharf Publication Trust of the Yeshiva University Press, 1994.

Engberg-Pedersen, T. "Philo's De Vita Contemplativa: A Philosopher's Dream." *JSJ* 30 (1999), 40–64.

Epictetus. *The Discourses as Reported by Arrian, the Manual, and Fragments*. Edited and translated by William A. Oldfather. 2 vols. LCL 131, 218. London: Heinemann, 1925–28.

Fallon, F. F. "The Law in Philo and Ptolemy: A Note on the Letter to Flora." *VC* 30, no. 1 (1976): 45–51.

Farrell, Joseph. "The Impermanent Text in Catullus and Other Roman Poets." In *Ancient Literacies, the Culture of Reading in Greece and Rome*, edited by William A. Johnson and Holt N. Parker, 164–85. Oxford: Oxford University Press, 2009.

Ferguson, Thomas C. K. "The Rule of Truth and Irenaean Rhetoric in Book 1 of 'Against Heresies.'" *VC* 55, no. 4 (2001): 356–75.

Fineman, Joel. "Gnosis and the Piety of Metaphor: The Gospel of Truth." In Vol. 1 of *Rediscovery of Gnosticism*, edited by Bentley Layton, 289–312. Leiden: Brill, 1980.

Finkelberg, Margalit, and Guy G. Stroumsa. *Homer, the Bible, and Beyond: Literary and Religious Canons in the Ancient World*. Leiden: Brill, 2003.

Finkelstein, David, and Alistair. McCleery. *The Book History Reader*. London: Routledge, 2002.

———. *An Introduction to Book History*. New York: Routledge, 2005.

Fisch, Menachem. *Rational Rabbis: Science and Talmudic Culture*. Bloomington: Indiana University Press, 1997.

Fitzgerald, William. *Martial: The World of the Epigram*. Chicago: University of Chicago Press, 2007.

Fowler, D. P. "Martial and the Book." In *Roman Literature and Ideology: Ramus Essays for J.P. Sullivan*, edited by A. J. Boyle. Bendigo, Australia: Aureal Publications, 1995.

Fraade, Steven. *From Tradition to Commentary: Torah and Its Interpretation in the Midrash Sifre to Deuteronomy*. Albany: State University of New York Press, 1991.

———. "Literary Composition and Oral Performance in Early Midrashim." *Oral Tradition* 4, no. 1 (1999): 33–51.

Frankfurter, David. "The Legacy of Jewish Apocalypses in Early Christianity: Regional Trajectories." In the *Jewish Apocalyptic Heritage in Early Christianity*, edited by James VanderKam and William Adler, 129–200. Van Gorcum: Fortress Press, 1996.

———. *Religion in Roman Egypt: Assimilation and Resistance*. Princeton: Princeton University Press, 1998.

Franz, Albert. "Erlösung Durch Erkenntnis: Zur Gnostischen Schrift Evangelium Veritatis." In *Glauben, Wissen, Handeln*, edited by Albert Franz, 219–31. Würzburg: Echter, 1994.

Friedman, C. "Laws of Mourning: The Tractate of Moed Katan and its Parallels." PhD diss., Hebrew University, 2008 [Hebrew].

Friedman, Richard Elliot. *Who Wrote the Bible*. New York: Summit Books, 1998.

Friedman, Shamma. "The Holy Scriptures Defile the Hands—The Transformation of a Biblical Concept in Rabbinic Theology," in *Minhah le-Nahum: Biblical and Other Studies Presented to Nahum M Sarna in Honour of his 70th Birthday*, edited by Mark Brettler and Michael Fishbane, 117–32. Sheffield: Sheffield Academic Press, 1993.

Gamble, Harry Y. *Books and Readers in the Early Church: A History of Early Christian Texts*. New Haven: Yale University Press, 1995.

———. "Marcion and the 'Canon,'" in *Cambridge Dictionary of Early Christianity: Origins through Constantine*, edited by Margaret M. Mitchell and Francis M. Young, 195–213. Cambridge: Cambridge University Press, 2006.

Gathercole, Simon. "The Nag Hammadi Gospels," in Die Nag-Hammadi-Schriften in der Literatur und Theologiegeschichte des frühen Christentums, edited by Jens Schröter, and Konrad Schwarz. 199-218. Tübingen: Mohr Siebeck, 2017.

Girardot, N. J. "Max Müller's Sacred Books and the Nineteenth-Century Production of the Comparative Science of Religions." *History of Religions* 41, no. 3 (2002): 213–50.

Gerhardsson, Birger. *Memory and Manuscript: Oral Tradition and Written Transmission in Rabbinic Judaism and Early Christianity*. Lund and Copenhagen: C.W.K. Gleerup and Ejnar Munksgaard, 1961.

Goldwurm, Hersch et al., eds. *Talmud Bavli: The Schottenstein Edition*. Brooklyn, NY: Mesorah Publications, 1990–2007.

Goodman, Martin. "Sacred Scripture and 'Defiling the Hands.'" *JTS* 41, no. 1 (1990): 99–107.

Goshen-Gottstein, Alon. *The Sinner and the Amnesiac: The Rabbinic Invention of Elisha ben Abuya and Eleazar ben Arach*. Stanford, CA: Stanford University Press, 2000.

Grafton, Anthony, and Megan Hale Williams. *Christianity and the Transformation of the Book: Origen, Eusebius, and the Library of Caesarea*. Cambridge, MA: Belknap Press of Harvard University Press, 2006.

Graham, William A. *Beyond the Written Word: Oral Aspects of Scripture in the History of Religion*. Cambridge, UK: Cambridge University Press, 1993.

Grant, Robert M. "Irenaeus and Hellenistic Culture." *HTR* 42, no. 1 (1949): 41–51.

———. *Irenaeus of Lyons*. London: Routledge, 1997.

Grobel, Kendrick. *The Gospel of Truth, a Valentinian Meditation on the Gospel*. New York: Abingdon Press, 1960.

Grottanelli, Cristiano. "On Written Lies," in *Homer, the Bible, and Beyond*, edited by Margalit Finkelberg, 53–62. Leiden: Brill, 2003.

Gruen, Erich S. *Diaspora: Jews Amidst Greeks and* Romans. Cambridge, MA: Harvard University Press, 2002.

Gurd, Sean Alexandre. *Work in Progress: Literary Revision as Social Performance in Rome*. Oxford and New York: Oxford University Press, 2012.

Habineck, Thomas. "Situating Literacy in Rome," in *Ancient Literacies: The Culture of Reading in Greece and Rome*, edited by William A. Johnson and Holt N. Parker, 186–232. Oxford: Oxford University Press, 2009.

———. *The Politics of Latin Literature: Writing, Identity, and Empire in Ancient Rome*. Princeton: Princeton University Press, 1998.

Hagg, Tomas. "Canon Formation in Greek Literary Culture." In *Canon and Canonicity: The Formation and Use of Scripture*, edited by Einar Thomassen, 109–28. Copenhagen: Museum Tusculanum Press, 2010.

Hahn, F. "Die Sendscheiben der Johannesapokalypse: Ein Beitrag zur Bestimmung prophetischer Redeformen," in *Tradition und Glaube: Das fruehe Christentum in seiner Umwelt*, edited by G. Jeremias, H. W. Kuhn, and H. Stegemann, 357–94. Gottingen: Vandenhoeck und Ruprecht, 1971.

Haines-Eitzen, Kim. *Guardians of Letters: Literacy, Power, and the Transmitters of Early Christian Literature*. Oxford: Oxford University Press, 2000.

Halbertal, Moshe. *People of the Book: Canon, Meaning, and Authority*. Cambridge, MA: Harvard University Press, 1997.

Hammer, Reuven. *Sifre: A Tannaitic Commentary on the Book of Deuteronomy*. New Haven: Yale University Press, 1986.

Handelman, Susan. *Slayers of Moses: The Emergence of Rabbinic Interpretation in Modern Literary Theory*. Albany: SUNY Press, 1983.

Hankinson, R. J., ed. *The Cambridge Companion to Galen*. Cambridge Companions to Philosophy. Cambridge, UK: Cambridge University Press, 2008.

Haran, Menahem. *The Biblical Collection*. Jerusalem: Bialik Institute, 1996 [Hebrew].

Harnack, Adolf. *Der Brief des Ptolemäus an die Flora*. SPAW.PH 1902.

———. *Das Neue Testament um das Jahr 200: Theodor Zahn's Geschichte des neutestamentlichen Kanons*. Freiburg: Mohr Siebeck, 1889.

Harris, Paul. "How Koran-Burning Pastor Set World Ablaze: Paul Harris Reports on the Background to an 'Execution by Fire' That Led to Fatal Rioting on Friday in Afghanistan," *The Observer*, April 3, 2011.

Harris, William V. *Ancient Literacy*. Cambridge, MA: Harvard University Press, 1989.

Harrison, S. J. "Deflating the Odes: Horace, Epistles 1.20." *CQ* 38, no. 2. New Series (1988): 473–76.

Hayes, Christine. *What's Divine About Divine Law?* Princeton and Oxford: Princeton University Press, 2015.

Hedrick, Charles W., and Robert Hodgson. *Nag Hammadi, Gnosticism, & Early Christianity*. Peabody, MA: Hendrickson Publishers, 1986.

Heger, Paul. *The Pluralistic Halakhah: Legal Innovations in the Late Second Commonwealth and Rabbinic Periods, Series Judaica* 22. Berlin and New York: De Gruyter, 2003.

Helderman, Jan. "A Christian Gnostic Text: The Gospel of Truth." In *Gnosis and Hermeticism from Antiquity to Modern Times*, edited by R. van den Broek and Wouter J. Hanegraaff, 53–68. Albany: State University of New York Press, 1998.

———. "Isis as Plane in the Gospel of Truth." In *Gnosis and Gnosticism*, edited by M. Krause, 26–46. Leiden: Brill, 1981.

Henrichs, Albert. "'Hieroi Logoi' and 'Hierai Bibloi': The (Un)Written Margins of the Sacred in Ancient Greece." *HSCP* 101 (2003): 207–66.

Hezser, Catherine. *The Talmud Yerushalmi and Graeco-Roman Culture*. Tübingen: Mohr Siebeck, 2002.

Hidary, Richard. *Dispute for the Sake of Heaven: Legal Pluralism in the Talmud*. Providence: Brown Judaic Studies, 2010.

Himmelfarb, Martha. "Torah, Testimony and the Heavenly Tablets: The Claims of Authority of the Book of Jubilees." In *A Multiform Heritage (Festschrift Robert A. Kraft)*, edited by B. G. Wright, 19–29. Atlanta: Scholars Press, 1999.

Holmes, Michael W. *The Apostolic Fathers: Greek Texts and English Translations*. Grand Rapids, MI: Baker Academic, 2007.

Holzhausen, Jens. "Irenäus und die Valentinianische Schule: zur Praefatio von *Adv. Haer.* 1." *VC* 55, no. 4 (2001): 341–55.

———. "Über Den Titel Von Nag Hammadi Codex I,3." *Zeitschrift für Antikes Christentum* 7, no. 1 (2003): 91–98.

Houston, George W. *Inside Roman Libraries: Book Collections and Their Management in Antiquity*. Chapel Hill: University of North Carolina Press, 2014.

———. "Tiberius and the Libraries: Public Book Collections and Library Buildings in the Early Roman Empire." *Libraries and the Cultural Record* 43, no. 3 (2008): 247–69.

Howard, Jennifer. "New Forms of Scholarship in a Digital World Challenge the Humanities," *Chronicle of Higher Education*, April 4, 2010.

Humphries, Caroline. "Judging by the Book: Christian Codices in Late Antique Legal Culture." In *The Early Christian Book*, edited by William E. Klingshirn and Linda Safran, 141–58. Washington, DC: Catholic University Press, 2007.

Hurtado, Larry W. *Destroyer of the Gods: Early Christian Distinctiveness in the Roman Empire*. Waco, TX: Baylor University Press, 2016.

———. "Oral Fixation and New Testament Studies? 'Orality,' 'Performance' and Reading Texts in Early Christianity." *NTS* 60, no. 3 (2014): 321–40.

Jaffee, Martin. "A Rabbinic Ontology of the Written and Spoken Word: On Discipleship, Transformative Knowledge, and the Living Texts of Oral Torah." *JAAR* 65, no. 3 (1997): 525.

———. *Torah in the Mouth: Writing and Oral Tradition in Palestinian Judaism 200 BCE–400 CE.* New York: Oxford University Press, 2001.

Jager, Eric. *The Book of the Heart.* Chicago: University of Chicago Press, 2000.

———. "Did Eve Invent Writing? Script and the Fall in 'The Adam Books'" in *SPh* 93, no. 3 (1996): 229–50.

Janowitz, Naomi. "The Rhetoric of Translation: Three Early Perspectives on Translating Torah." *HTR* 84, no. 2 (1991): 129–40.

Jansen, John. "Tertullian and the New Testament." *SecCen* 2, no. 4 (1982): 191–207.

Jastrow, Marcus. *A Dictionary of the Targumim, the Talmud Babli and Yerushalmi and the Midrashic Literature.* 2nd ed. Peabody, MA: Hendrickson Publishers, 2005.

Jeffrey, David L. *People of the Book: Christian Identity and Literary Culture.* Grand Rapids, MI: Wm. B. Eerdmans Publishing, 1996.

Jenott, Lance, and Elaine Pagels. "Antony's Letters and Nag Hammadi Codex I: Sources of Religious Conflict in Fourth-Century Egypt." *JECS* 18, no. 4 (2010): 557–89.

Johnson, Aaron. "Ancestors as Icons: The Lives of the Hebrew Saints in Eusebius' *Praeparatio Evangelica.*" *GRBS* 44, no. 3 (2004): 245–64.

Johnson, Bob. "Judge the Koran Day to Be Held in Gainesville, Florida," *Tampa Bay Examiner,* February 11, 2011.

Johnson, William. *Readers and Reading Culture in the High Roman Empire.* Oxford and New York: Oxford University Press, 2010.

———. "Toward a Sociology of Reading in Classical Antiquity." *American Journal of Philology* 121, no. 4 (Winter 2000): 593–627.

Johnson, William, and Holt N. Parker, ed. *Ancient Literacies: The Culture of Reading in Greece and Rome.* Oxford and New York: Oxford University Press, 2009.

Jonas, Hans. *The Gnostic Religion: The Message of the Alien God and the Beginning of Christianity.* Boston: Beacon Press, 1958; 2nd ed., 1963.

Kadari, Adiel. "'This One Fulfilled What Is Written in That One': On an Early Burial Practice in Its Literary and Artistic Contexts." *JSJ* 41, no. 2 (2010): 191–213.

Kaler, Michael. "The Prayer of the Apostle Paul in the Context of Nag Hammadi Codex I." *JECS* 16, no. 3 (2008): 319–39.

Kalmin, Richard. *Jewish Babylonia between Persia and Roman Palestine.* Oxford: Oxford University Press, 2006.

Kalvesmaki, Joel. "Italian Versus Eastern Valentinianism?" *VC* 62, no. 1 (2008): 79–89.

Karpp, H. *Schrift und Geist bei Tertullian.* Gütersloh: C. Bertelsmann Verlag, 1955.

Kelber, Werner. *The Oral and the Written Gospel: The Hermeneutics of Speaking and Writing in the Synoptic Tradition, Mark, Paul, and Q.* Philadelphia: Fortress Press, 1983.

Kenyon, Frederic G. *Books and Readers in Ancient Greece and Rome.* Oxford: Clarendon Press, 1951.

Ker, Walter C. A. *Martial: Epigrams,* rev. ed. LCL. London: William Heinemann LTD, 1968.

Kessler, Herbert L. "The Book as Icon." In *In the Beginning: Bibles Before the Year 1000,* edited by Michelle P. Brown, 77–103, 222–44. Washington, DC: Smithsonian, 2006.

Keith, Chris. "Early Christian Book Culture and the Emergence of the First Written Gospel." In *Mark, Manuscripts, and Monotheism: Essays in Honor of Larry W. Hurtado,* edited by Chris

Keith and Dieter T. Roth, 22–39. Library of New Testament Studies 528. London: Bloomsbury T&T Clark, 2014.

———. "Prolegomena on the Textualization of Mark's Gospel: Manuscript Culture, the Extended Situation, and the Emergence of Written Gospels." In *Memory and Identity in Ancient Judaism and Early Christianity: A Conversation with Barry Schwartz*, edited by Tom Thatcher, 161–86. Semeia Studies 78. Atlanta: Society of Biblical Literature, 2014.

Kim, Young R. *The Imagined Worlds of Epiphanius of Cyprus.* PhD diss., University of Michigan, 2006.

King, Karen. *What Is Gnosticism.* Cambridge, MA: Harvard University Press, 2005.

Kinzig, Wolfram. "καινὴ διαθήκη: The Title of the New Testament in the Second and Third Centuries," *JTS*, ns 45, no. 2 (1994): 519–45.

Kippenberg, Hans G., and Guy G. Stroumsa. *Secrecy and Concealment: Studies in the History of Mediterranean and Near Eastern Religions.* Studies in the History of Religions. Leiden: Brill, 1995.

Kittel, Rudolf. *Biblia Hebraica Stuttgartensia.* Editio funditus renovata adjuvantibus H. Bardtke [et al.] cooperantibus H. P. Rüger et J. Ziegler ediderunt K. Elliger et W. Rudolph. Textum Masoreticum curavit H. P. Rüger. Masoram elaboravit G. E. Weil. Stuttgart: Deutsche Bibelstiftung, 1977.

Klingshirn, William E., and Linda Safran. *The Early Christian Book.* CUA Studies in Early Christianity. Washington, DC: Catholic University of America Press, 2007.

Knütel, R. "Paulus, Iulius." In *Juristen: Ein biographisches Lexikon von der Antike bis zum 20. Jahrhundert*, edited by Michael Stolleis, 489–91. Munich: Beck, 2001.

Koep, Leo. *Das Himmlische Buch in Antike Und Christentum; Eine Religionsgeschichtliche Untersuchung Zur Altchristlichen Bildersprache.* Theophaneia; Beiträge Zur Religions- Und Kirchengeschichte Des Altertums. Bonn: P. Hanstein, 1952.

Koester, Helmut. *Ancient Christian Gospels: Their History and Development.* Philadelphia: Trinity Press International, 1990.

Kraft, Robert A. "Para-mania: Beside, Before and Beyond Bible Studies." *JBL* 126, no. 1 (April 2007): 5–27.

Kramer, David. *Mind of the Talmud: An Intellectual History of the Bavli.* New York and Oxford: Oxford University Press, 1990.

Kreps, Anne. "From Jewish Apocrypha to Christian Tradition: Citations of Jubilees in Epiphanius' Panarion." *Journal of Church History* 87, no. 2 (2018): 345–70.

———. "The Passion of the Book: The *Gospel of Truth* as Valentinian Scriptural Practice." *JECS* 24 no. 3 (2016): 311–35.

Krueger, Derek. *Writing and Holiness: The Practice of Authorship in the Early Christian East.* Philadelphia: University of Pennsylvania Press, 2004.

Krueger, Michael J. "P.Oxy. 840 Amulet or Miniature Codex?" *JTS*, new series 53/1 (2002): 81–94.

Krüger , Paul, and Theodor Momsen, eds. *Institutiones Digesta.* 16th ed. Berlin: Weidmann Verlag, 1954.

Kühn, C. G., ed. *Claudii Galeni opera omnia.* Reprint. Hildesheim: Georg Olms Verlagsbuchhandlung, 1830.

Lactantius. *Epitome Divinarum Institutionum.* Edited by Antonie Wlosok. Berlin: Walter de Gruyter, 1998.

Lampe, Peter, and Marshall D. Johnson, eds. *From Paul to Valentinus: Christians at Rome in the First Two Centuries.* Stadtrömischen Christen in Den Ersten Beiden Jahrhunderten. Minneapolis: Fortress Press, 2003.

Lang, Bernhard. "'The Writings': A Hellenistic Literary Canon in the Hebrew Bible." In *Canonization and Decanonization*, edited by Arie van der Kooij, K. van der Toorn, and Joannes Augustinus Maria Snoek, 47–66. Leiden: Brill, 1998.

Lardet, P. "Les Conditions de la mise en texte." In *Lieux de savoir*, edited by C. Jacob, 507–14. Paris: Albin Michel Press, 2007.

Larsen, Matthew. *Gospels Before the Book*. Oxford: Oxford University Press, 2018.

Lashier, Jackson. *Irenaeus on the Trinity*. Supplements to *Vigiliae Christianae* 147. Leiden: Brill, 2014.

Lattimore, Richmond, trans. and ed. *The Iliad of Homer*. Reprint. Chicago: University of Chicago Press, 1992.

Lauterbach, Jacob Z., ed. *Mekilta de-Rabbi Ishmael: A Critical Edition on the Basis of the Manuscripts and Early Editions with an English Translation, Introduction, and Notes.* Reprint. Philadelphia: Jewish Publication Society, 1976.

Layton, Bentley. *The Gnostic Scriptures: A New Translation with Annotations and Introductions.* Garden City, NY: Doubleday, 1987.

———. *The Rediscovery of Gnosticism, Vol. 1: The School of Valentinus*. Leiden: Brill; New Haven: Yale University Press, 1980.

Le Boulluec, Alain. *La Notion d'hérésie dans da littérature Grecque, IIe-IIIe siècles*. Paris: Etudes augustiniennes, 1985.

Leiman, S. Z. *The Canonization of Hebrew Scripture: The Talmudic and Midrashic Evidence*. Hamden, CT: Archon Books, 1976.

Lewis, Jack P. "Jamnia Revisited." In *The Canon Debate*, edited by Lee Martin MacDonald and James A. Sanders, 146–62. Peabody, MA: Hendrickson Publishers, 2002.

Lieberman, Saul. *Hellenism in Jewish Palestine*. 2nd ed. New York: Jewish Theological Seminary, 1962.

———. "The Martyrs of Caesarea," *Annuairv de I'lnstitut de Philologie et d'Histoire Orientales et Slaves* 1 (1939–44): 395–446.

———. *The Tosefta*. 5 vols. New York: Jewish Theological Seminary, 1955–1988.

———. "On Persecution of the Jewish Religion." In *Jubilee Volume in Honor of Salo Baron on the Occasion of his Eightieth Birthday*, edited by Saul Lieberman, 213–54. New York: Columbia University Press, 1975 [Hebrew].

Lim, Timothy H. "The Defilement of the Hands as a Principle Determining the Holiness of Scriptures." *Journal of Theological Studies* 61, no. 2 (October 1, 2010): 501–15.

Lim, Richard. *Public Disputation, Power and Social Order in Late Antiquity*. Berkeley : University of California Press, 1995.

Lookadoo, Jonathon. "Ignatius of Antioch and Scripture." *Zeitschrift Für Antikes Christentum* 23, no. 2 (2019): 201–27.

Lucchesi, Enzo. "Un nouveau complément aux *Lettres festales* d'Athanase." *AnBoll* 119, no. 2 (2001): 255–60.

Lucian. *Lucian*. Edited by Austin Morris Harmon, K. Kilburn, and Mathew Donald. Reprint. LCL 130. Cambridge, MA: Harvard University Press, 1968.

Lüdemann, Gerd. "Zur Geschichte Des Ältesten Christentums in Rom: Valentin Und Marcion; Ptolemäus Und Justin." *Zeitschrift Für Die Neutestamentliche Wissenschaft Und Die Kunde Der Älteren Kirche* 70, no. 1–2 (1979): 86–114.

Luijendijk, AnneMarie. "A Gospel Amulet for Joannia (P.Oxy. VIII 1151)." In *Daughters of Hecate Women and Magic in the Ancient World*, edited by Kimberly B. Stratton and Dayna S. Kalleres. New York: Oxford University Press, 2014, 418–43.

———. “Sacred Scriptures as Trash: Biblical Papyri from Oxyrhynchus,” *VC* 64, no. 3 (2010): 220.

Lundhaug, Hugo. “The Nag Hammadi Codies in the Complex World of Fourth and Fifth Century Egypt.” In *Beyond Conflicts: Cultural and Religious Cohabitations in Alexandria and Egypt Between the 1st and the 6th Century CE*, edited by Luca Acari, 339–58. Tübingen: Mohr Siebeck, 2017.

MacDonald, Lee Martin, and James A. Sanders. *The Canon Debate*. Peabody, MA: Hendrickson Publishers, 2002.

MacRae, Duncan. *Legible Religion: Books, Gods, and Rituals in Roman Culture*. Cambridge, MA: Harvard University Press, 2016.

MacRae, George W. “Gospel of Truth (I, 3 and XII, 2).” In *Nag Hammadi Library in English*, edited by Marvin Meyer and James Robinson, 37–49. San Francisco: Harper & Row, 1977.

Magnusson, Jörgen. *Rethinking the Gospel of Truth: A Study of Its Eastern Valentinian Setting*. Uppsala: Acta Universitatis Upsaliensis, 2006.

Malinine, Michel, ed. *Evangelium Veritatis [Supplementum]: Codex Jung F. Xvii[recto]-F. Xviii[verso] (p. 33-36)*. Studies from the C. G. Jung Institute, no. 6. Zürich: Rascher, 1961.

Malinine, Michel. Quispel. *Evangelium Veritatis: Codex Jung f.VIIIv-XVIv (p.16-32)/f.XIXr-XXIIr (p.37-43) / Puech, Henri-Charles*. Studien Aus Dem C. G. Jung-Institut, Zürich: Rascher, 1956.

Marjanen, Antti, and Petri Luomanen, eds. *A Companion to Second-Century Christian “Heretics.”* Leiden: Brill, 2005.

Markschies, Christoph. “Nochmals: Valentinus Und Die Gnostikoi: Beobachtungen Zu Irenaeus, Haer I 30,15 Und Tertullian, Val 4,2.” *VC* 51, no. 2 (May 1997): 179–87.

———. “New Research on Ptolemaeus Gnosticus,” *ZAC* 4, no. 2 (2000): 225–54.

———. *Valentinus Gnosticus?: Untersuchungen Zur Valentinianischen Gnosis; Mit Einem Kommentar Zu Den Fragmenten Valentins*. Wissenschaftliche Untersuchungen Zum Neuen Testament. Tübingen: Mohr Siebeck, 1992.

———. “The Canon of the New Testament in Antiquity.” In *Homer, the Bible and Beyond*, edited by M. Finkelberg and G. G. Stroumsa, 175–94. Leiden: Brill, 2003.

Marmorstein, Arthur. *Studies in Jewish Theology*. Oxford: Oxford University Press, 1950.

Martial. *Epigrams*. Edited by Walter Ker C.A. LCL 94. 95, 480. Rev. ed. London: William Heinemann LTD, 1968.

Martinez, Florentino Garcia. “The Heavenly Tablets in the Book of Jubilees.” In *Studies in the Book of Jubilees*, edited by M. Albani et al., 243–59. Tübingen: Mohr Siebeck, 1997.

Martyr, Justin. *Saint Justin: Apologies: Introduction, texte critique, traduction, commentarie et index*. Edited by A. Wartelle. Paris: Etudes Augustiniennes, 1987.

McKiraham, Richard. “The Nomos-Physis Debate.” In *Philosophy Before Socrates: An Introduction with Texts and Commentary*, 405–26. 2nd ed. Indianapolis and Cambridge: Hackett Publishing Company, 2010.

McCree, J Woodrow. “Valentinus and the Theology of Grace.” *Union Seminary Quarterly Review* 55, no. 1–2 (2001): 127–59.

McGuire, Anne. “Conversion and Gnosis in the Gospel of Truth,” *NT* 28, no. 4 (1986): 338–55.

Ménard, Jacques E. *L’Évangile de Vérité*. Leiden: Brill Archive, 1972.

———. “L’Evangile de Vérité et le Dieu caché des littératures antiques.” *Revue des Sciences Religieuses* 45, no. 2 (April 1971): 146–61.

———. *L’Évangile de Vérité. Rétroversion Grecque et commentaire*. Paris: Letouzey et Ané, 1962.

Metzger, Bruce M. *The Canon of the New Testament*. Oxford, UK: Clarendon Press, 1997.

Meyer, Elizabeth A. *Legitimacy and Law in the Roman World*. Cambridge, UK: Cambridge University Press, 2004.

Migne, Jacques-Paul. *Patrologiae Cursus Completus: Seu Bibliotheca Universalis, Integra, Uniformis, Commoda, Oeconomica, Omnium SS. Patrum, Doctorum Scriptorumque Ecclesiasticorum, Sive Latinorum, Sive Graecorum, Qui Ab Aevo Apostolico Ad Tempora Innocentii III (anno 1216) Pro Latinis Et Ad Concilii Florentini Tempora (ann. 1439) Pro Graecis Floruerunt. Series Graeca, in Quo Prodeunt Patres, Doctores Scriptoresque Ecclesiae Graecae a S. Barnaba Ad Bessarionem*, 1862.

Milgrom, Jacob. "The Priestly Laws of Santa Contamination." In *Sha'arei Talmon: Studies in the Bible, Qumran, and Ancient Near East Presented to Shemaryahu Talmon*, edited by Michael Fishbane, et. al., 137–46. Winona Lake, IN: Eisenbrauns, 1992.

Miller, Patricia Cox. *The Poetry of Thought in Late Antiquity: Essays in Imagination and Religion*. Aldershot, UK: Ashgate, 2001.

———. "'Words with an Alien Voice': Gnostics, Scripture, and Canon." *JAAR* 57, no. 3 (Fall 1989): 459–83.

Milikowsky, Chaim. "Reflections on Hand-Washing, Hand Purity and Holy Scripture in Rabbinic Literature." In *Purity and Holiness*, edited by M. J. H. M Poorthuis and J. Schwartz, 149–62. Leiden: Brill, 2000.

Moerman, Max D. "The Materiality of the Lotus Sutra: Scripture, Relic, and Buried Treasure." *Dharma World* 37, no. 3 (2010): 15–22.

Mortley, Raoul. "'The Name of the Father Is the Son' (Gospel of Truth 38)." In *Neoplatonism and Gnosticism*, edited by Richard T Wallis and Jay Bregman, 239–52. Albany: State University of New York Press, 1992.

Mueller, Dieter. "Prayer of the Apostle Paul." In *Nag Hammadi Codex I (the Jung Codex)*, edited by Harold Attridge, Nag Hammadi Studies XXII, 5–11. Leiden: Brill, 1985.

Müller, F. Max. *Introduction to the Science of Religion. Four Lectures Delivered at the Royal Institution with Two Essays on False Analogies and the Philosophy of Mythology*. London: Longmans, Gren and Co., 1882.

Munck, Johannes. "Evangelium Veritatis and Greek Usage as to Book Titles." *Studia Theologica* 17, no. 2 (1963): 133–38.

Musurillo, H. *Acts of the Christian Martyrs*. Oxford: Clarendon, 1972.

Myrvold, Kristina. *The Death of Sacred Texts: Ritual Disposal and Renovation of Texts in World Religions*. Farnham, Surrey, UK; Burlington, VT: Ashgate, 2010.

Nautin, Pierre. *Lettres et écrivains chrétiens des IIe et IIIe siècles*. Paris: Éditions du Cerf, 1961.

Moreschini, Claudio, and Norico Norelli. *Early Christian Greek and Latin Literature*. Translated by Matthew J. O'Connell, 2 vols. Peabody, MA: Hendrickson Publishers, 2005.

Mroczek, Eva. *The Literary Imagination in Jewish Antiquity*. New York: Oxford University Press, 2016.

Nagel, Peter. Codex apocryphus gnosticus Novi Testamenti: Band 1: Evangelien und Apostelgeschichten aus den Schriften von Nag Hammadi und verwandten Kodizes. Koptisch und deutsch. Tübingen, Mohr Siebeck, 2017.

Najman, Hindy. "Interpretation as Primordial Writing: Jubilees and Its Authority Conferring Strategies." *JSJ* 30, no. 4 (1999): 379–410.

———. *Losing the Temple and Recovering the Future: An Analysis of 4 Ezra*. Cambridge, UK: Cambridge University Press, 2014.

———. *Seconding Sinai*. Leiden: Brill, 2003.

———. "A Written Copy of Law of Nature: An Unthinkable Paradox?" *SPhilo XV* (2003): 107–18.

Nasrallah, Laura. *An Ecstasy of Folly: Prophecy and Authority in Early Christianity, Harvard Theological Studies 52*. Cambridge, MA: Harvard University Press, 2003.

Neusner, Jacob, ed. "The Oral Torah and the Oral Tradition: Defining the Problematic." In *Method and Meaning in Ancient Judaism*, 59–78. Missoula, MT: Scholars Press, 1979.

———. "Genesis Rabbah as Polemic: An Introductory Account." *HAR* 9 (1985): 252–65.

Nickelsburg, George. *1 Enoch 1: A Commentary on the Book of 1 Enoch, Chapters 1-36; 81-108*. Minneapolis: Fortress Press: 2001.

———. "Enochic Wisdom: An Alternative to the Mosaic Torah?" In *Hesed Ve-Emet: Studies in Honor of Ernest S. Frerichs,* edited by J. Magness and S. Gitin, 123–32. *BJS* 320. Atlanta: Scholars' Press, 1998.

Nickelsburg, George, and James VanderKam. *1 Enoch 2: A Commentary of the Book of Enoch Chapters 37–82*. Minneapolis: Fortress Press, 2012.

Niehoff, M. R. "Creation Ex-Nihilo Theology in Genesis Rabbah in Light of Christian Exegesis." *HTR* 99, no. 1 (2005): 37–64.

Norris, Richard A. "Irenaeus of Lyon." In the *Cambridge History of Early Christian Literature,* edited by Margaret M. Mitchell and Frances M. Young, 45–52. Cambridge, UK: Cambridge University Press, 2004.

O'Donnell, James Joseph. *Avatars of the Word: From Papyrus to Cyberspace*. Cambridge, MA: Harvard University Press, 1998.

Ong, Walter J. *Orality and Literacy: The Technologizing of the Word*. London: Routledge, 1988.

Origen. *Commentaire sur saint Jean*. Edited by Cécile Blanc. SC 120. Paris: Les Éditions du Cerf, 1966.

———. *Traité des principes*. Edited by H. Crouzel and M. Simonetti. SC 252, 253, 268, 269, 312. Paris: Cerf, 1978–1984.

Osborn, Eric F. *Irenaeus of Lyons*. Cambridge, UK: Cambridge University Press, 2001.

Pagels, Elaine. *The Gnostic Gospels*. New York: Random House, 1979.

———. "Irenaeus, the 'Canon of Truth,' and the Gospel of John: 'Making a Difference' Through Hermeneutics and Ritual." *VC* 56, no. 4 (2002): 339–71.

———. *The Johannine Gospel in Gnostic Exegesis: Heracleon's Commentary on John*. Nashville: Abingdon Press, 1973.

Parke, H. W., and B. C. McGing. *Sibyls and Sibylline Prophecy in Classical Antiquity*. London: Routledge, 1988.

Parmenter, Dorina Miller. "The Bible as Icon." In *Jewish and Christian Scripture as Artifact and Canon,* edited by Dorina Miller Parmenter, Craig A. Evans, and H. Daniel Zacharias, 289–310. London: T. & T. Clark, 2009.

Parvis, Paul. "Who Was Irenaeus? An Introduction to the Man and His Work." In *Irenaeus: Life, Scripture, Legacy,* edited by Sara Parvis and Paul Foster, 13–24. Minneapolis: Fortress Press, 2012.

Pauly, August Friedrich von, and Georg Wissowa. *Paulys Real-Encyclopädie Der Classischen Altertumswissenschaft: Neue Bearbeitung*. Stuttgart: J. B. Metzler, 1894.

Pearcy, Lee T. "The Personification of the Text and Augustan Poetics in 'Epistles' 1.20." *Classical World* 87, no. 5 (1994): 457–64.

Petrement, Simone. *A Separate God*. Translated by Carol Harrison. San Francisco: Harper & Row, 1990.

Plutarch. *Lives*. Edited by Bernadotte Perrin. LCL 7. Reprint. Cambridge, MA: Harvard University Press, 1967.

Perkins, Pheme. "What Is a Gnostic Gospel?," *CBQ* 71, no. 1 (2009): 104–29.

Petersen, William Lawrence. *Tatian's Diatessaron: Its Creation, Dissemination, Significance, and History in Scholarship*. Supplements to Vigiliae Christianae. Leiden: Brill, 1994.

Philo. *Philo with an English Translation*. Edited by F. H. Colson, et. al. LCL 1–9. Reprint. Cambridge, MA: Harvard University Press, 1929–1962.

Potter, David. *Prophets and Emperors: Human and Divine Authority from Augustus to Theodosius.* Cambridge, MA: Harvard University Press, 1994.

Price, R. M. "'Hellenization' and Logos Doctrine in Justin Martyr." *VC* 42, no. 1 (March 1988): 18–23.

Prowse, K. R. "Numa and the Pythagoreans: A Curious Incident." *Greece & Rome* 11, no. 1. Second Series (March 1, 1964): 36–42.

Puech, Henri Charles, and Gilles Quispel. "Les Écrits Gnostiques Du Codex Jung." *Vigiliae Christianae* 8, no. 1–2 (January 1954): 1–51.

Quasten, Johannes. *Patrology.* Westminster, MD: Christian Classics, 1983.

Quispel, Gilles. "Neue Funde Zur Valentinianischen Gnosis." *Zeitschrift für Religions und Geistesgeschichte* 6, no. 4 (1954): 289–305.

———. "Origen and the Valentinian Gnosis." *VC* 28, no. 1 (March 1974): 29–42.

———. *Ptolémée, Lettre à Flora, Analyse, texte critique, traduction, commentaire et index grec.* SC 24. Paris, 1966.

———. "The Original Doctrine of Valentinus the Gnostic." *VC* 50, no. 4 (1996): 327–52.

Patten, Robert. "When Is a Book Not a Book." *BIBLION* 4, no. 2 (Spring 1996): 35–65.

Plato. *Phaedrus.* Edited by C.J. Rowe. 2nd ed. Wiltshire, England: Aris & Phillips, 1988.

Pliny. *Letters and Panegyricus.* Edited by Betty Radice. LCL 55. Reprint. Cambridge, MA: Harvard University Press, 1972.

Rahlfs, Alfred, ed. *Septuaginta, editio altera.* Stuttgart: Deutsche Bibelgesellschaft, 2006.

Rankin, David. *From Clement to Origen: The Social and Historical Context of the Church Fathers.* Aldershot, UK: Ashgate Publishers, 2006.

———. *Tertullian and the Church.* Cambridge, UK: Cambridge University Press, 1995.

Rappe, Sara. *Reading Neoplatonism: Non-Discursive Thinking in the Texts of Plotinus, Proclus and Damascius.* Cambridge: Cambridge University Press 2000.

Rasimus, Tuomas. *The Legacy of John: Second-Century Reception of the Fourth Gospel.* Leiden: Brill, 2010.

Ray, Reginald A. "Buddhism: Sacred Text Written and Realized," In *The Holy Book in Comparative Perspective,* edited by Fredrick M. Denny and Rodney L. Taylor, 148–80. Columbia: University of South Carolina Press, 1985.

Reed, Annette Yoshiko. "Ευαγγελιον: Orality, Textuality and the Christian Truth in Irenaeus' *Adversus Haereses.*" *VC* 56, no. 1 (2002): 11–46.

———. "Retelling Biblical Retellings: Epiphanius, the Pseudo-Clementines, and the Reception-History of Jubilees." In *Proceedings from the 13th International Orion Symposioum: Tradition, Transmission, and Transformation, from Second Temple Literature through Judaism and Christianity in Late Antiquity, Hebrew University, Jerusalem, February 23, 2011,* edited by Menahem Kister, et. al., 304–21. Leiden: Brill, 2015.

———. "'Revealed Literature' in the Second Century B.C.E.: *Jubilees,* 1 Enoch and the Prehistory of the Biblical Canon." In *Enoch and Qumran Origins: New Light on a Forgotten Connection,* edited by Gabriele Boccaccini , 94–98. Grand Rapids and Cambridge: William B. Eerdmans, 2005.

Reymond, Eric D. "Wordplay in the Hebrew to Ben Sira." In *The Texts and Versions of the Book of Ben Sira: Transmission and Interpretation,* edited by Jean-Sébastien Rey and Jan Joosten, 37–38. Leiden: Brill, 2011.

Rimell, Victoria. *Martial's Rome: Empire and Ideology of Epigram.* Cambridge, UK: Cambridge University Press, 2008.

Ringgren, Helmer. "Gospel of Truth and Valentinian Gnosticism." *ST* 18, no. 1 (1964): 51–65.

Roberts, Colin H. *Buried Books in Antiquity; Habent Sua Fata Libelli.* Arundell Esdaile Memorial Lecture, 1962. London: Library Association, 1963.

———. *Manuscript, Society, and Belief in Early Christian Egypt.* Schweich Lectures of the British Academy; 1977. London: published for the British Academy by Oxford University Press, 1979.

Roberts, Colin H., and T. C. Skeat. *The Birth of the Codex.* London: Oxford University Press, 1983.

Robison, Andrew C. "The Evangelium Veritatis: Its Doctrine, Character and Origin." *JR* 43, no. 3 (July 1963): 234–43.

Roman, Luke. "The Representation of Literary Materiality in Martial's 'Epigrams.'" *Journal of Roman Studies* 91 (2001): 113–45.

Rönsch, Hermann, and August Dillman. *Das Buch der Jubiläen.* Leipzig: Fues's Verlag, 1874; reprint Amsterdam: Rodopi, 1970.

Rousseau, Adelin, and Louis Doutreleau, eds. *Irénée de Lyon: Contre Les Hérésies.* SC Nos 100, 101 152, 153, 210, 211, 263, 264, 293, 296. Paris: Les Éditions du Cerf, 1965–1982.

Rubenstein, Jeffrey. *Talmudic Stories: Narrative Art, Composition and Culture.* Baltimore: Johns Hopkins University Press, 1999.

Rudolph, Kurt. "Biblical Interpretation in the Gnostic Gospel of Truth from Nag Hammadi." *Theologische Rundschau* 55, no. 2 (April 1990): 113–52.

Runia, David. *On the Creation of the Cosmos According to Moses: Introduction, Translation and Commentary.* Leiden: Brill, 2001.

Rüpke, Jörg. *From Jupiter to Christ: On the History of Religions in the Roman Imperial Period.* Oxford: Oxford University Press, 2014.

Sabar, Shalom. "Torah and Magic: The Torah Scroll and Its Appurtenances as Magical Objects in Traditional Jewish Culture." *European Journal of Jewish Studies* 3, no. 1 (July 1, 2009): 135–70.

Sagi, Abraham. *The Open Canon: On the Meaning of Halakhic Discourse.* Kogod Library of Judaic Studies. London: Continuum, 2007.

Saldarini, Anthony J. "Last Words and Deathbed Scenes in Rabbinic Literature." *JQR* 68, no. 1 (July 1977): 28–45.

Salles, Catherine. *Lire à Rome.* Paris: Les Belles Lettres, 1992.

Sanders, James A. *From Sacred Story to Sacred Text: Canon as Paradigm.* Philadelphia: Fortress Press, 1987.

———. *Torah and Canon.* Philadelphia: Fortress Press, 1972.

Sandmel, Samuel. "Parallelomania" *JBL* 81, no. 1 (1962): 1–13.

Sanzo, Joseph E. "Magic and Communal Boundaries: The Problem with Amulets in Chrystostom, *Adv. Iud.* 8, and Augustine, *In Io. Tra.* 7." *Henoch* 39, no. 2 (2017): 227–46.

Satlow, Michael L. *How the Bible Became Holy.* New Haven: Yale University Press, 2014.

Sawyer, John F. A. *Sacred Languages and Sacred Texts.* Religion in the First Christian Centuries. London: Routledge, 1999.

Schafer, Peter. "Bereshit Bara Elohim: Bereshit Rabba, Parasha 1, Reconsidered." In *Empsychoi Logoi: Religious Innovations in Antiquity*, Studies in Honour of Pieter Willem van der Horst, edited by Alberdina Houtman, et. al., 267–89. Leiden: Brill, 2008.

Scheid, J. "Les archives de la piété. Réflexions sur les livres sacerdotaux." In *La mémoire perdue. A la recherchedes archives oubliées, publiques et privées, de la Rome antique*, edited by C. Nicolet. Paris: Sorbonne, 1994.

Schenke, Hans-Martin. *Die Herkunft des sogenannten Evangelium Veritatis.* Göttingen: Vandenhoeck & Ruprecht, 1959.

Schleicher, Marianne. "Accounts of a Dying Scroll: On Jewish Handling of Sacred Texts in Need of Restoration or Disposal." In *The Death of Sacred Texts: Ritual Disposal and Renovation of Texts in World Religions*, edited by Kristina Myrvold, 11–30. London: Ashgate, 2010.

———. "Artifactual and Hermenutical Use of Scripture in Jewish Tradition." In *Jewish and Christian Scripture as Artifact and Canon*, edited by Craig A. Evans, 48–65. New York: T&T Clark, 2009.

———."The Many Faces of the Torah: Reception and Transformation of the Torah in Jewish Communities." In Vol. 2 of *Receptions and Transformations of the Bible*, edited by Kirsten Nielsen, 141–58. Aarhus, Denmark Aarhus: University Press, 2009.

Schnabel, Eckhard. *Law and Wisdom from Ben Sira to Paul*. Tübingen: Mohr Siebeck, 1985.

Schniedewind, William. *How the Bible Became a Book*. Cambridge, UK: Cambridge University Press, 2004.

Schoedel, William R. "Gnostic Monism and the Gospel of Truth." In Vol. 1 of *Rediscovery of Gnosticism*, edited by Bentley Layton, 379–90. Leiden: Brill, 1980.

———. "Ignatius and the Archives," *HTR* 71, no. 1/2 (1978): 97–106.

Schofer, Jonathan. *The Making of a Sage: A Study in Rabbinic Ethics*. Madison: University of Wisconsin Press, 2005.

Schott, Jeremy M. "Heresiology as Universal History in Epiphanius's Panarion." *Zeitschrift Für Antikes Christentum* 10, no. 3 (2006): 546–63.

Schremer, Adiel. *Brothers Estranged: Heresy, Christianity and Jewish Identity in Late Antiquity*. Oxford: University Press, 2009.

Schwartz, Seth. *Imperialism and Jewish Society, 200 B.C.E. to 640 C.E.* Princeton and Oxford: Princeton University Press, 2001.

———. *Were the Jews a Mediterranean Society?: Reciprocity and Solidarity in Ancient Judaism*. Princeton: Princeton University Press, 2010.

Scott, James M. *Geography in Early Judaism and Christianity*. Society for New Testament Studies Monograph Series. Cambridge; New York: Cambridge University Press, 2002.

Scott, S. P. *The Civil Law*. 17 vols. Cincinnati: The Central Trust Company, 1932.

Seim, Turid Karlsen. *Johannine Echoes in Early Montanism*. Leiden: Brill, 2009.

Shutt, R. J. H. "*Letter of Aristeas*: A New Translation and Introduction." In *The Old Testament Pseudepigrapha*, edited by James H. Charlesworth, 2: 7–11. New York: Doubleday & Company, 1985.

Segal, Alan F. *Two Powers in Heaven: Early Rabbinic Reports About Christianity and Gnosticism*. Leiden: Brill, 1977.

Seo, Mira. "Plagiarism and Poetic Identity in Martial." *American Journal of Philology* 130, no. 4 (2009): 567–93.

Sherman, Charles Phineas. *Roman Law in the Modern World*. Boston: The Boston Book Company, 1917.

Smith, D Moody. "When Did the Gospels Become Scripture?" *JBL* 119, no. 1 (Spring 2000): 3–20.

Smith, Geoffrey S. "Constructing a Christian Universe: Mythological Exegesis of Ben Sira 24 and John's Prologue in the *Gospel of Truth*." In *Jewish and Christian Cosmogony in Late Antiquity*, edited by Lance Jenott and Sarit Kattan Gribetz, 64–84. Tübingen: Mohr Siebeck, 2013.

Snyder, H. Gregory. *Teachers and Texts in the Ancient World: Philosophers, Jews, and Christians*. London: Routledge, 2000.

Spisak, A. L. "Martial's Special Relationship with His Reader." In *Studies in Latin Literature and Roman History* 8, edited by C. Deroux, 352–63. Bruxelles: Latomus, 1997.

Stählin, Otto. *Clemens Alexandrinus: Stromata Buch I-VI*. GCS 15. Leipzig: Hinrichs, 1906.

Standaert, Benoit. "Evangelium Veritatis et Veritatis Evangelium: La Question du Titre et Les Témoins Patristiques." *VC* 30, no. 2 (June 1976): 138–50.

———. "Evangile de Vérité: Critique et Lecture." *NTS* 22, no. 3 (April 1976): 243–75.

Stark, Rodney. *Cities of God: The Real Story of How Christianity Became an Urban Movement and Conquered Rome*. San Francisco: Harper San Francisco, 2006.

Starr, Raymond J. "The Circulation of Literary Texts in the Roman World." *CQ* 37, no. 1 (1978): 213–23.

Stefaniw, Blossom. *Mind, Text, and Commentary: Noetic Exegesis in Origen of Alexandria, Didymus the Blind, and Evagrius Ponticus*. Frankfurt am Main: Peter Lang Verlag, 2010.

Steinsaltz, Adin. *The Talmud: A Reference Guide*. New York: Random House, 1989.

Stock, Brian. *Listening for the Text: On the Uses of the Past*. Parallax: Re-visions of Culture and Society. Baltimore: Johns Hopkins University Press, 1990.

———. *The Implications of Literacy*. Princeton: Princeton University Press, 1983.

Stone, Michael, and Matthias Henze, *4 Ezra and 2 Baruch: Translations, Introductions, and Notes*. Minneapolis: Fortress Press, 2013.

Story, Cullen. *The Nature of Truth in The Gospel of Truth and in the Writings of Justin Martyr: A Study of the Pattern of Orthodoxy*. Leiden: Brill, 1970.

———. "Ultimate Reality and 'The Gospel of Truth.'" *Ultimate Reality and Meaning* 4, no. 4 (1981): 279–96.

Strack, H. L., and Günter Stemberger. *Introduction to the Talmud and Midrash*. Translated by Markus Bockmuehl. Minneapolis: Fortress Press, 1996.

Striker, Gisela. "Origins of the Concept of Natural Law." In *Essays on Hellenistic Epistemology and Ethics*, edited by Gisela Striker, 209–20. New York: Cambridge University Press, 1996.

Stroumsa, Guy G. *The End of Sacrifice: Religious Transformation in Late Antiquity*. Translated by Susan Emanuel. Chicago: University of Chicago Press, 2009.

———. *Hidden Wisdom: Esoteric Traditions and the Roots of Christian Mysticism*. Leiden: Brill, 1996.

———."The Scriptural Movement of Late Antiquity and Christian Monasticism." *JECS* 16, no. 1 (2008): 61–77.

———. *The Scriptural Universe of Ancient Christianity*. Cambridge, MA: Harvard University Press, 2016.

Suetonius. *Lives of the Caesars*. Edited by John Carew Rolfe. LCL31, 38. Reprint. Cambridge, MA: Harvard University Press, 1997.

Svensson, Jonas. "Relating, Revering, and Removing: Muslim Views on the Use, Power, and Disposal of Divine Words." In *The Death of Sacred Texts*, edited by Kristina Myrvold, 31–54. Surrey: Ashgate, 2010.

Tabbernee, William. "Perpetua, Montanism, and Christian Ministry in Carthage C. 203 C.E." *Perspectives in Religious Studies* 32, no. 4 (2005): 421–41.

Tabernee, William. *Prophets and Gravestones: An Imaginative History of Montanists and Other Early Christians*. Peabody, MA: Hendrickson Publishers, 2009.

Tacitus, Cornelius. *Annals*. Edited by John Jackson. LCL 249. Reprint. Cambridge, MA: Harvard University Press, 1969.

———. *The Histories*. Edited by Clifford Herschel Moore and John Jackson. LCL 111, 249. Reprint. Cambridge, MA: Harvard University Press, 1986.

Tahir, Alfian ZM. "Holy Books Burned for Disposal Purposes," *Malaysian Reserve*, October 30, 2014.

Tertullian. *Adversus Marcionem*. Translated by Ernest Evans. Oxford Early Christian Texts. Oxford: Clarendon Press, 1972.

Thomassen, Einar. *Canon and Canonicity*. Copenhagen: Museum Tusculanum Press, 2010.

———. "From Wisdom to Gnosis." In *Colloque International "L'évangile Selon Thomas Et Les Textes De Nag Hammadi,"* edited by L. Painchaud and P.-H. Poirier, 585–98. Paris: Peeters, 2007.

———. "Gnostic Semiotics: the Valentinian Notion of the Name." *Temenos* 29 (1993): 141–56.

———."Notes pour la délimitation d'un corpus valentinien à Nag Hammadi." In *Les textes de Nag Hammadi et la problème de leur classification*, edited by Louis Painchaud and Anne Pasquier, 242–60. Quebec: Les Presses de l'Université Laval, 1995.

———. "Orthodoxy and Heresy in Second-Century Rome." *HTR* 97, no. 3 (July 2004): 241–56.

———. *The Spiritual Seed: The Church of the 'Valentinians.'* Nag Hammadi and Manichaean Studies. Leiden: Brill, 2006.

Theodor, J., and Ch Albeck, *Midrash Bereshit Rabbah: Critical Edition with Notes and Commentary*. 2nd edition. Jerusalem: Wahrmann, 1965.

Tiessen, Terrance L. *Irenaeus on the Salvation of the Unevangelized*. ATLA Monograph Series; no. 31. Metuchen, NJ: Scarecrow Press, 1993.

Tigchelaar, Eibert J. C. "Jubilees and 1 Enoch and the Issue of the Transmission of Knowledge." In *Enoch and Qumran Origins: New Light on a Forgotten Connection*, edited by Gabriele Boccaccini, 99–101. Grand Rapids, MI: Eerdmans, 2005.

Timbie, Janet. "Biblical Interpretation in the Gnostic Gospel of Truth from Nag Hammadi." *CBQ* 52, no. 1 (January 1990): 178–80.

Tite, Philip L. "The Two-Way Schema in Valentinian Paraenesis." *ARC* 33 (2005): 197–211.

———. *Valentinian Ethics and Paraenetic Discourse*. Leiden: Brill, 2009.

Too, Yun Lee. *The Idea of the Library in the Ancient World*. Oxford: Oxford University Press, 2010.

Toorn, K. *The Image and the Book: Iconic Cults, Aniconism, and the Rise of Book Religion in Israel and the Ancient Near East*. Leuven: Peeters, 1997.

Trevett, Christine. *Montanism: Gender, Authority, and the New Prophecy*. Cambridge, UK: Cambridge University Press, 1996.

Tuckett, Christopher M. "Synoptic Tradition in the Gospel of Truth and the Testimony of Truth." *JTS* 35, no. 1 (April 1984): 131–45.

Urbach, Ephraim E. *The Sages: Their Concepts and Beliefs*. Translated by Israel Abrahams. Cambridge, MA: Harvard University Press, 1987.

Vallée, Gérard. *A Study in Anti-Gnostic Polemics: Irenaeus, Hippolytus, and Epiphanius*. Studies in Christianity and Judaism. Waterloo, ON: Published for the Canadian Corporation for Studies in Religion by Wilfrid University Press, 1981.

VanderKam, James C., and William Adler. *The Jewish Apocalyptic Heritage in Early Christianity*. Compendia Rerum Iudaicarum Ad Novum Testamentum. Assen, Netherlands: Van Gorcum; Fortress Press, 1996.

Veyne, Paul. *A History of Private Life: From Pagan Rome to Byzantium*. Translated by Arthur Goldhammer. Cambridge, MA: Harvard University Press, 1992.

Visotzky, Burton L. "Genesis Rabbah 1: 1—Mosaic Torah as the Blueprint of the Universe—Insights from the Roman World." In *Talmuda de-Eretz Israel: Archaeology and the Rabbis in Late Antique Palestine*. Studia Judaica 73, edited by Steven Fine and Aaron Koller, 127–40. Boston: De Gruyter, 2014.

Wasserstein, Abraham, and David J. Wasserstein. *The Legend of the Septuagint: From Classical Antiquity to Today*. Cambridge, UK: Cambridge University Press, 2006.

Watson, Alan, trans. *Digest of Justinian*, 4 vols. Philadelphia: University of Pennsylvania Press, 1985.

Wellhausen, Julius. *Prolegomena to the History of Israel*. Translated by J. Sutherland Black and Allan Menzies. Edinburgh: Adam and Charles Black, 1885.

White, Peter. "Bookshops in the Literary Culture of Rome." In *Ancient Literacies, the Culture of Reading in Greece and Rome*, edited by William A. Johnson and Holt N. Parker, 268–87. Oxford: Oxford University Press, 2009.

Wilken, Robert L. "The Homeric Cento in Irenaeus, 'Adversus Haereses' I, 9,4." *VC* 21, no. 1 (March 1, 1967): 25–33.

Williams, G. D. "Representations of the Book-Roll in Latin Poetry." *Mnemosyne* 45 (1992): 177.

Williams, Francis E. "The Apocryphon of James." In *Nag Hammadi Codex I (the Jung Codex)*, edited by Harold Attridge, 13–54. Leiden: Brill, 1985.

Williams, Jacqueline A. *Biblical Interpretation in the Gnostic Gospel of Truth from Nag Hammadi*. Society of Biblical Literature Dissertation. Decatur, GA: Scholars Press, 1988.

Williams, Megan Hale, and Anthony Grafton. *Christianity and the Transformation of the Book: Origen, Eusebius, and the Library of Caesarea*. Cambridge, MA: Harvard University Press, 2006.

Williams, Michael A. *Rethinking "Gnosticism": An Argument for Dismantling a Dubious Category*. Princeton: Princeton University Press, 1996.

Wilson, Robert McL. "Note on the Gospel of Truth (33: 8-9)." *NTS* 9, no. 3 (April 1963): 295–98.

———. "Valentinianism and the Gospel of Truth." In Vol. 1 of the *Rediscovery of Gnosticism*, edited by Bentley Layton, 133–41. Leiden: Brill, 1980.

Wimbush, Vincent L. *Theorizing Scriptures: New Critical Orientations to a Cultural Phenomenon*. New Brunswick, NJ: Rutgers University Press, 2008.

Winsbury, Rex. *The Roman Book: Books, Publishing and Performance in Classical Rome*. London: Duckworth, 2009.

Wintermute, O. S. "Jubilees: A New Translation and Commentary." In *The Old Testament Pseudepigrapha*, edited by James H. Charlesworth, 2: 35–142. New York: Doubleday, 1985.

Wisse, Frederik. "The Nag Hammadi Library and the Heresiologists." *VC* 25, no. 3 (1971): 205–23.

Wolfson, Elliot R. "Inscribed in the Book of the Living: Gospel of Truth and Jewish Christology." *JSJ* 38, no. 2 (2007): 234–71.

Wollenberg, Rebecca Scharbach. "The Book That Changed: Narratives of Ezran Authorship as Late Antique Biblical Criticism." *JBL* 38, no. 1 (2019): 143–60.

———. "The Dangers of Reading as We Know It: Sight Reading as a Source of Heresy in Early Rabbinic Traditions." *JAAR* 85, no. 3 (2017), 709–45.

Wray, Judith Hoch. *Rest as a Theological Metaphor in the Epistle to the Hebrews and the Gospel of Truth: Early Christian Homiletics of Rest*. Atlanta: Scholars Press, 1998.

Wright, Benjamin. "The Apocryphal Ezekiel Fragments." In *The Apocryphal Ezekiel*, edited by Michael Stone, Benjamin Wright, and David Satran, 19–21. *Early Judaism and Its Literature 18*. Atlanta: Society of Biblical Literature, 2000.

———. "The Wisdom of Ben Sira or Sirach." In *New Interpreter's Bible One Volume Commentary*, edited by David L. Petersen and Beverly R. Gaventa. Nashville: Abingdon, 2014.

———. "Translation Greek in Sirach in Light of the Grandson's Prologue." In *The Texts and Versions of the Book of Ben Sira: Transmission and Interpretation*, edited by Jean-Sébastien Rey and Jan Joosten, 78–84. Leiden: Brill, 2011.

———. *The Letter of Aristeas: 'Aristeas to Philocrates' or 'On the Translation of the Law of the Jew.'* Commentaries on Early Jewish Literature. Berlin: De Gruyter, 2015.

———. "Translation as Scripture: The Septuagint in Aristeas and Philo." In *Praise Israel for Wisdom and Instruction: Essays on Ben Sira and Wisdom, the Letter of Aristeas and the Septuagint*. Leiden: Brill, 2008, 297–313.

Wyrick, Jed. *The Ascension of Authorship: Attribution and Canon Formation in Jewish, Hellenistic, and Christian Traditions*. Harvard Studies in Comparative Literature. Cambridge, MA: Harvard University Press, 2004.

Yadin, Azzan. *Scripture as Logos: Rabbi Ishmael and the Origins of Midrash*. Philadelphia: University of Pennsylvania Press, 2004.

Young, Frances M., Lewis Ayres, and Andrew Louth. *The Cambridge History of Early Christian Literature*. Cambridge, UK: Cambridge University Press, 2004.

Van der Horst, Pieter. "Ancient Jewish Bibliomancy." *JGRChJ* 1, no. 1 (2000): 9–17.

———. "Sortes: Sacred Books as Instant Oracles in Late Antiquity." In *The Use of Sacred Books in the Ancient World*, edited by L. V. Rutgers, P. W. van der Horst, H. W. Havelaar, and L. Teugels, 143–73. Leiden: Brill, 1998.

Van der Kooij, Arie, K. van der Toorn, and Joannes Augustinus Maria Snoek, eds. *Canonization and Decanonization*. Studies in the History of Religions. Leiden: Brill, 1998.

Van der Toorn, K, ed. *The Image and the Book: Iconic Cults, Aniconism and the Rise of Book Religion in Israel and the Ancient Near East*. Louven: Peeters, 1997.

Van Groningen, B.A. "ΕΚΔΟΣΙΣ," *Mnemosyne*, Fourth Series, 16, no. 1 (1963): 1–17.

Von Harnack, Adolf. *History of Dogma*. Translated by N. Buchanan. New York: Dover, 1961.

Van Henten, Jan Willem. "Jewish and Christian Martyrs." In *Saints and Role Models in Judaism and Christianity*, edited by Marcel Poorthuis and Joshua Schwartz, 163–82. Leiden: Brill, 2004.

Von Rad, Gerhard. *Genesis: A Commentary*. Translated by J. H. Marks. Philadelphia: Westminster Press, 1961.

Zahn, Theodor. *Geschichte des neutestamentlichen Kanons*. 2 vols. Erlangen: A. Deichert, 1889, 1890.

Zeitlin, Solomon. "A Historical Study of the Canonization of the Hebrew Scriptures." *PAAJR* 3 (1931–1932): 121–58.

INDEX

ACKNOWLEDGMENTS

This book features ancient authors who were executed, wrapped in their own books. Thank you to many people, who kept me wrapped up in this book through trying times, and saw me through to a happy conclusion.

Ellen Muehlberger has been a constant source of wisdom and support from this book's inception to its final form. She has also taught me the true meaning of revision. Daniel Boyarin has shown me that philology is the basis of everything. During the last stages of the book, his comments, from keen observations on wording to large structural recommendations, gave the book a sharper focus. I first encountered the *Gospel of Truth* as a graduate student at UC Berkeley, where I studied Coptic with David Johnson, of blessed memory. I will never forget his kindness and generosity as a scholar, or the hours the two of us spent translating the *Gospel of Thomas*, the *Gospel of Phillip*, and of course, the *Gospel of Truth*. The translations in this book are based on those meetings.

I wish to thank several scholars who read drafts and offered advice at various stages of this project, including Jon Bailiff, Susie Bright, Francis Borchardt, Dylan Burns, Malcolm Choat, Sara Feldman, Stephen DeBacker, Helen Dixon, Jay Garfield, Ilgi Evrim Gerçek, David Hollenberg, Andrew Hui, Young Richard Kim, Karen King, Kristina Lucenko, Emmanuel Mayer, Eva Mroczek, Rachel Neis, Guy Stroumsa, Stephen Shoemaker, Jacqueline Vayntrub, Martin Weissman, Rachel Yuen-Collinridge, and Jason Zurawski.

I would like to thank Jerome Singerman, Derek Krueger, Virginia Burrus, and the editors at University of Pennsylvania Press for shepherding the book through its last stages, even during the worst of the COVID-19 pandemic.

I am grateful to the Dolores Zohrab Liebmann Foundation, the Mellon Foundation, the Jean and Samuel Frankel Center for Judaic Studies, the Michigan Center for Early Christian Studies, Yale-NUS College, the Oregon Humanities Center, and the College of Arts and Sciences at the University of Oregon for their support.

Finally, I would like to thank my family. My parents and sister encouraged an early interest in religious studies. Max Mortimer, along with Tiger the Second and Pertinax Polydactylis, have been exacting overseers of my work. Marty Weissman provided unwavering support for this project from the beginning and lent his savvy editorial eye and typing skills to the final draft.

CPSIA information can be obtained
at www.ICGtesting.com
Printed in the USA
JSHW052030220222
23247JS00001B/1